DISCARDED RABBITS:

The Growing Crisis of Abandoned Domestic Rabbits

and How We Can Help

Lucile Moore with

Debby Widolf

Foreword by Michael Mountain

Front cover photo and back cover art by Debby Widolf

To the memory of my mother and father, who loved all animals,
To Siegfried and Roy, my Las Vegas golf course rabbits,
To all the other rabbits who do share and have shared my life;
I dedicate this book to you all, with love. — *Lucile Moore*

To my rabbit Rosebud, who started my journey, and to those human helpers, present and future, who will continue to champion the work of saving the lives of discarded rabbits.— *DebbyWidolf*

Table of Contents

Part II: Rescuing Large Groups and Colonies of Rabbits

FOREWORD

Princess was sitting by the swimming pool in the house we were renting in Phoenix, Arizona. The cute white rabbit had arrived earlier that scorching summer afternoon in 1979, burrowing under the fence from an adjacent, empty five-acre lot, looking for something to drink.

We made her comfortable and weren't quite sure what to do next, especially when, the following day, this friendly girl was joined by a larger, pale brown rabbit who wanted something to eat but didn't want much to do with Princess or anyone else. He was altogether quite reclusive, so we called him Howard Hughes after the famously eccentric and reclusive aviation entrepreneur of that time.

A couple of days later, Howard Hughes dug a warren in the backyard and gave birth to six white baby bunnies. Oops! We renamed "him" Harriet Hughes, and took Princess to the veterinarian, who confirmed that "she" was, in fact, not a princess but a prince. Neutered that same day, Prince Princess rejoined his family at home, and once Harriet's babies were weaned, she and they were also fixed.

That might have been the end of the story, except that word had apparently gotten around the adjacent empty lot, and more rabbits were now burrowing under the fence and starting to dig a more extensive warren that was quickly becoming inaccessible even to the longest of human arms. Long story short, and before the situation got seriously out of control, we managed to round up the various families and take them to a small sanctuary out of town where my friend Faith Maloney was caring for a few dozen homeless dogs and cats and finding new homes for many of them.

Five years later, the sanctuary moved to a new home in the glorious red-rock canyon country of Southern Utah, where it would grow into

Best Friends Animal Sanctuary, the largest companion animal sanctuary in the United States and a driving force in the budding no-kill movement of the 1990s.

Best known for its work with dogs and cats, Best Friends was also caring for horses, donkeys, pigs, birds and rabbits. One day in 1996, Faith got a call from a woman in Las Vegas who needed some help with "some rabbits" in her backyard.

"How many do you have there?" Faith asked.

"Well, umm, I guess maybe about 150," the woman admitted.

When, the following day, Faith and her colleague Chandra, our bunny manager at that time, drove down to Vegas, about 250 miles from Best Friends, to assess the situation, they stepped into a sea of fur and counted 167 rabbits.

"Why didn't you get them neutered?" Faith asked.

"I didn't know you could do that," the woman offered.

Two days later, we returned with a truck and loaded up 177 rabbits. Five hours later, back at the sanctuary, we unloaded 185.

While racing to get ahead of nature taking its course, there was a certain element of humor to the rapid growth in numbers –some light-hearted jokes about rabbit reproduction that helped break the stress of the whole situation. Our veterinarian, faced with spay/neutering hundreds of rabbits (more were still being born), got himself a new username on AOL with the handle "drbunnyman."

All in all, the much-reported Las Vegas Bunny Rescue was probably the largest rabbit rescue on record. But it paled in comparison to the situation we undertook eight years later when Debby Widolf was manager of our rabbit department and a woman in Reno, Nevada, called for help.

When Debby and her team arrived in Reno, the situation that presented itself was grim: more than 1,200 rabbits barely able to move around in the small backyard and under the woman's trailer – burrowing, and in some cases dragging themselves around the house. Many were sick and injured. The entire scene was horrific and a struggle against time: renting land for a temporary rescue center, bringing in fencing and housing, setting up a veterinary center and creating staff accommodation for all the people who would be needed to save as many of these sad lives as possible.

The local authorities told us they'd rescued rabbits from this woman before. She was a classic animal hoarder. A few years earlier, the animal control department had taken her to court to ask for a ruling that would stop her from collecting and breeding any more rabbits. But the judge had literally laughed the matter out of court, saying that it was a big joke that anyone would be paying attention to rabbits.

As word spread in the news media, I ran into similar laughter on talk shows around the country. Some of it was well-meaning, but there were also jokes about bunny stew and fur coats. If it had been dogs or cats, there would have been none of that. But rabbits . . .

Whenever I hear of rabbit rescues and hoarding situation like in the Reno case, they always seem to engender jokes and laughter. Not all of this is unpleasant; it includes the warm-hearted chuckles of the people who do care about these animals and are working so hard to save them. And some of it doubtless stems from the fact that there's something slightly ambivalent in our whole relationship to rabbits. Perhaps related to the fact that we humans are ourselves seriously overpopulating our planet.

While they are the third most common pet in the United States, most rabbits are not born to be pets. Cottontails are born wild and remain wild. Some domestic rabbits are born, raised and sold to be food or to be used in cruel, invasive, laboratory experiments. (In 2016, approximately 140,000 rabbits were used in USDA-licensed vivisection experiments in the United States, compared to about 60,000 dogs and 18,000 cats.)

Thousands of years before we humans ever took in rabbits as pets, they were thought of as symbols of fertility. In pre-Christian versions of Easter, rabbit icons and symbology were all part of the annual spring celebrations of rebirth and sexuality that live on in modern society through Easter bunnies.

From baby bunnies to cartoon bunnies to energizer bunnies to Easter bunnies, rabbits are cute and whimsical. And their whiskers twitch. But while they're adorable, they need all the same long-term care as any other pet. And when the fun of a super-cute bunny purchase wears off, they often find themselves being dropped off, frequently into empty lots to fend for themselves, as had been the case with Prince Princess and Harriet Hughes.

And that's definitely not funny.

While the no-kill movement has made great strides toward ending the killing of homeless dogs and cats, rabbits remain somewhat overlooked in local and national campaigns. Some advances have been made, like the fact that several of the large pet store chains that stopped selling dogs and cats several years ago are no longer selling rabbits, either.

But without the same kind of support that today's large and well-funded no-kill organizations provide for local spay/neuter and adoption programs on behalf of dogs and cats, rabbit rescue and protection groups find themselves to a large extent having to go it alone.

Fortunately, this hasn't fazed people like Debby Widolf and Lucile Moore in their efforts to bring rabbits into the mainstream of the no-kill movement. This book will be an invaluable help to anyone with a heart for these marvelously engaging animals.

Michael Mountain

Michael Mountain is the former President of Best Friends Animal Society. He is co-founder of the Whale Sanctuary Project, which is building a model sanctuary where captive whales and dolphins can be rehabilitated and live permanently in their natural environment.

PREFACE

In 2017 the death of my father just short of his 101st birthday ended a 25-year stint of family caregiving that included my mother, a brother and my father. Like many long-term family caregivers, I suddenly found myself with a little free time again. I thought about writing another rabbit book and asked my friend and fellow rabbit rescuer and advocate, Debby Widolf, if she had any ideas. "You may be sorry you asked," Debby replied, and proceeded to suggest a book on what she felt to be the greatest challenge ahead for rabbit advocates and rescuers: the exponentially increasing number of abandoned domestic rabbits, especially the colonies that have developed from rabbit 'dumpsites.'

I hesitated at first, for although I was certainly aware of this growing problem, colony rabbit rescue was not my area of expertise. But after a little preliminary research I agreed to tackle a book such as Debby suggested with the provisos that I expand the scope of the book to include multiple aspects of rescue and that she be a part of the project and help me find experienced rabbit rescuers willing to donate their time and knowledge. Debby agreed and we began our search for contributors. Caroline Gilbert, a long-time rabbit rescuer and founder of what is now The Rabbit Sanctuary, Incorporated, of Simpsonville, South Carolina, was one of the first to agree to share her wealth of knowledge, and many others followed.

The book became a collaborative effort in the best sense of the word. People of widely different backgrounds in animal and rabbit rescue put aside their differences of opinion on various rabbit topics in order to benefit rabbits as a whole by sharing ideas, how-to, failures and successes in dealing with the rapidly growing problem of dumped domestic rabbits. Contributors ranged from people who are widely known in the field of animal rescue, such as Faith Maloney (a co-founder of Best Friends Animal Society) to individuals who donated pictures of much-loved rescued companion rabbits, and from internationally known established authors like Dr. Linda R. Harper to those who have never before written anything for publication.

While most of the contributors have been active in rescue for a decade or more, I am pleased that several people just starting out in rescue contributed as well. And because I feel it important to emphasize that those who foster and/or adopt rescued rabbits are just as much a part of rescue as those who initially save rabbits, I have included their stories as well.

Every contribution, from the smallest to the largest, added something of value to the finished volume. Nor were contributors the only ones who helped with this book. Debby and I give special thanks to Victor Gutschalk for his steadfast computer tech support through the writing of this book and for his brilliant design, building, and maintenance of the www.dontdumprabbits.org website.

I feel I need to emphasize that the fact a person contributed to this volume does not mean that the contributor agrees with everything presented in the book. Rescuers from many backgrounds who have different philosophies about rabbit rescue and rabbit care donated their time and work to this project. Debby and I felt that a wide variety of contributors would offer a wide variety of examples, options, and possible solutions, but this means that not every contributor will agree with everything presented by other contributors or by Debby and me. Debby and I owe a huge debt of gratitude to each and every person who donated to this project for the sake of the rabbits we all love.

I initially came up with the title "Abandoned: The Growing Crisis of Dumped Domestic Rabbits and How We Can Help," but Debby suggested the main title should be "Discarded Rabbits." I feel her wording expresses the casualness with which the lives of many abandoned domestic rabbits are tossed aside, and we changed the title to its current wording.

We had originally intended the book to be out in the fall or winter of 2018, but in late spring of 2018 I was evacuated from my home due to a fast-moving human-caused forest fire that ended up destroying many homes in my area. I got out with my companion animals and little more. For three days my property was shown as burned on the official burn maps, and I did not learn until I returned a week later that the fire itself had missed my property by a scant twenty yards. However, there was much heat damage to my property, and dealing with that plus three more fire scares ended up delaying completion of this volume by several months.

I would not feel this book was complete without taking a paragraph to thank the many "bunny people" who offered me assistance – prayers, emails to politicians about animals evacuees were forced to leave behind, and offers of clothes, household goods and places to live – during those days I thought I had been left essentially destitute. Thank you. Your help and concern meant more than I can say.

INTRODUCTION

It was our goal to cover as many aspects of rabbit abandonment and rescue as possible, from the causes to potential solutions. We wished to have useful information for everyone, from beginners who have never rescued a dumped rabbit to highly experienced rescuers who have been involved in multiple rescues of large colonies. To that end we covered topics ranging from the causes of rabbit abandonment to specifics on how to organize the rescue of a colony of feral rabbits. Many of the contributors shared personal stories of rescues rather than focusing on a particular aspect of rescue. Debby and I felt these stories were valuable, for they show readers the wide variety of rescue situations that may be encountered and describe failures and successes from which others can learn. To make it easier for readers to find what they are looking for we divided the book into three parts: Part I: The Problem and Potential Solutions; Part II, Rescuing Large Groups and Colonies of Rabbits; and Part III, Individual Rescue of Dumped Rabbits.

Inevitably, there were subjects that had to be left out. This is not a book specifically about medical care, so for the most part we have left medical topics out, although we do have sections on zoonoses, parasites, and common diseases and injuries found in abandoned rabbits. At the same time, although we tried to limit repetition we needed to give different information on the same subjects to experienced rescuers and novice rescuers, and also to group rescuers and individual rescuers. Therefore, we address many of the same subjects in Parts II and III, but the information presented is tailored to fit the two different types of rescue.

In Part I we address some of the causes of the high number of rabbits that are abandoned, the scope of the problem, why people dump their rabbits, what really happens to rabbits that are abandoned to fend for themselves, and why shelters and re-homing are not enough. Then contributors Faith Maloney, a co-founder of Best Friends Animal Society, and Caroline Charland, the founder of Bunny Bunch Rabbit Rescue, address the issue of rabbit hoarding. In Chapter 3 Debby Widolf presents a case study of a rabbit dump in Las Vegas. Chapter 4 contains strategies for educating various sectors of the public about rabbits and rabbit abandonment. In Chapter 5 we discuss what things and information it is good to have on hand so that time will not be lost when abandoned rabbits are discovered.

Part II focuses on the rescue of large numbers of rabbits and colonies of rabbits. First we address the initial steps to take when a large group or colony of abandoned/feral rabbits is discovered, followed by a chapter on managing large numbers and/or colonies of rescued rabbits. Topics covered include housing, feed, finding placements for rabbits, fundraising, common medical and behavioral problems in rescued rabbits, and how to transport rabbits. Several contributors share their experiences on these topics. Chapter 8 has a discussion of trap-neuter-return/release for feral domestic rabbit colonies, presenting the pros and cons. We end part II with a chapter on the Reno Rabbit Rescue of 2006, presenting the story from the viewpoints of four different people.

Part III is for those who are or might be involved in individual rescue, even those who have never rescued a rabbit before. We include basic information on capturing, feeding, and caring for rabbits, along with many stories of personal rabbit rescue. We also address adopting rescued rabbits, for the adopters of rescued abandoned rabbits are just as much a part of rescue as those who capture them. Included in the section on adoption is information on adopting a small group of rescued colony rabbits for a backyard or country property (micro-colonies). At the end of Part III we look at staying strong in rescue and caring for ourselves. Two eminently qualified people, Davida Kobler (long-time House Rabbit Society Educator, Fosterer, and Chapter Manager) and Linda R. Harper, PhD, (founder of Blessed Bonds), generously contributed pieces for this section.

We have four appendices: one on online resources, the second a list of low-cost neuter and spay generously contributed by Judy Books, a third listing classes of antiparasitic agents, a fourth giving signs of selected digestive disorders, and the fifth appendix is for fun – a story of the eighteenth-century lagomorphs advocate, William Cowper. The appendices are followed by the contributor biographies, a selected bibliography, and index.

An important note on some wording decisions we made for this volume:

i. Rabbits are often referred to as "he," "she," and "who," not "it," "which" and "that" because many of those who donated their efforts to this book view rabbits as fellow sentient creatures. However, usage will not be consistent because of the multiple contributors to this volume.

ii. The word "unaltered" encompasses both unspayed females and unneutered males, and to "alter" a rabbit may refer to either a spay or neuter.

iii. Many of the people involved in animal rescue try to avoid the terms "pet" and "owner," using instead the terms "companion animal" and "caregiver," respectively. It is not feasible for us to follow this convention everywhere in this book because some of the articles or stories we quote use those terms and many of the laws relating to animals include those terms.

Evonne Vey contributed the artwork on pages 4, 7, and 212; the rest of the art contained in the book is by Debby Widolf. With the exception of photos by Debby and myself, which were placed wherever they were needed, for the most part the photos in each piece are by the author of that piece or another person associated with that rescue. There were a few exceptions: a photo from Adrienne Lang's story was used to illustrate a section on broken limbs, a photo by Kim Dezelon was placed in a section on feeding, a photo of Meg Brown's 14-year-old rabbit Bear put at the end of the Contributor's section and one of the rescues Sugar and Spice at the end of the bibliography.

A final note: all rabbit photos in this volume are of rescued rabbits.

PART I:

THE PROBLEM AND POTENTIAL SOLUTION

CHAPTER 1: THE DOWNSIDE OF POPULARITY

Not so long ago rabbits were an unusual companion animal; a situation that has changed drastically over the last twenty years or so. Rabbits are now the third most popular mammalian pet in several countries, including the United States (estimated 6.2 million pet rabbits) and United Kingdom (estimated around 1 million). Rabbit medicine is greatly advanced from what it was a scant generation past, and veterinarians experienced with rabbits are no longer as difficult to find as they once were.

However, there is a downside to rabbits' increased popularity: an exponential increase in the number of abandoned rabbits. And many – if not most – of these unwanted rabbits are not turned in to a shelter or rescue but are let loose to fend for themselves. The actual numbers of dumped rabbits are unknown and essentially unknowable, for most published figures for abandoned animals don't list rabbits separately but lump them under "other," and surrender counts are usually counts of animals turned in at shelters and humane organizations. It is not possible to account for the numbers of rabbits, cats, and other animals that are simply let loose. Still, surrender numbers from shelters can give some idea of the numbers of rabbits that are given up. Researchers who did a study of four shelters in the US in 2012 found rabbits were usually the third most surrendered pet (although birds occasionally took this place). In the UK the author of an article in *Metro* reported that four out of five rabbits bought as pets near Easter are abandoned or die within a year. In 2017, the Rabbit Welfare Association and Fund (RWAF) estimated that 67,000 rabbits go through re-homing shelters in the UK each year, a figure that was almost double the 2006 RSPCA estimate of 35,000 rabbits abandoned each year.

There is no way to know how many rabbits are turned loose, but members of rabbit rescue organizations across the country have been reporting higher and higher numbers of rabbits literally abandoned to fend for themselves. A summary of the findings of the Make Mine Chocolate! Rabbit Rescue Survey completed in 2010 included the comment that "A worrying large (and increasing) number of rabbits enter rescue as a stray/dumped." One shelter in the Chicago area noted in 2011 that they were seeing a big increase in the number of pet rabbits released into the wild and that most of them had bite wounds, abscesses, and parasites. Another Chicago area shelter reported taking in 83 rabbits that had been abandoned outside in one year. A rescuer in Georgia estimated that thousands of domestic rabbits are let loose in that state each year, and another rescuer in Northern California believes that about 2/3 of abandoned rabbits in that area are simply let go to fend for themselves.

However beautiful and lush a spot may appear to the person who releases a rabbit, many of these rabbits released into the wild soon die. Those fortunate enough to find adequate food and shelter may survive for a while and be joined by other rabbits. If any are unneutered, breeding will add yet more rabbits to the colony. Some colonies of domestic feral rabbits have grown so large and become such a problem to the municipalities where they are located that they have made the news. "The Problem that Valdez just can't shake: An infestation of bunnies," "Bunnies have town hopping mad," "Calgary councilor thumps residents for feeding feral rabbits," and "Feral rabbits overtake Cannon Beach and no agency has responsibility," read some story headlines. I even found an article about a feral domestic rabbit problem in Helsinki, Finland, in which it was noted even the cold winters did not noticeably reduce the numbers because the rabbits found enough food in gardens and at bird feeders to survive.

Why Rabbits are Abandoned

Why are so many domestic rabbits given up to shelters or turned loose? The 2006 study by the RSPCA listed owners losing interest, a move, and behavior problems as common reasons. The *Make Mine Chocolate! Rabbit Rescue Survey* of 2010 reported that 36% or rabbits entering rescues in the UK are surrendered within the first six months of ownership, and 59% within the first year. The top reason (34%) for surrendering a rabbit was a child losing interest and no longer wanting the rabbit. In the 2012 study of four US shelters, most rabbits were given up because the owners no longer wanted to take care of them. A researcher in Sweden found that the top three reasons given for surrendering rabbits in that country were lack of time (35.8%), owners are moving (16.6%), and allergies (13.2%). The author of a 2016 article that appeared in the *Telegraph* reported that 80% of bunnies bought specifically at Easter will be given up or die from neglect within a year. The Massachusetts SPCA reported the top three reasons given for surrendering rabbits to them were a child losing interest, the owners had too many rabbits, or the people surrendering the rabbit claimed they were bringing in a stray. In a 2018 UK study, researchers found that younger rabbits tended to be given away for rabbit-related reasons and older rabbits for human-related reasons. In most studies in both the US and UK the majority of surrendered rabbits were unaltered adults.

All the studies on reasons rabbits are surrendered rest on the assumption the person surrendering the rabbit is telling the truth, of course. But if one assumes that at least most are telling the truth it appears that a child losing interest and lack of time and/or desire to care for the rabbit are the most common reasons for surrender. Given that most surrenders are unaltered adults, not wanting to pay for a spay or neuter may be another reason, as may behavior problems stemming

from the rabbit's unaltered state. Two other things that any shelter operator will tell you affect a surrender are the size and breed of the rabbit. In general, fewer small, lop-eared rabbits are surrendered than larger, up-eared, all-white or all-black rabbits.

A final reason for surrender has to do with rabbits' status among the general public, i.e. the perception of rabbits as a "starter pet." When children (or adults) become bored with a rabbit, the family often adopts a dog or cat. The rabbit is then either surrendered or neglected. Authors of a 2006 study found that dogs receive far more attention and have far more money spent on them than cats. How much further down the ladder would be the poor rabbit! There is a hierarchy among pets, and dogs are unquestionably at the top. If people would spend even one-quarter the time and money on their rabbits they do their dogs, they might discover that rabbits, although different, can also be entertaining, affectionate companion animals. But until the general public is better educated about rabbits they will continue to be displaced by more common pets.

The Fate of Rabbits Let Loose to Fend for Themselves

Those of us who are active in rabbit rescue know that unfortunately rabbits are often viewed as disposable pets – small, inexpensive, easy-to-care-for and short-lived (although none of those perceptions are true).Rabbits are often brought into a home on a whim and as casually tossed out to fend for themselves. Many otherwise bright people honestly believe that rabbits will be just fine fending for themselves. They're not. One of the best posters on abandoned rabbits I've seen pictures a young rabbit sitting amongst vegetation with the caption "Could you survive on your own in the wilderness with no supplies?

Neither could I. Please don't dump me."

Rabbits formerly kept as companion animals do not have the survival skills that native rabbits have honed throughout their lives, and their coloring often makes them easy targets for predators. Nor do they know where to find food, water and shelter in an unfamiliar area. If any are fortunate enough to find food and shelter, they may yet fall prey to disease, parasites or wild predators, be struck by vehicles, savaged

by dogs, or intentionally killed by people who do not like them in their gardens or on their property. No, domestic rabbits are not "just fine" fending for themselves. Stephen Guida, an experienced rabbit rescuer and volunteer with Brambley Hedge Rabbit Rescue of Phoenix, Arizona, tells about the fates of some of the abandoned rabbits he has seen:

Some of my Experiences with Dumped and Abandoned Rabbits

by Stephen Guida

I can remember back in 2010 Brambley Hedge Rabbit Rescue began hearing reports of a number of domestic rabbits running loose in a greenbelt area, a tract of relatively open space between housing developments. We went to get a look at the situation and found approximately eight to ten rabbits, mostly Lionheads, which had been abandoned in the area. Capturing them is always a challenge, since rabbits are smart and fast, and can dash into yards and under fences before anyone could even get close. We found a neighbor on the side of the greenbelt who had video from her surveillance camera. It showed a woman and a young girl pull up in a car, removed a large cage from the back of their car, and dump out a number of rabbits by the side of the road. The rabbits looked quite young, and were momentarily dazed at the freedom suddenly thrust upon them. Slowly they dispersed through the neighborhood. We tried capturing them over the next week, and were able to bring four or five of them to our shelter. The others gradually disappeared, either taken by predators or migrated to another area. We later found out that every community in the area has their own laws and regulations regarding the dumping of domestic animals, and we were deeply frustrated to learn that even if we could identify and locate the woman who did the dumping, she would be immune from any legal prosecution since the community had no laws covering such an action.

Where the dumping actually occurs has other ramifications. One rabbit dump occurred in July of 2012, in a county park that is part of a local waterway. The area was quite arid that time of year and ridden with gullies, washes, and steep hills. We estimated about 12-15 domestic rabbits were loose in the area, including about 4-5 very young ones. The terrain made trapping the rabbits extremely difficult, and the native vegetation was mostly wide, squat shrubs and bushes, bristling with thorns. The rabbits could run under them and hide with great ease, and trying to get them out from under the bushes was nearly impossible. The weather was quite brutal, and we could only mount our rescue efforts in the early morning before the heat got too extreme. When the temperature started edging close to 100 degrees and it was only 10a.m., we had to call it a day. The whole area was extremely dry and food very scarce. I remember cornering one young rabbit in a small hole, where it was trying to hide, huddled next to a dead sibling. I was able to save that one, but I think we were able to rescue only five out of the group. Eventually they all disappeared.

Rabbit dumps in the city itself present unique challenges. Rabbits abandoned in a neighborhood quickly map out many escape routes for themselves. They can quickly dash from one yard to another, under fences and gates. Of course we cannot enter anyone's property to try and capture the rabbits without their express permission, and not everyone is inclined to give it. One rescue operation began in a person's large, relatively open yard, but the rabbits were able to run under a fence into the neighbor's yard, which was wall-to-wall abandoned cars.

Again a situation that was perfectly suited to the rabbits' ability to dart under the cars and easily run from one to the other, and very difficult for the human rescuers. City rabbit dumps are fraught with danger, not only from predators such as dogs and cats, but occasionally coyotes will come into town seeking a meal. Depending on the area, hawks and owls are also a very serious danger. Vehicular traffic is everywhere, and many rabbits end up being run over by a car.

Human attitudes toward domestic rabbits and abandonment situations can be very frustrating and vexing. Many people do not understand the difference between domestic and native rabbits, and think that any unwanted rabbit can be released into the outdoors, where they think they will meet up with a pack of native rabbits and live happily ever after. In some cases no amount of arguing will convince them that things like that never happen, and domestic rabbits are woefully unable to cope with the very harsh conditions of the desert. The heat is lethal to them, they are not adapted to the environment, they do not know where the sources of food and water are, and the many different predators almost guarantee they will live short, brutal lives. One time we received reports of domestic rabbits loose on a local golf course. While there were sources of food and water for them, most of them where white rabbits with multicolored markings, and as such they were highly visible to predators. We talked to the owners of the golf course but they insisted that the rabbits "belonged" there, despite the fact that they were domestic, not native. They refused to allow us to capture the rabbits and take them to safety. The rabbits roamed off the golf course and into the surrounding neighborhood, but again the resident we contacted said they really enjoyed having "their" rabbits in the neighborhood, in spite of the fact that they did nothing to feed or care for the rabbits, and would not allow us to try to capture the rabbits.

Perhaps the saddest and most frustrating kind of rabbit abandonment I have ever had to deal with was when people move out of their home, and leave their pet rabbit(s) behind. They move out all the furniture and the only thing they leave in the house is their pet rabbit, INSIDE a cage, with a small amount of food and water. It is unfathomable to me how anyone could do that to an innocent, defenseless animal that presumably they once cared for. It is so galling to know that there are options for a rabbit in that situation, in the form of the local humane society or rabbit rescue groups, where at least the rabbit will be cared for and given an opportunity to find a new home. But how people can leave a rabbit behind in a completely empty house, with ZERO chance of survival, and facing a gruesome, horrible, lingering death due to starvation and lack of water, is something I would never understand no matter how many lifetimes I have. It's these kind of situations, where the casual cruelty and ignorance of humans is on full display, that stay with animal rescuers for a long time, and make us realize the great potential for evil in this world.

Community Rabbits

Some of the rabbits dumped to live on their own in the wild or in parks and empty lots do manage to survive for at least a while. If any of these are unaltered, which they often are, they may breed and add to the colony. People who see the rabbits living on their own may dump more at the same site, and the colony grows. Domestic rabbits living in these colonies are known by several terms: feral rabbits, colony rabbits, community rabbits. (Technically the feral rabbits are the domestic rabbits born in the wild; the domestic rabbits that are dumped are abandoned pets.) But even though the rabbits in these colonies manage to live, it is not an easy existence. Many are thin and malnourished, most have evidence of fight or predator wounds, abscesses, bone breaks, disease and parasites.

If the colony rabbits persist long enough or the colony becomes large enough, the rabbits may cause problems for local landowners, businesses, or governments. Feral domestic rabbits in Texas are now listed as an invasive species, and are described as aggressive foragers who reproduce rapidly and out-compete native mammals for scarce resources. The feral rabbits in Helsinki, Finland are said to have caused costly damage to parks and buildings. Local officials in Langley, Washington complain that the rabbits burrow in the football fields, destroy the foundations of buildings, and pose health risks. And in many cities from Stockholm, Sweden to Calgary, Alberta, feral rabbits are considered a problem because of the damage they do to landscaping.

Unfortunately, the means taken to control or eradicate these feral rabbits may not be what many would consider humane. Some – most often on private property – are poisoned. Other rabbits are rounded up and killed. Officials of one Washington town have considered releasing raptors to help control feral rabbit populations, and in Alaska many of the feral rabbits captured and turned in by residents near Juneau were euthanized and fed to raptors. In Stockholm rabbits were shot and their bodies (along with those of other unwanted animals) burned as biofuel to heat homes. And in countries where European rabbits (descendants of released rabbits) caused extensive damage to agriculture and native ecosystems, such as Australia and New Zealand, diseases such as rabbit viral hemorrhagic disease and myxomatosis have been introduced to kill rabbits.

It cannot be denied that feral domestic rabbit populations that get out of control can present a difficult problem for governments to solve. But we in animal rescue remember what others ignore – these rabbits did not choose to be abandoned and live wild. They were dumped and abandoned by irresponsible humans who are not held to account for their ignorance and/or cruelty. The humans suffer no adverse consequences for their deeds. The rabbits do.

Why Shelters and Re-homing are Not Enough

Many of those who contributed to this book work tirelessly to rescue and find homes for abandoned rabbits. Some rescue individuals or small groups of dumped rabbits, others have participated in huge colony rescues, all with the goal of saving the lives and finding homes for as many of the abandoned rabbits as possible. The ideal would be for all dumped and feral domestic rabbits to be rescued, go to shelters, and eventually be adopted out to good homes where they would receive the love and care they deserve. *The reality is that this is not going to happen.* Some abandoned rabbits will find a happy ending through the efforts of dedicated rescuers and committed animal lovers, but there are not enough rescuers, not enough shelters, and not enough people who appreciate the unique qualities of rabbits to adopt the huge numbers of unwanted domestic rabbits.

Many multi-species shelters do not accept rabbits, and those that do rarely, if ever, allocate the same resources to rabbits as they do to dogs and cats. Rabbits are not as popular as dogs and cats and this means rabbits don't have as high an adoption rate, which translates to higher cost per animal to maintain rabbits until they are adopted. Medical costs too are often higher for rabbits than dogs and cats, so many multi-species shelters are reluctant to take rabbits. One humane society that took captured feral rabbits from the Juneau area and tried to find homes for them was soon in a bad financial position because so few residents in the area had any interest in adopting rabbits. Even among those interested in adopting rabbits not everyone adopts from a shelter. The authors of a 2015 study of UK rabbit owners reported that only about 29% of rabbits were adopted from shelters.

Rabbit-only shelters are overwhelmed with calls to take unwanted rabbits and must either turn them away or take on more than the shelter is equipped to handle. In the latter case over-stretched space and other resources may lead to sub-standard care, burnout of volunteers, and sometimes even the eventual closure of a much-needed shelter.

Human impatience factors in as well. In one case a woman asked a shelter to take several rabbits. The shelter did not have room at the time, but the woman was asked to wait and promised that the shelter would work to make room. The woman tired of waiting and turned the rabbits loose.

What, then, is the answer? There is no single answer, but there are many partial answers. Of these, education is the most important. We must employ more effective methods of educating the general public about the consequences of dumping rabbits, and better prepare adopters for the realities of caring for rabbits. Beyond education, we must implement new strategies for placing, housing, and caring for the thousands of rabbits that are rescued. If we implement enough of these strategies we **can** help many of these unwanted, discarded rabbits.

Why Rescue?

Some might wonder why we rabbit rescuers and advocates are even willing to try and take on such a daunting challenge. The answer lies with the nature of the rabbits themselves and our love for them. We want each unwanted discarded rabbit to have a chance at a fulfilling life, a life that can be as fulfilling for the person who takes that rabbit into his or her home as for the rabbit:

I'm Still Learning from Mimmo

by Mac Morrison

Sometimes animals come into our lives and we are forever grateful to have known them – not just for being cute or fun but for the lessons we learned as the result of knowing them. Mimmo was like that. No one who ever got to know him ever doubted that he was a Teacher in a bunny suit. Most of us were changed permanently by his love. To this day I contend he was a wise being who knew what he was doing…

Mimmo came into rescue when a veterinarian called us and asked if we would take him on. He had been brought in after being starved and allowed to tangle his legs in chicken wire, and now he had severe infections in both hind legs. His cruel owners refused treatment, asking the vet to euthanize him. But after they left, the doctor sat with this poor rabbit, who gazed at him with great affection and then kissed him on the hand. The vet decided that if this rabbit was trying so hard to live he would give him a chance.

So Mimmo came to us after multiple surgeries and antibiotics and lived on clean towels in our bathroom. He had soft brown eyes like a fawn, and what seemed like a slight smile on his face. He greeted me with enthusiasm and great joy whenever he saw me. As his legs became more functional he would try to spin and dance around me, and would lay in my arms after his dose of medicine and leg soaking and snuggle and kiss my hands.

This was our beginning but I soon came to see that his love for humanity in general was a gift. Mimmo was about to change my perception of the world and teach me about love in ways I didn't know I needed.

As Mimmo grew stronger and more healed he was moved into my bedroom where he began sleeping on the bed with me. I made steps for him and he would climb up and lay next to my head on the extra pillow. In the middle of the night he would wash my face, and sometimes fall asleep so soundly that he would roll off the bed. I began padding the edges of the bed with towels so he wouldn't hurt himself.

Then came Scooter. She was a six- week-old white baby rabbit who had been thrown away the day after Easter and apparently attacked by a creature that almost killed her. She was found on a sidewalk and brought into the vet who called us. "I don't think there's any chance she'll make it" he said. She had been torn up, legs broken, head half-smashed. I brought her home, laid her on clean towels in a cat cage and got her to eat a little something.

Then Mimmo saw her. He ambled up and reached in, washing her little face. It was the first time I saw real animation in her eyes. He lay down near the cage and refused to leave. I brought him a bed to lay on and he was like a guardian, watching over her. And miraculously, over days and weeks, Scooter began to heal. Like Mimmo, she would never have full use of all her legs, but she was growing and eating and her head had stopped swelling. She would lie against the cage next to Mimmo, trying to use his warm side as a pillow.

Over months as she healed we let her out of the cage and she and Mimmo had to live in a large X-pen because the world was too hazardous for her to navigate. They would spend hours kissing and lying together.

One of our young volunteers was a girl who had a disability and she especially loved Mimmo and Scooter because of their "crippled legs". I told her that vets sometimes had to put down animals with severe injuries and she replied, "But look at how Mimmo and Scooter are so full of love! What if someone said that about me? I have crippled legs too!" She helped me to see the value of a life well lived – even if all the moving parts were not there or didn't work perfectly.

Mimmo loved to visit with friends and he seemed to especially care for those who were in some way wounded. My friend who was going through a devastating divorce. My friend who had been diagnosed with cancer. A volunteer who had never been able to have a loving relationship due to some mental illness. Children who came to see the rescue bunnies from a foster home. Mimmo's open-hearted and joyful greeting often took them aback. They had never had a rabbit look them square in the eye with such a kind and discerning gaze! He would lay in their laps until they had to leave, giving them gentle kisses and cuddles.

And Mimmo changed me. Like him, I had lived through an abusive relationship. Like him, I had become wounded in ways I never thought

I could recover from. Like him, I wanted the world to see my good heart and love, but I feared all they saw was the brokenness. In the back of my mind, I feared that no one would love me because I wasn't "whole" and perfect.

What I realized was that Mimmo was showing me I lesson I had heard before but never truly believed – true love casts out fear. Real and genuine love transcends our failings and hurts. And that love can heal and mend if we are open to it. Having an open and giving heart in spite of past wounds can be the hardest thing to allow…and yet, in spite of everything Mimmo trusted me. He knew I was committed to him. If I made mistakes he was quick to forgive me, because he recognized that my heart was in the right place.

Then one sunny Saturday morning I was in a devastating four car collision, hit by a drunk driver who pinned my car in the middle of crashing steel. Miraculously, I lived through it, but the next two years I would spend in and out of a wheelchair, doing physical therapy and struggling to remember the names of things. Strangely, I had no fear about this. I see now – looking back on it – that Mimmo's example of bravery and perseverance had really inspired me.

I worked my way out of that wheelchair with hard work, pain and a few tearful days. And Mimmo was my buddy through it all, sitting for hours in my lap, ever happy to see me and exuding his special brand of goofy love.

Mimmo and his beloved Scooter lived with me for a total of seven years – far outliving all predictions and enjoying every moment of their lives. Mimmo never lost his smile, his joyful greetings, his love for everyone – no exceptions.

In November of 2004 he began to suffer. At first he could not get up and hobble on his back legs as he had done since his recovery. He could only lie on a blanket with a diaper, and I had to hand feed him. The vet said he would not live long. We put him on painkillers knowing that his time was limited. Soon he could not hold his head up. My partner and I were devastated. We could see the happy look in his eyes for us, the spark of love was still strong… and yet, we knew he was suffering. The day we took him to the vet to be euthanized was maybe the hardest day of my life. He wanted so desperately to live that it took three shots to stop his heartbeat.By then, everyone in the room was sobbing openly as we said goodbye.

We brought his body home so that Scooter could say farewell. She lay next to his body, trying to keep him warm and revive him with kisses. She kept looking at me as if to ask, "Where did he go?" After a few hours, we had to take his body away. She lay staring off into space.

It's been all this time and yet I can remember his joyful greeting as if it were yesterday. The lessons he taught me about courage, self-forgiveness and love will stay with me forever. I hope that where he is now he is whole and happy, jumping and playing in the grass in a perfect place with a God who knows him well.

Perfect love does cast out fear. Mimmo understood that better than so many of us humans.

And, even now…I'm still learning from Mimmo.

CHAPTER 2: HOARDING

A chapter on hoarding in a book about abandoned rabbits may at first glance appear misplaced. But the unfortunate reality is that most rabbits in hoarding situations, although ostensibly receiving care, have in fact been abandoned to terrible living conditions and ill health. Hoarding not infrequently leads to more literal abandonment as well. Rabbits may escape from a hoarder or unaltered rabbits may breed and a colony develop on a hoarder's property. Even in cases where the hoarder keeps the rabbits indoors, rabbits may breed and increase to the point that indoor rabbits live feral lives. One rescuer was called in to a case where the rabbits in a hoarder's home had invaded every piece of furniture and were essentially surviving as feral rabbits inside the house.

Debby and I were very fortunate to have two highly experienced and respected people in animal rescue contribute pieces for this chapter: Faith Maloney, co-founder of Best Friends Animal Society, and Caroline Charland, founder of the Bunny Bunch Rabbit Rescue and Bunny Bunch Boutique.

Best Friends Animal Society is a nationwide animal rescue and advocacy organization and operates the largest sanctuary for homeless animals in the United States. Faith Maloney, a co-founder of Best Friends, is a consultant on animal care at the sanctuary in Kanab, Utah, and advises people around the world on how to start sanctuaries. Faith has interacted with many hoarders over her long career in animal rescue. In the following piece she explains what hoarding is and what signs to watch for.

Hoarding Rabbits: What were they Thinking?
by Faith Maloney

My first experience with animal hoarding happened, in of all places, Las Vegas. Who would expect to see a single rabbit in Las Vegas, much less hundreds? But it was 1996, and I got the call at Best Friends Animal Society that a lady in Las Vegas had a lot of rabbits in her yard and needed some help. A team of us drove down to take a look. The house was modest and situated on a back street, far from the hustle and bustle of Las Vegas life, but the front yard was teeming with rabbits of all ages, sizes and colors.

She said she did not know rabbits could be spayed or neutered, but I knew it was a lie. As a dog breeder, she did know about the birds and bees and how it all worked. She just didn't want to spay or neuter them. She really, really liked seeing baby rabbits running around her front yard. They were filling some kind of a hole in her life. It's not at all uncommon.

Rabbits seem to be an easy target for animal hoarders. They reproduce quickly so there are always going to baby rabbits around. I think we can all agree that baby rabbits are extremely cute. In this case, this woman's mental illness of animal hoarding was being satisfied at the expense of the lives of nearly 200 miserable rabbits.

Animal Hoarding is defined as: An individual possesses more than the typical number of companion animals. The individual is unable to provide even minimal standards of nutrition, sanitation, shelter and veterinary care, with this neglect often resulting in starvation, illness and death.

Hoarders fool themselves into thinking they do what they do out of the love of rabbits, or cats, or dogs, or whatever animal it is, when in fact, it's a compulsion that has little to do with love. Since they've fooled themselves, they also fool those around them. The Las Vegas woman was known in her area as the bunny lady. So, when a family needed to give up the pet rabbit they had bought to celebrate Easter who do they think to contact? The bunny lady of course. Unwittingly, the public contributes to the pain and suffering of that rabbit thinking they are helping.

I've talked with many, many animal hoarders over the last forty years and it still seems to come as a surprise to a lot of them that one person alone cannot adequately care for 200 animals of any kind. When we long for all that life running around us, we don't want to have to think out the logistics, it seems. But once the veil is lifted, and light is shone on the true living conditions of these animals, most people do seem to understand it. And once we have that understanding we can make different choices.

Exposure to this knowledge is the key. Letting the light shine into this very dark aspect of human nature that causes endless suffering to countless animals. People need to know this.

Animal hoarding is a sickness, so we do need to have some compassion for the perpetrators, but we cannot stand by and let them do it again and again. Psychologists acknowledge that this condition is very hard to treat. In the Las Vegas case the lure of those baby bunnies was like a drug to the woman. Others may see themselves as 'the only hope' of every animal, the only one who really loves them. The triggers might be different, but the results are always the same. Animals are going to pay a high price as a result of a damaged mind.

Cues we should all be looking for if we suspect animal hoarding:

- The individual has numerous animals but cannot say the total number of animals in their care. That's not normal; even people with many pets know the number. Another is they take any opportunity to acquire more and more, even though they are full beyond their capacity for care. The number of animals alone should not be seen as proof of animal hoarding because some people have the resources to care for more than a few animals. But it can be a red flag.

- Another sign of hoarding is that the person's environment is trashed and they rarely if ever let anyone come in to the home. There is a strong smell of ammonia, and floors may be covered with dried feces, urine, vomit, etc. Home service providers need to be aware of animal hoarding as they might be called in to fix plumbing or repair a furnace when others are kept out.

- The animals in a hoarder's care are emaciated, lethargic and not well-socialized. The condition of the animals is very revealing.

But care needs to taken to not accuse someone of lack of care when the animal in question has a known condition and is under medical care. Having a sick animal or two does not mean one is neglectful. But if *all* the animals are sick, and there are many, or there are some other clues in place, then it needs further examination.

Another sign is that the person usually, though not always, neglects personal care and stays away from other people. They may smell like animal urine. However, animal hoarding is a hidden crisis and some people conduct a normal life outside of the home. Their co-workers are shocked when the truth comes out as they presented well in the work place. But deteriorating grooming and dirtiness can be a sign to take a further look at how their animals are being cared for.

Yet another indication is that the individual insists that all of their animals are happy and healthy – even when there are clear signs of distress and illness. This belief is common in the hoarder's mind. And is often followed by statements that the animals love only them. (In other words, nobody else can adopt any of the animals because of this very close, monogamous relationship they're having. Despite, perhaps, the hoarder not being able to remember all of their names.)

Every year in the United States, a quarter of a million animals fall victim to hoarding. Rabbits can breed rapidly so the numbers can grow quickly when they end up in the grip of an animal hoarder. They are quiet so can be hidden from neighbors more easily than other animals. If we suspect someone is hoarding rabbits we need to contact the local authorities who can make sure the rabbits are rescued and the hoarder is offered psychological help. It's the best we can do for the rabbits we love.

Caroline Charland founded Bunny Bunch Rabbit Rescue in 1984, and Bunny Bunch Boutiquein 1986. Her examples of hoarding cases she has been involved with illustrate the wide variety of such cases and can provide experienced rescuers with hints on how to handle difficulties that may arise in dealing with hoarding situations. After reading Caroline's contributions Debby and I were amazed at how she is able to handle the volume of work she does, especially considering she also has a special interest in caring for disabled rabbits. Thank you Caroline!

Rabbit Hoarding and Abandonment
by Caroline Charland, Bunny Bunch Rabbit Rescue

Over the last thirty years of doing rabbit rescue I have encountered many rabbit hoarding and abandonment cases; the smallest hoarding case being twenty rabbits and the largest being over five hundred rabbits. In every situation the rabbits suffered, whether it was from neglect, being killed by predators, or, in one case, being killed by a person. I am leaving out a lot of the horrible details in the cases below as I want as many people as possible to read this article and learn from it. Below are brief descriptions of some of the hoarding cases I have dealt with:

San Dimas, California. Backyard Hoarder

The first hoarding case I ever did was when fifty-five rabbits were confiscated by animal control from someone's back yard. The rabbits were kept outside in hutches and most of them were adults. Animal control called us to see if we could take the rabbits if the owner agreed to sign them over to Bunny Bunch. (If the rabbits had gone to the local shelter it would have caused the rabbits at the shelter to be euthanized to make room for the new ones.) The hoarder did sign them over and Bunny Bunch took in all the rabbits. Afterwards the person who had hoarded the rabbits started coming to Bunny Bunch events, asking about her rabbits. Hoarders tend to have mental illness and can be hard to deal with as they don't seem to understand reality.

Chino, California 300 Abandonment

We received a call from animal control asking if we could take on a case where hundreds of rabbits were living loose in a neighborhood. The houses were all horse properties so they had a lot of land. One of the neighbors had moved out and left behind several rabbits. The rabbits of course bred and soon there were hundreds. One of the neighbors cared about the rabbits and was kind enough to let us build temporary rabbits enclosures on her property so we could keep the rabbits there during this rescue. It can be hard to catch rabbits that have been born outside, but you can't give up. You have to catch every single rabbit or else there will be hundreds more. We even dug up the burrows looking for babies so no one was left behind.

Pasadena, California Hoarding Case

I was called by someone who would frequent Bunny Bunch events. He said he had become ill and wasn't able to take care of all his rabbits anymore and asked if Bunny Bunch could take some. I said we could, and he drove twenty rabbits to my house that night. After seeing the rabbits were not in good shape I asked about visiting the rest of his rabbits. He refused. Later I received a call from one of his relatives. The man had been taken by ambulance to the hospital, as he needed physical and mental help. I went to the home with some of our Bunny Bunch volunteers and it was absolutely terrible. The smell of rabbit urine in the house was so unbearable we had to wear masks. The rabbits were living in cages that had not been cleaned for months. Dead rabbits were found left with live rabbits. These poor rabbits needed to get out right away. Bunny Bunch rescued many of them, and I believe some went to the local city shelter which has a good program in place for rabbits.

Northern California Breeder/Hoarder

This was a case where a breeder was out of control and not caring property for the rabbits. The breeder signed the rabbits over to Bunny Bunch and Animal Control took care of the legal matters with the breeder/hoarder. If I remember correctly about seventy rabbits were transported down to Bunny Bunch. These rabbits were mostly in good health but were badly in need of grooming.

Ontario, California Resident

Animal Control called us to help with this case. A man had been buying rabbits from the swap meet and keeping them in tiny cages, eachwith its own padlock, in his back yard. I felt it was obvious he must have suffered from mental illness, in fact I was surprised he was able to live alone. He had about thirty rabbits which he did not want to give to Animal Control, so he was given the option of giving them to Bunny Bunch. If he would not release them either to Bunny Bunch or Animal Control they would have been confiscated by Animal Control, and it would then have become a court case. This would mean that the rabbits would not be able to be rescued or adopted until the court case was settled, which could take many months. I accompanied Animal Control to the man's home and was able to persuade him to sign over his rabbits to Bunny Bunch.

Hollywood, California Front Yard Rescue

I received a call from a person who had bought six rabbits for his son about a year earlier. When the son lost interest and neither the son nor the father wanted to care for the rabbits the man let them loose in his front yard. Needless to say by the time we were called there were between fifty to sixty rabbits digging tunnels under the pathways and sidewalks. Bunny Bunch volunteers went out with exercise pens and were able to catch every one of them. The man who had let the rabbits loose in his yard asked if we would pay him so he could get back the money he had paid for the six rabbits he bought from a breeder. I of course said no. He then stole the exercise pens we had on his property for catching the rabbits.

Van Nuys, California Breeders/Hoarders

I received a call from Animal Control telling us there was a house with hundreds of rabbits in bad conditions in tiny cages in a back yard. I contacted the resident and made arrangements to go to the home. It was horrible! All the rabbits were outside in tiny, stacked, poop-filled metal cages. Many rabbits were ill. Two people owned all these rabbits; they had bred them and shown them for years, so many of the rabbits were older. One owner wanted us to take all the rabbits, but the other owner was not on board with that. After some convincing I was able to get them to sign over the older and sick rabbits to us. About twenty left that day to go to Bunny Bunch, and another rabbit rescue took quite a few. Bunny Bunch later made several trips back to get the rest.

Pomona, California Trailer Rescue

I received a call from our local Animal Control shelter saying they just confiscated sixty-plus rabbits that were being kept in two trailers by a hoarder. The shelter needed the rabbits to be moved from their facility because they did not have room for them and could only keep the rabbits for three days before their time would be up. I went to the shelter to assess the rabbits. Most of them were in good shape; their weight was good and they weren't too dirty, but some had ear mites and some had health problems.

Three days to figure out what to do with sixty plus rabbits! Bunny Bunch always has two hundred or more rabbits in our care so it's not an easy task to take more in. None of the rabbits from the hoarder were spayed or neutered, some had newborns and of course some would probably give birth in the next few days. I of course didn't want the rabbits to die so I got to work making arrangements to take them all in. I took two mums with babies and the rabbits with health problems, filling up the back of my car with carriers, and took them with me. I would return the next day for the rest.

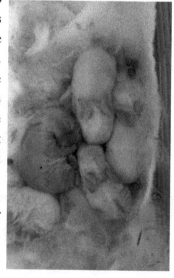

The Mum's and babies, plus the rabbits with health problems went to my house. I set up groups by sex at our Montclair rescue center in our classroom, quarantining them from any other rabbits. Because they were not spayed and neutered yet, the same sex groups had trouble makers that had to be separated out. They were all treated for ear mites and weregiven health checks. I then started making calls to the volunteers who foster for us; everyone came through for the rabbits and room was made for all of them. Spay and neuter appointments were set up right away, photos were taken, they were all given names, and files were made for each rabbit.

The following week a couple of men came to our rescue center. We felt something was off, for they were asking strange questions. We came to find out one was the person who had had all of these rabbits in his trailers. He was an older man, and apparently he had kept females in one trailer and males in the other. He had names for some of them. He had

been told by Animal Control that we had his rabbits and he wanted them back. Upon asking why he had all these rabbits he stated that he had started with a few and would find homes for their offspring. He did take them to the same rabbits vet we use when they had health problems. He had had a heart attack and while in the hospital the person feeding his rabbits put them all – males and females –together. In his own way the man loved his rabbits and was sad not to have them. Again we are dealing with someone who is thinking they are doing something good, without realizing the harm being done to the rabbits.

I was able to convince the man that the rabbits were better off with Bunny Bunch; that they would all be spayed or neutered, get vet care and eventually find homes as indoor rabbits. I told him he could come and visit his rabbits by appointment. I would never allow him to get back any of his rabbits and was relieved that the situation did not get out of hand. I only hope that Animal Control will check on a regular basis to make sure that the man does not get more rabbits. But that end is out of my control.

Westminster, California U-Haul Rabbits

I received a call from a man who said he had a lot of rabbits that needed a place to go right away. Animal Control had given him a certain amount of time for him to find homes for all of his rabbits. He said he

had over one hundred at his home and his time was up to find them homes. Bunny Bunch was over-loaded with the rabbits we already had in our rescue, plus we had just taken in the rabbits from the trailer hoarder case. But I still needed to find out how I could help, so I got his address and set up a time to go and see exactly what the situation was. My husband Tim and I prepared to go to the house that evening after Bunny Bunch had closed. We were just walking out the door when the hoarder called and said the rabbits were no longer at his house but were now in a different city (out of the jurisdiction of where he lived, so Animal Control for that area could no longer confiscate the rabbits). He gave me the new address and told me he had all the rabbits in the back of a U-Haul truck parked in a neighborhood outside his friend's house.

We drove to the new address and saw the U-Haul truck parked in the street with the back door rolled up. There were about thirty baby bunnies in a long wire cage on the grass next to the sidewalk; the rest were in the truck. I stepped into the back of the truck to get a good look at the rest. I felt sick; some of the rabbits were running loose, others were in horrible, filthy, rusty, tiny metal cages which must have been the same ones they had been living in inside his house. The rabbits were thin and dirty, and none were spayed or neutered.

I knew Bunny Bunch was full, but there was no way I could leave these rabbits to be dumped. I had to come up with a plan. I had to be pleasant and friendly to the two owners of the rabbits in order to get them to trust me, so I could help these rabbits. In their eyes there was nothing wrong with the way the rabbits were being kept. Again I am dealing with people with a mental illness. One of the owners started telling me how much he loved his rabbits and didn't want to give them up. He also told me that he was the one that was on the news last year when the local shelter confiscated two to three hundred rabbits from this home. I now knew who he was. The problem was that Animal Control left him with twelve rabbits and didn't require that they were spayed or neutered. So he just started letting them breed and collected more.

I decided to take the rabbits that were in the worst shape. I got an owner release signed so the rabbits we were taking then belonged to

Bunny Bunch. I told the owners that we would be back in the morning to get the rest of the rabbits. Even though Bunny Bunch did not have room I had to come up with a plan to save the rest of the rabbits.

We got home around 11p.m., and after doing health checks and giving needed medical care, I got the rabbits set up into pens and settled in at my house. I found out who did the Animal Control for that city. Thank goodness I knew who they were. I was in luck, for it was run by an exotic vet we used for our rabbits. However, Icould not reach them that night so I called the police department and was told they were all busy and to call back in the morning.

At 6 a.m. I called the owner of the rabbits telling them not to move the truck and that we would be coming back. That would buy us some time. I got hold of the police department and Animal Control. The police sent cars to surround the U-Haul truck so the people could not take off with the rabbits. Animal Control showed up and took the rest of the rabbits to their shelter where the vet assessed and sexed the rabbits. They were safe! The hoarders were charged with one hundred and twenty-five counts of animal cruelty. Bunny Bunch took in more of the rabbits from Animal Control as space permitted.

Volunteer/hoarders

I have encountered several individuals over the years who want to volunteer with rabbit rescues that are actually hoarders. You can generally tell early on that there is something that is not quite right about them. They can be well educated, well-spoken people so don't let that fool you. But they are often dressed in older clothes that are not very clean. Their cars tend to have a lot of junk filling up the whole car. They are often very helpful and will even bring donations, but rescuers beware! I have found that once it is recognized by the rescue that something is not quite right, the person disappears and moves on to another rescue. Often that rescue is so thankful to have a volunteer the person is accepted and the same cycle starts again.

The problem is these people keep pulling rabbits from shelters and hoarding them in their homes. Some go to the exotic vets with their animals when they are sick, but they don't tend to have much money so they often rack up bills at the vet's office that will go unpaid. They then are refused service and the rabbits don't get treated.

The conditions the rabbits are kept in are terrible. They are often in small cages that are not cleaned, or the rabbits are all living together, pooping and peeing where they please in a room of the house or apartment (nearly always rented). Once the landlord finds out, Animal Control is called.

I have known several of these hoarders over the years. Time after time I see other rescues try to help them by taking all their rabbits in and cleaning up the hoarder's home only to find a few months later the home is a mess again and full of rabbits not being cared for.

Helping rabbits in hoarding situations

How do we help rabbits in circumstances like these? It's a hard situation all around. Rabbits suffer and die because of these people. The problem is the people suffer from mental illness, and when you take away their rabbits they get more. In their own minds they think the rabbits are better off with them than in any other situation. The people often want recognition and praise from others, and they do not want to give up their rabbits.

Another problem is where will these rabbits go when rescued? Here in Southern California we have a terrible problem with homeless rabbits. Bunny Bunch normally has about two hundred rabbits all time in our adoption centers and in foster homes. We have hundreds at all times waiting to come in. We generally get over ten calls a day to take in rabbits that are unwanted by the people that have them, have been found dumped in parks, or from city and county shelters that are over-full and asking for help so they don't have to euthanize. Bunny Bunch has a very successful rescue, we have wonderful foster homes, lots of volunteers, and two rescue/adoption centers, and many great homes are found for our rescued rabbits. So we are sometimes able to take on hoarder cases as room permits.

The rabbits from hoarding situations need to get to safety the quickest way possible. How do you do that? For a hoarder case you need to get the hoarder to trust you. As hard as this may be you have to be nice to them, listen to their stories about their rabbits and how much they love them and how great they care for them. Even though you are seeing terrible conditions, bringing this up could scare them off and prevent you from rescuing the rabbits. Once you have the hoarder's trust you need an owner release form for them to fill out, signing all the rabbits over to your rescue. It's a good idea to come up with a plan right away so you can get the rabbits out of there, the sooner the better.

It is also good to work with Animal Control. They can take care of the legal part of the abuse and neglect and take the abusers to court for animal cruelty. It is important to stay in touch with Animal Control after everything is completed; reminding them to go to the home to make sure no more rabbits have been taken in.

Once the rabbits come to Bunny Bunch, I sex and do health checks on all of them. They are named, photographs taken, and a file made for each rabbits. We then set the rabbits up in exercise pens with beds and litter boxes full of hay. In some cases, we house same sex groups together and get them all spayed and neutered right away (apart from any

that are not well enough for the operation). We nurse the sick rabbits back to health. One particular rabbit comes to mind as I write. She gave birth in a carrier in the back of my car on the way home from a hoarding case. She had a broken front leg and a huge abscess on the other front leg. But she fed all of her babies and they all survived. Her broken leg had to be amputated. Rabbits have a strong will to survive; and they can learn to trust humans even after going through horrible abuse.

It is heart-wrenching to deal with any kind of animal abuse. I have seen things that keep me up at night, and that I will never be able to forget. But staying positive, being able to work well with all kinds of people, and keeping the end goal in mind keeps me going. Every single rabbit deserves kindness and a wonderful home.

CHAPTER 3: RABBITS KILLED AT LAS VEGAS DUMPSITE

As Faith Maloney commented in her Chapter 2 contribution, "Who would expect to see a single rabbit in Las Vegas, much less hundreds?" One would not think the hot desert climate would be conducive to domestic rabbits; in general they do not do well at temperatures above 84° Fahrenheit, and temperatures in southern Nevada can climb to over 100 degrees. Yet not only does Las Vegas have a feral domestic rabbit problem, it is a long-standing one that keeps growing. The rabbits, like the people, survive by staying mostly in the city where introduced plant species and buildings provide some protection from desert heat.

I first became aware of the feral rabbits in Las Vegas about ten years ago when rescuers were attempting to find homes for rabbits that had been living on a golf course. I offered to adopt one, and ended up with two (bringing the number of my personal rabbits up to fourteen at that time). Many of those rabbits were captured and saved, but it did not end the problem, for more rabbits kept being  dumped, and golf courses were popular dumping sites. News stories about abandoned rabbits on golf courses appeared again in the years between 2011 and 2014, and there were reports of rabbits being dumped in places other than golf courses, such as parks and empty lots. By 2016 one internet story had the headline "Rabbits dumped in abundance across Las Vegas Valley," and in 2017, "Abandoned Bunnies are Multiplying and Taking Over Las Vegas."

Rabbit advocates and rescuers were not idle during these years. On the contrary, they were working tirelessly to combat the dumping itself and to rescue rabbits that had been dumped. Yet the problem kept getting worse. Why weren't they successful? There were many reasons: sufficient donors could not be found to finance enough large educational campaigns such as Debby Widolf's "Don't dump rabbits" billboards; there were conflicts with local businesses and government; the rescuers themselves could not always agree on the best way to deal with the problem; there were not enough shelters to take the rabbits and not enough volunteers.

Debby and I had already begun working on this book when one of the Las Vegas feral rabbit colony situations turned into tragedy as many feral colony rabbits died horribly; apparently killed by people that were upset the colony of rabbits was there. Early on there was an attempt to poison the rabbits; later a text message conversation between volunteers reported an attempt to kill the rabbits by dumping antifreeze on the rabbits' food. But the worst killings occurred in February. "Outrage Follows Mysterious Mass Bunny Murder," read a February 2018 headline. Initial reports stated that over two dozen rabbits died by poisoning, but at the time of this writing necropsies have revealed many of the rabbits had major trauma and were possibly beaten to death. It is also now suspected that the actual number of rabbits killed may be much higher than originally thought, as reports have come in that some of the dead rabbits may have been removed from the site shortly after being killed.

Because this particular dumped/feral rabbit colony case involved so many of the difficulties rescuers find in such cases around the globe, we felt that a detailed case study of this Las Vegas colony would be useful to include in Part I of this book. It illustrates both how such a situation arises and many of the problems and pitfalls involved in attempting to rescue rabbits at a large colony and dump site.

Las Vegas Feral Rabbit Colony Case Study
by Debby Widolf

As a rabbit advocate and former manager of the Best Friends Animal Society's Bunny House in Kanab, Utah, I became aware of the plight of abandoned domestic rabbits in Las Vegas in 2008. I received a phone call that year asking if we had room to take in rabbits that had been dumped on a golf course in Las Vegas. Thus began my introduction to the colonies of rabbits that had developed as a result of irresponsible and illegal dumping on golf courses in and around the city. Little did I know that during this same period a state mental health facility in Las Vegas released several unspayed and unneutered domestic rabbits on the large grounds surrounding the buildings. It has been reported that staff of the health facility thought the presence of the rabbits would be entertaining for their patients. Perhaps a well-intended idea, it was one that had not been researched as to either short term or long term consequences of releasing domestic rabbits to survive on their own in an especially hostile environment.

Rabbits, being prey animals, reproduce prolifically and can produce as much as a litter per month, each litter usually comprised of five to ten kits. Even though most of these young ones do not live to see their first year, reproduction begins early in those that do survive, and the numbers of rabbits can quickly grow even when conditions are dire. It is estimated that the population at the mental health grounds contained around 1,000 rabbits at its peak!

The mental health facility was not the only site in Las Vegas with colonies of feral rabbits. Many parks, such as the Floyd Lamb State Park, have developed feral rabbit populations due to the dumping of rabbits. As numbers grow, rabbits move from dumping sites into neighborhoods. One rabbit rescue volunteer, Dave Schweiger speaks about feral domestic rabbits in his neighborhood in NW Las Vegas and others throughout the city. His family trapped the feral rabbits, had them spayed or neutered and then returned them to their property to stop the breeding. Some were also adopted and five went to an out of state rescue for re-homing. The actual number of abandoned rabbits in the Las Vegas area is unknown, however a fair estimate over the past ten years is in the thousands. The Nevada Society for the Prevention of Cruelty to Animals spokesperson stated that the SPCA in Las Vegas has 100 plus rabbits waiting for homes and adoption rates are only around twelve per month, and they do not have room to take in all the rabbits needing a space in the shelter.

Looking out over a grassy park populated with abandoned rabbits may appear pastoral, but what one sees is highly deceptive. Rescue volunteers report that during the spring and fall the properties provide some grasses and maybe water from sprinklers, but once the brutal weather of summer and winter arrives the rabbits suffer without assistance from volunteers. Domestic rabbits do not have the means to survive extreme weather conditions, attacks from predators, illnesses, traffic deaths and the evil actions of some humans. Rescuers often pay out of pocket for the food and vet care they provide the rabbits. A report from 2016 found that in one of the dump sites rabbits had been poisoned, and extreme injuries were seen, sometimes resulting in rescuers having to take rabbits to a vet to have them euthanized.

Over the ten-year time period the colony at the mental health facility grew the rescues and grassroots volunteers were not idle, but there was only so much they could do. In the earlier years of the state mental health facility rabbit dumpsite, little help or funding was available. In 2015 the state of Nevada provided funds to a local animal rescue to "fix" the rabbit situation. But the money was only enough to relocate, spay/neuter, and provide necessary vet care for around 200 rabbits. These rabbits then stayed at the rescue until placement could be found with other rescues and shelters, most of which are always at capacity. While this resulted in less rabbits at the dumpsite for a short time, the population was soon back where it had been, and the suffering from exposure and lack of food continued, although volunteers never ceased doing what they could to alleviate the rabbits' plight.

Other people were more interested in eliminating the rabbits than helping them. On June 11, 2017, volunteer rescuers discovered "poison boxes." Metal boxes which contained poisoned food were attached to the sides of buildings at the site. The entrances to the poison traps were large enough for the smaller and younger rabbits to enter. Equally tragic was that other animals such as birds, squirrels and small pets could also eat the poisoned food.

Rescuers knew that if they spayed and neutered rabbits at the mental health facility it would help keep the population from growing until a more permanent solution could be found. However, they were informed by authorities that this would not be allowed, for returning rabbits to the site after they had been spayed or neutered would constitute abandonment, which was against the law. (Whether this was actually correct is debatable; see "Legal Issues" in Chapter 5.) Prevented from taking this action, volunteers continued to care for the rabbits as best they could.

In early 2018 another crisis developed. According to some reports, complaints about the rabbits at the facility led to local government taking more action. On January 10, 2018, an employee working in one of the buildings on the state property where the site was located removed the water and food bowls volunteers had put out for the rabbits. She was contacted about her actions, but again removed the rabbits' food and water dishes during the night after they had been replaced by volunteers. The situation was eventually resolved, but time that volunteers needed for finding shelters to take the rabbits and care for the injured ones was set back by this cruel and insensitive action.

In February 2018, a state department of health team reported that the rabbits at the mental health facility could potentially be a risk for spreading disease to humans. Signs were posted on the property warning people not to go near or to feed the rabbits. This claim that the public was in danger from zoonotic diseases carried by rabbits was refuted by many whose work required knowledge of animal - human transmission of identified diseases. Veterinarian Nicole Smee, who is the founder of "All Creatures Sanctuary" in Las Vegas, and works with the group "Bunnies Matter in Vegas Too," stated that one of the diseases if concern, tularemia, is not currently in the state of Nevada.

Perhaps the statement from the department of health was being used to open the way to remove and/or destroy the rabbits. Whatever the intent, the report worked to spread doubt and fear among the general public and complicated rescue efforts. But volunteers continued their efforts, publicizing the rescue and searching for shelters willing to take the abandoned rabbits.

The week following the posting of the warning signs, rescue teams were preparing to transport some rabbits to out-of-state rescues where they would be put up for adoption. On February 18, 2018 as the volunteers showed up to feed the dumpsite rabbits, they were devastated to find that dozens of rabbits were dead. Hands shaking, volunteer rescuer Stacey Taylor, founder of "Bunnies Matter in Vegas Too," took a video of the deceased rabbits, saying, "We are looking at the bodies of our friends." Erin Urano, founder of "Rusty and Furriends of Dumpsite Bunnies," found that a rock-built memorial she and volunteers had put up commemorating rabbits that had passed away at the dumpsite had been ripped apart during the night of the killings.

Initially it was suspected that the rabbits had been poisoned, and several of the dead rabbit's bodies underwent necropsies to try and determine the cause of death. Results of the necropsies indicated that the rabbits died of traumatic wounds likely caused by being clubbed to death. Rescue efforts went into crisis mode to get as many rabbits off the property quickly before more tragedies occurred. March 12, 2018, a reward of $5,000 was offered for information leading to the arrest and conviction of the person/s involved in the slaughter of the rabbits. Outrage spread across the country and abroad by animal advocates. The perpetrators have not been found as of this writing.

During February, March and April 2018, major transports went across the United States from Las Vegas, taking the rescued rabbits to no-kill shelters to find adoptive homes. Rescue groups started online fundraising sites to help pay for the transports. The House Rabbit Society awarded a $1,000 grant to the effort and sent Dawn Sailer of the House Rabbit Society chapter in Indiana to Las Vegas to help spearhead the transport efforts and placements. Lisa White and her team from Bunderground Railroad, along with independent transporters Jodie and Rodney, planned routes, prepared the rabbits, loaded vans, and drove through some inclement weather conditions to get the rabbits to safety. House Rabbit Society chapters across the nation helped by hosting the drivers and rabbits overnight as the transports passed through their states. Many others did much to make the transports happen.

I am writing this paragraph and the next not as criticism of any one person or group involved in this rescue, but rather as a learning tool and reminder. Transporting the large numbers of rabbits presented challenges: some logistical and financial, others caused by lack of communication, that occasionally resulted in hurt feelings and frustration in volunteers. Rescue work can cause tremendous stress that pushes volunteers to their limits. Sometimes when the differences among individuals or groups are unresolved, they splinter off and begin to work in parallel, each pursuing their goals, which appears to be what happened in Las Vegas. Progress can still be made when this division occurs, but without a workable connection to others interested in helping rabbits we will lose our collective power to make change and meet challenges.

Individual rescuers and rescue groups encountered numerous other challenges while attempting to help the abandoned rabbits at the mental health facility. As is often the case in animal rescue, personalities and differences in expectations also led to problems, as did lack of communication and miscommunication. It is understandable these difficulties occur in situations where volunteers are under great emotional stress. However, when frustrations spill over into social media gossip and attacks, this can drive volunteers away and result in diminishing donations and a lack of cooperation from outside officials and organizations. These tactics must stop if we are to reach our goal of saving rabbits' lives. Animal rescue requires a strong knowledge of one's own skills and limitations and also the ability to put yourself and your ego aside to focus on the goal of saving lives.

The hard work and devotion of those involved in the Las Vegas mental health facility dumpsite rescue resulted in many rabbits being adopted to loving and safe homes thanks to the established groups and grassroots individual rescuers and volunteers. The stories are all different as each rabbit brings his or her own individual essence to their new homes. There is "Lolo", a lovely Harlequin rabbit that was born at the dumpsite and had never had a home with humans. Her new human mom worked at one of the buildings on the property and volunteered to help feed the bunnies. On her birthday, she gave herself the gift of adopting little Lolo. What a gift of love for both! "Willow" was adopted and her new home reports that she is still leery of trusting people, which is not uncommon for an abandoned rabbit. "She is not a lap bunny, but she is loved and has found her home for life," says mom. And there is "Bella," whose person says that Bella rescued her. They live together in Los Angeles.

We must also remember the ones that didn't make it. "Vegas," rescued but suffering the effects of poisoning, died shortly after rescue. Frances was also rescued but was suffering from starvation and dehydration. Despite efforts to treat her, her body was beyond repair. Little Coda was found in horrible shape from major injuries and passed away four days later. These and so many others are a testament that domestic rabbits are not meant to survive on their own. More abandoned rabbits die than are rescued. Let us not forget them or the caring people that risk their hearts to provide care and kindness.

When writing this story about the rabbit rescue efforts in Las

Vegas, Nevada, I did my best to present it as a case study, that is, a look at what happened through my contact with those "on the ground," news articles, research, my own personal experiences, and what I have learned from involvement in the rescue of large numbers of abandoned domestic rabbits. There was much information to filter through, many conflicting reports about events and timelines, plus the differing perspectives of the individuals involved. I followed this rescue effort for several years and have great admiration for those who gave so much of themselves to save the lives of the rabbits. This story will continue with its lessons learned, the sorrow, and the triumphs. It is how we grow and become our best selves to help the rabbits and all animals on our journey.

Postscript December 2018: To date 700 rabbits from the mental health facility dumpsite have been rescued! Currently there are no abandoned domestic rabbits living at this site. Rescuers are now focusing on Floyd Lamb Park in Las Vegas, where several hundred more discarded rabbits need help.

CHAPTER 4: EDUCATION

Education is the single most important weapon in fighting the growing number of dumped rabbits. Dealing with the individual dumps and feral colonies is necessary, but the only hope of having a lasting impact on the problem of abandoned rabbits is through education and a change in the way rabbits are perceived. With the general public we must fight both the mistaken perception that rabbits are easy-care inexpensive starter pets, and we must also combat the idea that rabbits will be "just fine" if let loose to fend for themselves. We must also persuade those who are active in animal advocacy and rescue in general that expanding programs to include rabbits as well as more popular pets can be a positive public relations move and bring in donations from a new sector of the animal-loving public.

As I write these words I can imagine a few readers feeling a little indignant about now, thinking of the educational websites different rabbit organizations work hard to maintain which attack many generally-held misconceptions about rabbits and enlighten readers about the true nature of rabbits. Many of these websites are quite good, but the truth is they are not enough. If they were, the problem of dumped rabbits would not be increasing as it is and surrenders to shelters would not be so high. Our reach must be expanded, and in particular in must be expanded beyond the internet.

There are three primary targets for educational efforts:

- Current and potential adopters of rabbits
- General public
- Directors of multi-species shelters and rescue organization

If any of these groups are left out, the effects of such education will be limited. We need to reach out beyond those people who are inclined to search out information on rabbits. We must change enough in our educational programs that we also reach those who rarely think about rabbits and never go looking for websites that focus on rabbit care because they don't think they need to for "just a rabbit."

Educating Current and Potential Adopters of Rabbits

Most educational efforts by rabbit advocates and rescuers have been directed toward current and potential adopters of rabbits. They are the easiest to reach because they have an interest in rabbits, and this audience can also be reached with little financial outlay because they are the ones likely to go to rabbit websites and buy books about rabbits. However, it needs to be remembered that a fairly large proportion of this group believe that rabbits are starter pets and easy-care pets, and people who have that perception of rabbits will not usually think about looking for websites and books about rabbits because they don't think there is that much to learn. Yet if their attention can be captured they might well be open to learning more about rabbits as companion animals for life. Two methods for catching their attention are:

- *Printed material* made available at veterinary offices, shelters and humane organizations
- *Classes* about rabbits and rabbit care

Printed material

In this age of smart phones and internet not many think of using printed materials such as brochures and handouts to reach an audience. But a pile of brochures or leaflets at a veterinary office, shelter, or humane organization works much like the racks of candy where a person stands in a grocery check-out line. You may not have been intending to pick it up, but there it is so you *do* pick it up.

Information on a leaflet or brochure should be concise and useful, and presented in an eye-catching manner. The whole point of such printed material is to get the attention of the person and then direct them to other places (such as your organization's website) where they can find more detailed care information. Topics for brochures could include care basics, rabbits as companion animals, community/feral rabbits (see Debby's brochure on www.dontdumprabbits). Many veterinarians and directors of humane societies and/or shelters will be happy to allow a person to leave printed educational material if it is well-done.

Classes on rabbit care

People often welcome the opportunity to learn through a workshop or class where they can interact with others and ask questions. Rabbit organizations and shelters in many metropolitan areas already offer occasional classes on rabbit care, but such classes tend to be rare in smaller cities and towns. If no such classes are currently offered in your area, try to start one. The directors of many shelters and other humane organizations are open to such a class if asked. If there are any existing programs on dog and cat care, ask to include a presentation on rabbits. If a class is part of a joint presentation on other pets, it may help to educate those not specifically interested in rabbits as well those who are contemplating adopting one. Debby Widolf suggests that attending local humane society board meetings can be a way to educate the board members about rabbits and persuade them to include rabbits in community programs and events.

Offering a class on rabbit care through a humane society or shelter is not the only option. Adult education is a greatly under-utilized tool for reaching both current and potential adopters of rabbits. Most communities have some kind of continuing education or adult education programs, as do many colleges and universities, and are very open to including classes or workshops on a variety of topics. Offer to do a class on rabbit care in the spring, and explain the reasons it is important that people be educated about the nature of rabbits and their proper care. An advantage of offering a class through an adult education program is that these classes are often promoted through class schedules sent to all postal customers in a large area. This gives the potential of reaching many people who might not ever hear about a class offered at an animal shelter or through a humane organization.

To demonstrate how effective a class on rabbit care can be, long-time rabbit rescuer Meg Brown shares her experience. It happened that at the time Debby and I were gathering materials for this book Meg was involved in presenting just such a class on rabbits and rabbit care. Meg and a woman who runs a spay-neuter clinic had gone out for a meal, and the director commented about how many of the people who had rabbits knew so little about them and their care. She then floated the idea of a class presented through the human society in the area on rabbits. Of course Meg immediately jumped on this suggestion and before long the class was in the planning stage.

Meg and her co-presenters, Bonnie Selke and Erica Winnie, planned a two-hour class, as the feeling was that a longer class might put some people off or lead to boredom. An attractive poster advertising the free class was left at veterinary offices, shelters, and supermarket boards, and the class was also promoted on Facebook. They next prepared a list of the points they wished to cover. Because I felt this list was quite comprehensive, I am reproducing a slightly edited version here with the presenters' permission:

- What you should know before you adopt
- How rabbits are different from cats and dogs
- How I can help my bunny get comfortable in his new home
- Why a bunny needs to live inside and not out in a hutch
- What housing needs to be set up before bringing a bunny home
- Bunny-proofing your home – bunnies chew!
- Why spaying and neutering is essential for the rabbit's health and behavior
- The diet that is needed for optimal health
- How to litter train a rabbit
- The benefits, costs and commitment necessary when adopting a rabbit
- Giving the rabbit attention and time
- Getting to know what the rabbit's body language means
- How to set up exercise pens for your rabbit
- Playtime in a bunny-proofed area
- Times of day rabbits are naturally active.
- Petting your rabbits on their terms

- ᵛ Why most rabbits don't like being picked up
- ᵛ How to safely pick up a rabbit when it is necessary for nail-trimming and trips to the vet
- ᵛ How to tell when your rabbit is ill
- ᵛ Choosing a vet
- ᵛ Making arrangements for rabbit care when you go away
- ᵛ Rabbits are a 10-year or longer commitment

Meg and the other presenters later expanded this list into a detailed outline and prepared a power point presentation. They also made up a simple manual of rabbit care based on the outline to hand out to attendees. To add interest, the presenters planned a free raffle and set  up a table with an attractive basket holding the prizes, which included a copy of *The Forgotten Rabbit* by Nancy Furstinger and a stuffed toy rabbit. All attendees were given a chocolate rabbit as part of their mention of the Make Mine Chocolate! campaign. They also had live rabbits at the class, and gave demonstrations on safe handling, nail-trimming, and brushing. During the break water, coffee, and an assortment of vegan snacks were available.

But the most interesting thing about this class was how successful it was. The first class only had room for fifteen, and it filled up quickly (the second class had room for thirty). The planned part of the class took two hours, but over 90% of the participants stayed for about another hour afterwards to ask questions and share with other people who had attended. Some of the people who had taken the class were so fascinated with rabbits that even after learning how difficult their care could be they adopted a rabbit after the class; others (and these were considered just as much of a success as the first group) decided that rabbits were not for them after all.

The feedback from the class was so overwhelmingly positive that the humane society shelter that sponsored the class asked Meg to present a sessions for training of twenty shelter staff. Another class was planned for the public, this one to be held in June in order to be available to those who had gotten a rabbit at Easter, possibly entitled "I got a rabbit for Easter – now what do I do?" Furthermore, the classes were so positively received that the shelter asked Meg and her co-presenters to make the class an annual spring event.

Hands-on classes such as the one Meg, Bonnie and Erica did can have a much greater and more lasting effect than information passively available on the internet, valuable as that can be. Such classes are especially good for people who are beginners with rabbits. I wish rabbit advocates across the country would have such classes available at least once during the spring in every community. Meg has generously offered to share her experience in presenting these classes to anyone who is interested. See her bio in the contributors section for her email.

Reaching the General Public

One of the greatest challenges for rabbit advocates is educating the general public about rabbits and dumping. Many in this audience have very little or no interest in rabbits and are hard to reach. The most direct way to reach this huge audience directly is through media advertising, which can cost a great deal of money. Very occasionally there may be an opportunity to interest the news media in a story about dumped rabbits, but in general anything that reaches big audiences costs big money. At the same time, this is an audience that must be reached if rabbit advocates and rescuers are to have an impact on the growing problem of dumped and abandoned rabbits.

Television

Without doubt, television is the surest way to reach the general public. It is also quite expensive, especially for a well-done, professional spot. I contacted a person I know who has worked in advertising and marketing for over 30 years, and at the time of this writing production costs for a 30-second spot range from around $10,000 to a million for Super Bowl level ads, with the average being around $300,000 to $400,000. However, it is sometimes possible to find a person or production company (usually a small company just starting up) that will donate their services or charge only for out-of-pocket costs if the spot is for a cause the person really believes in or if they think there is an opportunity to produce an outstandingly creative Public Service Announcement (PSA) that could win them awards. It will take research to find such companies, but they are out there. Do your homework before making an appointment to talk to anyone at a company; be prepared to explain what message you want to get across in the spot you are hoping to have done and why it is important.

Production costs are not the only costs in getting an ad on television; air time is another expense. Again, this varies from a few hundred for a late-night spot on a local station with a limited audience, to over a million for a thirty-second ad during the Super Bowl. In order to reach a large enough audience for the ad to do any good, it is necessary to pay several thousand.

While it is possible to research production companies and stations selling air time, it is better to have professional assistance if possible. Ask members and volunteers with your rabbit or animal organization and find out if any of them have relatives or friends who have such experience and might be willing to offer advice.

Billboards and other signage

There are several alternatives to television advertising, including billboards. Debby Widolf was able to fund billboards in Las Vegas for her "don't dump rabbits" campaign and shares her knowledge:

Don't Dump Rabbits Billboard Campaign
by Debby Widolf

In 2015 I began to follow the story of the large numbers of abandoned domestic rabbits in Las Vegas, Nevada. A state-owned property in the city came to be known as the "dump site" for unwanted domestic pet rabbits. There were also several other sites such as golf courses in and around Las Vegas where domestic rabbits were abandoned. The numbers of rabbits in crisis was ever growing, and I wanted to raise awareness that rabbit abandonment is not just cruel, it is against the law. It is now illegal in all fifty states to abandon pets or any domesticated animal. I targeted Las Vegas for a billboard campaign; setting out with the idea of a bold, dynamic, superhero type of billboard that would speak loudly for the abandoned rabbits. As I have limited computer and design skills, I turned to a friend that loves animals and is an amazing web graphic designer. He understood exactly what I wanted, and although he does not want public credit for his design and volunteer help with the campaign, he will always have my appreciation!

I decided to do a "CrowdRise" campaign to help raise money for the costs to install the billboards beginning in December 2015. (CrowdRise helps nonprofit organizations create a campaign for charity online.) I soon found out a lot about the hefty cost of putting up billboards! But with the combined help of the chapter manager of the Las Vegas House Rabbit Society, the National House Rabbit Society and the people that donated to the CrowdRise campaign, we were on our way! The first billboard went up in March 2016. The 14x48 foot board with its bold graphics sent

out a powerful message about rabbit abandonment being against the law. The location was super, near the convention center in Las Vegas. More signs were to come in the form of "digital boards," the first of which went up in April 2016 and was rotated among seven locations. The "don't dump rabbits" billboard campaign was completed by May 2017. We were successful in putting up one large roadside billboard along Interstate 15 and multiple digital billboards, including a ten-week run prior to Easter in 2017.

Many rescue groups and organizations have used billboards, signs on buses and taxi cabs and digital signs, and they can all be very effective educational tools. The cost of a large roadside billboard varies greatly between cities and the location, rising into the tens of thousands of dollars a month in some areas. There are advertising companies that will give non-profits discounts on the cost for signage. Others want an empty space to be filled with an ad and might offer free or discounted space until a full paying customer comes along. In this case, you will not have control over how long your billboard will remain.

Go bold with your educational signs; send gripping and dynamic messages to reach your audience. It is also crucial that signage includes a website to let people know where to go for additional information or help. It was my personal experience that the digital boards and signs were more efficient, had lower costs and greater versatility, but traditional billboards are also effective, as are the signs on buses, taxicabs and other vehicles. Costs for vehicle signs vary, with full wraps (advertising around the whole bus or other vehicle) and large signs on the sides (kings) being the most expensive, while smaller signs on the sides (queens) and vehicle backs (tails) cost slightly less. Ads can also be placed on cards within a bus interior. The cost varies with the area – in some towns and small cities bus ads can cost as little as $150 a month, while in large cities the cost may reach as high as $6,500 per month. Vehicle ads need to be uncluttered and simple because the audience is moving – a person needs to be able to take your message in at one glance.

Billboard messages and other signs work, and they reach a large audience. I was extremely fortunate and am grateful to have had great support from many who believed the "don't dump rabbits" billboard campaign worthwhile and were willing to volunteer or donate to help abandoned rabbits through education.

Finding big-money contributors

There is no way around the fact that reaching the general public – a public that for the most part is not particularly interested in rabbits – takes big money. People who donate relatively small amounts of money are the bread and butter of most animal organizations, and it is these donations organizations count on to pay basic bills. But there is rarely anything left over to fund a costly television spot or billboard. So how does one find such contributors? It takes two things: a special person who enjoys social interaction and the challenge of finding such contributors, and it takes time because a personal relationship must be established with potential contributors.

Donations of $5,000.00 or more are usually considered large for animal organizations. Sometimes a person who will donate at the lower end of this range can be found among an organization's current supporters. Look at those who might occasionally be listed in the business or social news of the community. And look at older, retired supporters. Sometimes they will be willing to make a one-time larger donation for a special project. A personal approach is the key. Visit the person or make a personal phone call. And if you get the donation you hoped for, **always** send a hand written thank-you and keep them updated on the progress of the project for which you solicited the money.

The first hurdle in getting the really large donations is finding a person who is willing and able to devote the time to cultivating big donors and has the gift of easy social intercourse. If you are fortunate there will be a person already in your organization who has the necessary skills. Look for someone who is interested in society, who knows who the local movers and shakers are and where they are to be found. If there is no member in your organization who fits this description, look at your volunteers. If no one fits the job, then ask your members and volunteers if they know anyone who has these skills and might be willing to donate the time. *Once you find that person, let this be the person's only job, don't ask him or her to be cleaning litter boxes or feeding animals.* It is important not to overwhelm volunteers, and a good fundraiser is hard enough to find that you do not want him or her to burn out on other tasks.

Once the right person has been found, the next step is to identify possible donors. Follow celebrities who are animal advocates on Twitter. Check your state and local news for stories on businesspeople, politicians, and celebrities interested in animal welfare. If you are really fortunate, perhaps one or two of these people are already on your list of contributors. After a potential large donor has been identified the first approach needs to be made through an appointment. These are busy people, and it should never be assumed they will appreciate being buttonholed at a social affair or on the street. And they should always be approached with a specific request. What are you hoping to do? Fund a billboard or television spot? Why? What will it cost? How will you do it? How much are you hoping that person will donate? Have all your facts and figures ready. But be positive; don't say your whole campaign will go under if you don't receive a certain amount immediately. Guilt is not going to work. And remember to listen as well as talk – pay attention to what the potential donor is saying, don't just be thinking about what you are going to say next.

After the initial contact has been made, contact must be continued if the initial meeting was at all positive. Make sure you thank the person for their time and donation, if you received any. Sending a brief written note of thanks often makes more impact than a phone call or email. And keep in touch. Most manuals on fundraising suggest contacting donors about four times a year, but not over once a month. Don't take up too much of the person's time, but send a short email detailing progress on the project the person donated to, letting them know their gift made a difference. These relationships have to be cultivated. It is the personal touch that makes them successful. Finally, don't expect to get a huge donation right away. The average time from first contact to the big donation you really want is eighteen months.

Unfortunately, because finding large donors takes so very long and requires a person with special social skills, it has been almost entirely ignored by most rabbit shelters, rescues and other organizations. In my opinion this must change if we are to have any hope of impacting the dumped rabbit crisis, for this is the only way we can effectively reach the general public. I wish every single rabbit organization in this country would make an effort to find a person to cultivate big donors and get educational messages out through television, billboards, and other mass advertising. Then we might truly have a chance of helping to reduce the numbers of discarded rabbits.

Educating CEOs of Large Multi-species Shelters

Most large multi-species rescues and shelters do not have all their animals housed equally. It is an unfortunate fact that in most such shelters rabbits are treated as a poor relation, with lesser quarters and with less money for their care. Little effort has been made by rabbit advocates to persuade the CEOs of such large multi-species shelter to expanding their small mammal programs and to make the point that having model rabbit facilities able to house larger numbers of rabbits in better circumstances could be a positive public relations move and actually bring in donations from a new sector of the animal-loving public.

When I first wrote this section into our book outline, I envisioned listing strategies for persuading corporate officers and managers of such large multi-species shelters to allocate more resources to domestic rabbits. What I did not expect was the attitude expressed by many of those in the upper echelons of those shelters. I had expected them to be open to seeing possible financial advantages of having state-of-the-art rabbit facilities. They were not. Responses ranged from the statement that rabbits were only a "blip" on the screen compared to other animals, that rabbits were still mostly viewed by the public as farm animals, and finally, that it was up to rabbit advocates to get the general public to *demand* good rabbit facilities that were comparable to those of dogs and cats before it would be economically feasible for a shelter to build such facilities.

I do not accept the above excuses. There has been a large enough increase in the number of pet rabbits (at the time of this writing they are and have been for many years the third most popular mammalian pet) and enough publicity about them that I believe the majority of the public is already aware of rabbits as pets and only needs further education and examples of good rabbit care. Witness the Budweiser "Friends are waiting" public service announcement/commercial released May 1, 2018 on YouTube that clearly shows a rabbit living a wonderful life as a cherished companion. That commercial alone demonstrates that many people in this country are aware of rabbits as pets. In my personal opinion, the commercial illustrates the essence of the wonderfully close relationship that can develop between house rabbit and human better than anything else I have ever seen online, and it does it in one minute and fifteen seconds.

No, it is not the lack of understanding by the general public that rabbits can be pets; it is – in my personal opinion – the intransigence of many of those decision-makers in the large multi-species shelters that keeps rabbits and other small mammals being treated as poor relations. I believe that they are so focused on the more popular dogs and cats and reap so much money from them that they are unwilling to even consider giving more room and resources to less popular pets such as rabbits and guinea pigs.

I understand shelters and other animal organizations must raise money to keep going. But what I believe these multi-species shelters are missing is the potential to use a state-of-the-art rabbit facility as a *draw* for donations. Many people with rabbits would donate, and some largely, to such a project. Rabbits – due to what is often called their "cuteness factor" – are always a draw to the general public. I have seen this myself at fairs where the rabbit quarters are often packed nearly solid with visitors while the quarters for other animals have only handfuls of visitors. A model area for rabbits at a large multi-species shelter, one with adequate space, toys, and other enrichment, could educate the public about proper rabbit care and rabbits' value as companion animals in a relatively painless manner. Seeing rabbits and other small mammals treated as lowest on the totem pole only reinforces the idea many of the general public hold that rabbits and other small-mammal pets are low-care disposable pets that they do not need to treat as well as they do their dogs and cats.

However, given the current attitude about rabbits and other small mammal pets among large shelter and rescue CEOs, I suspect it will take tremendous effort by rabbit advocates to persuade those with power at large multi-species shelters to take a chance for the sake of animals other than dogs and cats. How sad that employees at a large beer company apparently have more understanding of the nature of rabbits and their potential as companion animals than the CEOs of a preponderance of the multi-species shelters and other organizations supposedly in existence to help animals of many species, not just two.

Special Topics in Education

Children

However we rabbit advocates and rescuers deplore the fact, rabbits, Easter and children are firmly linked in the public's mind. And despite efforts to diminish this link, every Easter rabbit rescuers and shelter volunteers brace themselves for the yearly onslaught of unwanted rabbits. Kim Dezelon from Brambley Hedge Rabbit Rescue in Arizona describes this yearly phenomenon in the Phoenix area:

Overpopulation of Domestic Rabbits in the Phoenix Area by Kim Dezelon

When Easter approaches, domestic rabbit rescue groups in the Phoenix area brace for a deluge of dumped rabbits after the holiday has come and gone. Brambley Hedge Rabbit Rescue has been involved in many dump situations throughout our 32 years. It happens in parks, neighborhoods, backyards, and even in the desert as families tire of their "Easter rabbits" and decide the simplest way to be rid of an unwanted rabbit is to

let it go.

The process of trying to catch these rabbits is a difficult one. It involves many volunteers who are experienced in the process but even more patience and luck. Rabbits are prey animals that will run for cover when frightened, especially out in open spaces. If the rabbits are successfully caught the next steps taken can be equally difficult and may involve intense medical treatments. BHRR's first step with captured rabbits is bringing them to our rescue. Volunteers assess their health, and if veterinary care is needed the rabbit immediately sees our "rabbit-savvy" vet. Medical issues in dumped rabbits may range from minor superficial wounds to more serious broken legs or open gashes.

BHRR is not only involved in rescuing dumped rabbits, but as of late has assisted the Arizona Humane Society in hoarding houses where rabbits were discovered with broken legs. Many of these rabbits had their legs crushed and our vet was not able to save the leg. In those cases amputation takes place and hopefully the rabbit can be rehabilitated and go on to find a loving home. This must be a family that is experienced and prepared to care for a disabled rabbit for its entire life. In 2017 alone, BHRR rescued three rabbits needing amputation surgery and two more rabbits having surgery to implant metal rods. The recovery of these bunnies can be long, but BHRR is committed to insuring the bunnies can go on to live a "normal" life.

Brambley Hedge Rabbit Rescue recognizes the importance of educating the public in an effort to minimize Easter purchases of rabbits, dumping, and hoarding situations. BHRR works tirelessly with local humane groups in Phoenix, Tucson, and Yuma, sharing our experience and knowledge of proper rabbit care. To that end we make it crystal clear that domestic rabbits are not appropriate for many families, and ultimately most families. It takes unique individuals who are patient, financially prepared, and willing to take time every day to care for the rabbit its entire life.

At Easter time we see the results of an increase of rabbit purchases from pet stores and backyard breeders. Inaccurate care information, or even worse, no care information, is provided to the family buying the rabbit. Many such rabbits are young, not spayed or neutered, and end up being kept in a small cage outside. Rabbits that survive for even a few months and are relinquished to a local humane society are the lucky ones. Many other rabbits are simply "set free" by people who think domestic rabbits can live in the wild just as cottontails do.

BHRR, along with other domestic rabbit rescues across the country, takes part in a campaign during the Easter season called "Make Mine Chocolate." This campaign encourages families to purchase  chocolate or stuffed bunnies for an Easter gift instead of live rabbits. Should the appropriate time come (preferably not at Easter) for a family to consider bringing a rabbit into the family, the campaign recommends adoption as the best option as opposed to purchasing a rabbit.

Whether rabbits should be adopted out to families with young children is a question of some debate. There is little doubt that many rabbits that are taken into families to be a child's "learner" or "starter" pet end up neglected or abandoned, and because of that many rabbit rescue organizations discourage or prohibit adoptions into families with young children. This is particularly true of those given at Easter and other holidays. As Lisa Carrera, a volunteer at the Reno rabbit rescue of 2006 put it:

> Not every family that loves a tiny bunny or chick at holiday time or as a birthday gift comprehends what it actually takes to properly care for these innocent, reliant, precious animals, and that's part of the problem. Roughly 95 percent of all bunnies given at Easter do not live beyond their first year of life. Not long after adopting or purchasing a bunny, it's all too likely the rabbit will be allowed to "escape", get dropped off at a local shelter, dumped in the desert or left on a golf course as boredom and the monotony for caring for the bunnies occurs. Rabbits can also die due to lack of proper nutrition, forceful handling, or falling prey to other pets.

Still other shelters and rescues allow adoptions by families with young children because of the need to find homes for so many rabbits. I recommend that such shelters at least be selective when considering adopting a rabbit out to a home with young children. One of the best determiners I have found for deciding whether to adopt a rabbit out to a family with children is to ask the parents this question: **"Would you be interested in adopting this rabbit if not for your children?"** Because in the majority of cases where a rabbit is adopted for a child, that child quickly loses interest once the cuteness factor wears off and they realize a rabbit is not like a dog or a cat. The care of the rabbit is then left to the parents. It is vitally important the parents understand this.

Some shelters and rabbit rescues require the purchase of specific books on rabbit care before a person can be approved to adopt a rabbit (and I'm honored my own book *A House Rabbit Primer* has occasionally been so used). I think this is a good idea that can be expanded to children, and I would suggest that if a family with a fairly young child is being considered, they should be required to buy and read aloud to their child a book such as Nancy Furstinger's *The Forgotten Rabbit* or Quan Myers' *Silly Pilly, Lilly and Mr. Wally*. Children often learn better from an illustrated story that holds their interest, and both these books teach important facts about the nature and care of rabbits.

Nancy Furstinger's *The Forgotten Rabbit* is the story of Bella, a rabbit gotten as an Easter present but soon left to herself. The bunny begins to starve from physical and emotional neglect but is saved by a girl named Rosalita who takes Bella to be her cherished companion. The book is written so that children age five and up can easily understand the points the author makes about rabbit nature and care, and illustrations by Nancy Lane help readers visualize each episode in Bella's life. Read more about *The Forgotten Rabbit* at www.nancyfurstinger.com

Silly Pilly, Lilly, and Mr. Wally by Quan Myers is the story of three rabbits who each have a different start in life but, after exciting adventures, end up together at a special rabbit rescue where they share a wonderful "rabbitat" and live happily ever after. Colorful illustrations by Thomas Block appeal to children, and Quan conveys her lessons on bunny nature and proper care in a simple non-preachy fashion.

The above books will help educate the parents as well as children about rabbits. I have noticed that sometimes rescues and shelters will gloss over the challenges of having a rabbit in the home to families interested in adopting. While I understand the desire to adopt out as many rabbits as possible, at the same time I don't think much is accomplished if the same rabbit is back again (or worse, dumped to fend for itself) within six months because a family was unprepared for the reality of living with a rabbit. The books I mentioned can help children *and* their parents learn something about rabbits before they adopt. Make them required reading.

Tone, attitude and inclusiveness

When Debby and I began this book project we discussed how blunt and honest we should be. We ultimately decided that if we were not honest we would be doing our potential readers a great disservice, for we learn as much from failures as we do successes. In that spirit I am going to be very honest and tackle what will be a rather touchy subject for many: the tone and attitude with which we interact with those who do not completely share our beliefs and value systems. I have placed this topic in the chapter on education because how we talk to people affects how well we can teach and how open they will be to what to say. It also affects whether we will be able to learn from others, and ultimately determines whether we will be able to work with others toward our goal of reducing the number of abandoned rabbits.

During my years of rabbit rescue and advocacy I have never become a member of any particular rabbit organization, although I have donated time and money to many. My primary reason for this was my need to maintain my scientific integrity: I had to be free to write what I learned in my research whether that information supported published guidelines of rabbit organizations or not. But I also had another reason: I wanted people of any rabbit background to feel free to contact me because the core of all my rabbit work is the individual rabbit. When a rabbit needs help I don't care where that rabbit came from, I just want to give whatever assistance I can.

Because of my independent status, I have been in an ideal position to observe and learn from people of many backgrounds. One of the things I learned was that most people who have a rabbit in their home – whether they call the rabbit a pet or a companion animal and whether they adopted their rabbit from a shelter or bought it at a pet shop – are interested in learning how to give that rabbit better care. But they don't want to be talked down to and they particularly don't want to be branded as lesser people or made to feel guilty because they did not adopt their rabbit from a rescue organization or shelter. Not only do people not learn if approached in this manner, they often become angry and turn against the organization the person represents. I once spoke to a person who became so upset at her reception by members of one rabbit organization that she dubbed them "rabbit Nazis" and told me they appeared to think only they knew anything about rabbits and everyone had to do exactly what they said or else. Amazingly, several years later another person – not even in the same state as the first – gave this same organization the identical epithet. We are doing something wrong if that is how we come across.

In another situation I know of a volunteer at a rescue was trashed by other volunteers for not being vegan. Yet results from the studies on plants by researchers in plant science over the last ten years appear to support the premise that plants are also sentient beings. Despite not having a central brain, it has been demonstrated through various studies by different researchers that plants are capable of self-recognition and recognition of relatives, remembering, learning, and avoiding discomfort. They also appear to have senses analogous to our sight, hearing, taste and touch. For example, in one experiment a chemical ecologist played a *recording* of a caterpillar munching on leaves and plants reacted to the sound by marshalling a chemical defense. In another experiment plants learned, remembered, and acted on what they learned at a future time. If more evidence is found that supports the theory of plants as sentient, conscious beings, those of us who are vegans will have to re-think our stance. Will it be concluded it is acceptable to eat sentient life forms that can't talk or walk, but not those that vocalize or can walk, swim or fly? How would that be justifiable? I am old enough to remember when many scientists thought mammals like cats and dogs could not feel pain as we do. Our understanding of life and sentience changes all the time. Given that fact, should not the focus on the above-described volunteer have been on her willingness to donate time and money to help rabbits rather than her diet?

Having a different background does not preclude having a genuine love for animals. My own family is a case in point. One of my grandfathers was a Wyoming rancher who raised cattle for sale and  horses, particularly appaloosas, because they were his passion. My other grandfather was a medical doctor. Ranchers and medical doctors tend to have extremely practical outlooks on life and a deep understanding that death is an inescapable part of life. To outsiders they may appear cold and unfeeling, but that is usually far from the truth. My gruff rancher grandfather personally cooked breakfast for his barn cats every Saturday morning and he was trampled and injured twice because his horses loved him so much they would fight over who got to be closest to him.

Another person I know of comes from a family that breeds limited numbers of rabbits. Yet this woman takes the time to record the ear tattoo of each rabbit that leaves their home and gives the numbers to the local humane society. If any of their rabbits are taken in by the humane society the family is notified and they take them back for re-homing. Should not this woman's efforts be applauded and other breeders encouraged to do the same? We may oppose breeding, but we need to be willing to work with those who do not think as we do in our efforts to combat the rising numbers of abandoned rabbits.

I believe that if we are to solve the immense problem of dumped rabbits we must be more inclusive. That does not mean abandoning our own beliefs or stance on various issues; it means being willing to listen and to accept that others may not share our values. Let us try and find common ground so we can work together with all those who share at least one of our important values – a love for rabbits. Only by such inclusiveness do we have any chance of stemming the tide of discarded rabbits.

CHAPTER 5: BEING PREPARED FOR A RESCUE

Until rabbit advocates and rescuers are able to institute wide-reaching educational campaigns that will slow the dumping of domestic rabbits, it is an unfortunate reality that rabbits will continue to be abandoned and that a percentage of these dumps will develop into colonies. Given this fact, those who are involved in rabbit rescue should take the time to educate themselves on and prepare themselves for issues that may arise if they or their organization are called upon to participate in a large rescue. Some of these issues are dealt with in the next chapter on the initial steps to take upon the discovery of a colony of dumped rabbits. But there are others that should be researched or dealt with ahead of time so valuable time is not lost during an actual rescue. Five of these are:

- What to have on hand
- Finding and keeping volunteers
- The lost arts of appreciation and consideration
- Legal issues in rescue
- Zoonoses

What to have on Hand

Any person involved in animal rescue or rabbit advocacy may be asked – at any time – to help rescue stray, dumped or feral rabbits. It is important to be prepared so that valuable time is not lost running around trying to locate items. Exactly what will be needed will depend upon whether a single stray, several, or a whole colony needs to be rescued, but there are items that can come in handy for any rescue. The following list will not contain everything that might be needed, but will give a good start for rescuing both single and multiple rabbits:

- Small animal carriers and collapsible carrier
- Multiple cardboard cat carriers – these can be stored flat (for emergencies; not meant for long-term use).
- Heavy gloves and latex gloves
- Exercise pens or wire panels
- Flat sheets (helpful in rounding up rabbits)
- Towels and blankets (for lining carriers and calming and warming rabbits)
- Phone that takes good pictures or a camera (to document the rescue and take pictures of the rabbits for their files)
- Computers to start files on each rabbit
- Flashlights
- Medium-sized live traps
- Large soft-rimmed net with ¼" or smaller holes and a long pole
- Several animal surrender forms
- Copies of local laws on abandonment and animal cruelty
- Names and phone numbers of good rabbit vet
- Basic medical supplies (sub-Q fluids, vet wrap, gauze, scissors)

Shelters or large rabbit organizations that might be called upon to be helped in very large rescues should have volunteers research the following:

- The names and phone numbers of any veterinarians who might be willing to give a discount or do spays and neuters *pro bono* for abandoned or feral rabbits.
- Names and phone numbers of volunteers who might be willing to assist in a large rescue.
- Names and phone numbers of volunteers or organizations that would be willing to lend live traps or other equipment.
- Addresses of possible buildings or other facilities where large numbers of rabbits could be housed temporarily, along with the owners' names and phone numbers.

Actions that should be taken early once a large rescue has begun will be addressed in Chapter 6; the above lists are of things that should be obtained beforehand.

Finding and Keeping Volunteers

Volunteers are the lifeblood of any rabbit shelter or rescue organization. Without them, many organizations could not function. They are particularly needed in coping with any large rescue, yet finding and keeping good volunteers can be problematic. Why? The truth is, it is often easier for harried directors of shelters and rabbit organizations to call upon a few good existing volunteers than to search for new ones matched to specific tasks. Moreover, it is easy to take the good volunteers for granted, simply because they are good and can be relied upon. But if such good volunteers are overburdened, with time many will burn out and quit.

There are three keys to finding and keeping good volunteers:

- Match the person to the volunteer position
- Don't overburden the volunteer with duties
- Say "thank you" frequently

Two demographics that can be especially lucrative when seeking volunteers: university students and retired people. College students are often energetic, motivated, good with social media, love animals, and may enjoy volunteering, especially if they are allowed to volunteer small amounts of time around their classes and other activities. They may be ideal volunteers for many internet/social media tasks, such as posting updates on a rescue, and since they often love interacting with animals, they can be ideal helpers for adoption days. This group of potential volunteers can easily be reached through the internet. Try posting notices of volunteer opportunities on social media and on university/college websites.

When I was younger I worked in adult education, and because of what I learned during those years I believe retired persons are a very under-utilized pool of volunteers. While some may be limited in the physical work they can do or be unable to drive, many have special skills they would be pleased to offer. Not to mention that many of them now have the time to give! Although some retired persons may not like computer work, others are very computer-savvy and may be perfect for researching legal information or sending out thank-you notes or emails for donations and offers of help. Searches for retired volunteers should not be limited to online social media however; try leaving brochures at local senior centers and senior-oriented businesses and housing. Many senior centers and retirement homes have a central board in their recreational area or public area where a notice about volunteer opportunities could be left.

In my opinion the greatest failing of rescues and shelters regarding volunteers is having too few volunteers with too wide a variety and number of tasks given to them. This often leads to frustration, burnout, and a high turnover of volunteers. Not to mention the organization loses reliable and hard-working volunteers! By seeking volunteers for specific, limited tasks only, an organization can grow a larger volunteer base with people who have specialized skills. Offering planned, comprehensive training for volunteers with no rabbit experience can also be helpful. Some volunteers may feel unsure and uncomfortable if the training they receive is haphazard or on an "as needed" basis. And ask for feedback. Give volunteers an opportunity to submit such feedback anonymously. Volunteers need to be made to feel they are part of a team that is working together; a valued, appreciated part of that team!

A good way to start the search for volunteers is to have a page on the organizational website titled "volunteer opportunities." There list each *specific* volunteer opportunity, along with a detailed list of tasks the volunteer will be expected to perform, plus any requirements, such as having transportation. Following are a few volunteer job opportunities notices that anyone is welcome to use, most created by Debby and myself, but a few based (with permission) on a rabbit group's website:

Position: <u>Foster Home Coordinator</u>
Tasks: Help recruit foster homes for rabbits, do home safety visits, set up the foster home with initial supplies and rabbits, make sure everything is going smoothly with the foster homes and the rabbits are healthy, report back to the group manager
Requirements: Vehicle, physical ability to handle required tasks
Skills needed: Computer skills, clear communicator, good organizational abilities, knowledgeable about rabbit care.
Good match for: Students, employed adults, as can make own schedule
Notes: This does not necessarily involve fostering, just managing the foster rabbit program.

Position: <u>**Rabbit Fosterer**</u>

Tasks: Help abandoned rabbits by fostering. Snuggle, exercise and care for our bunnies until they find forever homes. Please note we advocate for indoor, cage-free (or 2-4 hours of supervised free roam time) homes for our domestic bunnies.

Requirements: Previous experience caring for rabbits is preferred but not necessary. Will train.

Skills: Knowledgeable about rabbit care or willing to learn.

Good Match For: People who work from their homes, retired persons, part-time workers, individuals and families dedicated to helping animals.

Position: <u>**Transporter**</u>

Tasks: We need transporters to help with picking up and delivering supplies and taking sanctuary and foster rabbits to the veterinarians and to adoption venues.

Requirements: Must have a valid driver's license, a good driving record, a vehicle that is in good repair, and be at least 21 years of age. Must be 100% reliable! Some lifting is involved.

Skills: Good basic rabbit handling skills, ability to maintain safety of rabbits during transport, able to drive safely in varied weather and traffic conditions.

Good Match For: People with a flexible schedule.

Position: <u>**Fundraiser**</u>

Task: To help raise approx. $3,000 per month to pay for neuter, veterinary and other costs for our rabbits.

Requirements: No specific requirements.

Skills: Previous experience fundraising (grant writing, networking, connection to local community events) may be helpful but is not necessary.

Good Match For: Creative and enthusiastic individuals who enjoy a challenge.

Position: <u>**Helpers for weekly Saturday adoption events**</u>.

Tasks:
1) Set up pens, table, and put rabbit in pens with litter boxes and toys.
2) Socialize the rabbits and assist adoption counselors
3) Help break down at the end of the event

Requirements: Willing to learn the adoption requirements of the rescue. Some lifting is involved.

Skills: Must know how to safely handle a rabbit and be able to monitor the interactions between the rabbit and people at the event, and able to address any safety concerns.

Good Match For: Rabbit-experienced university students, people with Saturdays free, 55+ age group

Position: <u>Litter box and cage cleaners</u>
Tasks: Dump, clean, and refill litter boxes; clean the cage or enclosure floors, replace bedding,
Requirements: Safe rabbit-handling skills. Bending, reaching, kneeling and ability to lift 20 pounds. Good ability to work as a team member.
Skills needed: Good at following directions and effective communication with coordinator. Good observer and attention to details (needs to notice and report changes in litter habits and other behavior; must be careful there is no contamination between areas).
Good match for: Parents working with older children, students, community service workers, those that are in good physical condition.

Position: <u>Researcher</u>
Tasks: To research local laws regarding animals and make hard copies of such laws. Keep abreast of any animal-related laws up for vote, both at municipal and state level.
Requirements: Computer and internet access,
Skills needed: Good computer skills, ability to network with other organizations and individuals.
Good match for: Students, 55+ age group, homebound individuals, anyone who enjoys research and helping animals.

The Lost Arts of Appreciation and Consideration

I fear this section may be skimmed or skipped by many readers, yet its importance is incalculable because it affects so very many aspects of rescue. Appreciation and consideration are critical in dealing with authorities, volunteers, and donors, to name just three. Too often managers of shelters and rescues are truly unaware of the importance of appreciation and consideration and how the lack of them hinders rescue efforts. Directors and managers may focus so intently on the overwhelming tasks in rescue that they are oblivious to the effects of failing to be appreciative and considerate.

I also believe a certain amount of this lack comes because of who we are and what we do. I receive many emails and phone calls asking me for help with rabbits and other animals. Most of those phone calls and emails come laden with three assumptions:

1) That I will agree to help.
2) That I will give away my knowledge for free.
3) That I don't need to be thanked, because, after all, I am an "animal person" and that's what we do – help animals.

There are exceptions; of course, people who are considerate enough to ask instead of demand and who are scrupulous about letting me know they appreciate my time and knowledge. And while the truth is I help almost anyone who asks precisely because I *am* an "animal person," who do you think gets the extra help or extra donation when I can afford it? That's right, because I am human and like being appreciated as much as the next person.

I am far from the only "animal person" who tends to give and give of time, knowledge, and money. Most of us do. But this very willingness to give leads to us being taken for granted. Volunteers at rescues often end up with the least pleasant jobs and put in long hours. Harried shelter and rescue managers, overwhelmed with pressing tasks, may feel gratitude for the volunteers but forget to say those two simple and immensely effective words; "thank you." There are also other ways to show appreciation to volunteers, such as an annual "volunteer appreciation day" or picnic.

Appreciation and consideration come into fundraising for rescues as well. I found one site where the words "thank you" were called "the forgotten fundraising tool." The focus of shelter/rescue directors is on obtaining enough money to cover needed food, housing, and veterinary services for rescued rabbits, and many might protest they do not have the time to thank each person who donates. Here is where that retired or homebound volunteer would be perfect – have them send out emails or cards of thanks to donors, leaving other shelter workers free to attend to more physical tasks at the rescue itself.

Routine fundraising should also be done with these two attributes in mind. Since the internet has become the favored way of fundraising, many of us receive emails soliciting donations for animal causes. If your organization or shelter sends out emails to solicit donations, *please* have the consideration to limit the number sent to each person! I once contacted an animal organization I had supported for over twenty years asking a business question. I did receive a response to my business question, but it soon became obvious that my email had been taken and put on their list for soliciting donations. I began to receive multiple emails a day, to the point they were a problem for me. I became so irritated I ceased donating to this organization that I had supported for over twenty years. Now I give a little extra to those organizations that don't overwhelm me with emails.

When I told friends and fellow rescuers that I was including this section in the book, I was surprised at the overwhelmingly positive response. They all told me it was needed. To a person they had experienced a lack of gratitude either for donations of money or time spent volunteering, or both. They also told me stories about other people they knew who had stopped donating to an organization after not receiving a thank-you for a donation. I believe many shelters and rescues have no idea how many steady donors and volunteers they are losing because of a failure to express appreciation for the money and time that is given to their organization.

Remember:

- ✓ Say the words "thank you" frequently and from the heart.
- ✓ Be considerate; don't overwhelm volunteers with too many tasks or donors with too many requests for funds.

Legal Issues

Legal issues are bound to come up in one form or another during a rescue, especially a large one. Because laws vary so widely from area to area, the information in this section is mostly general, and may or may not apply in your locality. Use the information in this section with caution, and always seek qualified legal advice from a professional for your specific rescue situations.

Know your local laws

Because laws vary so widely state-to-state and municipality to municipality, it is critical that the members of any animal shelter and/or rescue organization research the laws applying to animals in their area. This would be a great task for one of those computer-savvy volunteers from a senior center (see the sample volunteer position ad in the volunteer section above). Whoever is found to research laws, make sure they print out copies as well as save the website where the information was found. Make multiple copies of any statutes that might come into play often and have them ready in clearly-labeled files where any volunteer can easily obtain one.

I cannot over-emphasize the importance of having printed copies of pertinent laws on hand. I had my own experience with how useful this can be. In one place I lived I kept chickens, because I liked having the eggs and because I found them beautiful and loved getting to know them and their different personalities. I had a very secure area for my chickens to be nights, but most days I liked to let them out for a while as I kept watch. I began to have a problem with my neighbor's dogs harassing them, and several times had to open my gate and chase the dogs off. This puzzled me, for I had gone to the effort and expense of putting up a very secure fence around my 40-acre property. I could not understand how the dogs were getting in and out, and  walked the fence multiple times looking for weak spots but finding none. I was very worried about the dogs, for I had known a woman who had over 30 chickens killed when two dogs broke into the beautiful enclosure she had built, went into a frenzy, and slaughtered every one.

One day as I was keeping watch on my chickens I happened to be in a spot where I could see through the trees to my eastern fence and saw a man on my neighbor's property lift his dog up and let it go on my side! I stopped only to grab a paper from a file in my car and marched purposely through the trees. "Hey," I shouted, "what do you think you are doing?" What it turned out he thought he was doing was letting his dogs have a little fun chasing my chickens! I first explained to him that my chickens meant just as much to me as his dogs meant to him – something he clearly could not comprehend – and that I would not stand by to watch his dogs attack my chickens on my own property; that in future I would capture his dogs and turn them in or do whatever else was necessary to stop his dogs from harassing and/or harming my chickens on my land. "You can't do that!" the man exclaimed, clearly outraged. "Oh yes I can," I informed him, holding out the paper, "and furthermore I have the legal right to pursue your dogs off my property for as far as necessary in order to take whatever action is needed to keep them from continuing to harass my chickens." After this incident I no longer had trouble with his dogs chasing my chickens.

I seriously doubt the above-described confrontation would have been half as effective if I had thrust out a smart phone or tablet and started punching it to bring up the appropriate webpage. And if I had simply told him of the law I am certain he would not have believed me. (The law was a state law originally drafted for the protection of livestock, which included chickens and rabbits. Don't overlook the fact that sometimes laws pertaining to livestock can actually be used to help protect rabbits and other animals.) Having the actual law printed on a paper I could give the man so he could read it for himself and look up the statute for more information if he chose was very effective.

Meg Brown relates another circumstance where having a printed-out copy of a law was effective, this one involving rabbits:

Route 50

by Meg Brown

On my way to the spay/neuter clinic one morning about four years ago I was surprised to see a black bunny running near the road across the street.I asked the women at the clinic if they knew what was going on with the rabbit, and was told that the people across the road apparently had three bunnies and that they "let them out to play."

Concerned that one would be injured by a vehicle, I walked over to the home where I was quickly dismissed by the owners and told to mind my own business. "We do this every day. They come back when we call them. They like it."

Letting bunnies "out to play" in an open area and expecting that they'll come when you call is not something that I would advocate in the best of situations. But on a busy road like RT 50, it's a death sentence for the rabbits and a sure set-up for a vehicular accident.The man and woman shooed me off their property.

I did not feel I could leave without doing something about this situation, so I called the local police who said that I needed to call the sheriff's department. I did, and then waited a good hour for an officer to show up. During that hour, I watched no less than eight vehicles swerve to avoid hitting the bunnies who were running in the road.

When the officer from the sheriff's department finally arrived, I told him about the situation. He spouted something about it being none of my business, clearly annoyed he had to drive 45 minutes to deal with bunnies. "It's not against the law. They own the bunnies. They can do anything they want with them," the officer said, rolling his eyes in exasperation.

"Actually Sir, Mr. _____," I responded, looking at his badge and making a point of writing down his name, "it IS against the law." I then pulled out a copy of Article 26 of the Agriculture and Markets Law relating to cruelty to animals. I pointed out the section I had highlighted, 355 Abandonment of Animals, which stated that "A person being the owner or possessor or having charge or custody of an animal who abandons such an animal or leaves it to die in a street, road or public place, or who allows such animal, if it becomes disabled, to lie in a public street, road, or public place more than three hours after he receives notice that it is left disabled is guilty of a misdemeanor, punishable by imprisonment by not more than one year or by a fine of not more than one thousand dollars or by both."

"Not providing an enclosure for these bunnies to keep them out of the road is considered abandonment," I finished. The officer said that I was stretching the law. It was not until I played the following card that a bell rang in his mind and he realized the implications if he did not take action.

I said: "Mr. _____, if you are not worried about the bunnies, surely you are worried about the people driving who narrowly avoided one accident after another, swerving to avoid hitting them. As I waited for you to arrive, I counted eight vehicles crossing the line to avoid them. There WILL be an accident. I guarantee it. I am reporting this to you now, Mr. _____. I am sure that you don't want to have an injury or death of a person hanging over your head. I'll be following up with your supervisor to report what we have spoken about. Thank you for your time."

He glared at me; then walked over to the house. I could see him speaking with the couple. A few days later, the people who had the rabbits went into the spay-neuter clinic and asked if there was someone who could help them to re-home their bunnies.

The Department of Agriculture and Markets in New York State writes many legally binding articles, which are often not known, let alone enforced, by officials such as local police or sheriff's departments. It is helpful to be informed of, learn, and carry copies of some of the basic animal cruelty laws in your glove compartment. And be proactive in urging your legislators to strengthen the animal cruelty and abandonment laws.

Abandonment

Some legal definitions of abandonment focus on intent; the intent to withhold or deprive an animal of necessary care and/or the intent to relinquish ownership. Others are more general, defining abandonment as deserting or forsaking an animal without securing another owner, or leaving an animal used to being provided for to provide for itself.One definition reads (in part): "A person commits the crime of animal abandonment if the person intentionally, knowingly, recklessly, or with criminal negligence leaves a domestic animal at a location without providing for the animal's continued care." Know the exact definition in force in your municipality.

The issue of abandonment does not often arise in connection with single rescues, but frequently arises in large-colony rescues and trap-neuter-return (TNR) situations where it may be used by officials to prevent rescuers from helping colony rabbits. This may be done by claiming that if rabbits are removed from a colony or dump site for spaying or neutering or other medical treatment and then returned, the rescuer returning the rabbit is guilty of abandonment.

However, I found opinions by several attorneys who took issue with the use of abandonment laws to prevent rescuers from aiding feral and dumped rabbits. One pointed out that if the rabbits are returned to their original location, the rescuer cannot be accused of abandonment because the rescuer is improving the living conditions and health of the rabbits. Another attorney pointed out that feral/dumped animals are not owned, and caregivers are not owners. They lack the rights of ownership and therefore cannot be held accountable for actions that imply ownership, such as abandonment. Remember, officials themselves often do not know the precise wording of laws and how they may be applied. Sometimes officials may be looking for ways to intimidate rescuers and/or caregivers from providing care in a situation the officials would rather deal with in a different way, such as euthanization.

Unfortunately, if abandonment becomes an issue in a rescue it may be necessary for the rescuer to hire or search for a volunteer attorney to deal with the situation. But, once again, it may help simply to have the official local definition of animal abandonment printed out and available to volunteers.

Laws vary in other countries as well as the US. Rescuers in areas of western Canada have noted that rabbits may be classified as pets, wildlife, or agricultural, depending upon the circumstances and the governmental entity involved. This can cause much confusion and difficulty for rescuers.

Sometimes laws were such that they were essentially impossible to enforce. For example, a rabbit was not considered wildlife until it had been free-roaming for thirty days. Therefore, if a rabbit was removed or killed under designation as wildlife, unless it had been free-living for thirty days the removal would not have been legal. But clearly in a large group or colony of rabbits it would in many cases be essentially impossible to determine which rabbits had been free-living for thirty days and which had not.

Laws also made it more difficult for rescuers to save rabbits than dogs and cats as no permits were required to rescue a stray cat or dog but were required for rabbits.

Ownership

In many states and municipalities of the US pets and other domestic animals are considered the property of the person or organization which has them, which person or entity is the "owner." To be an owner of an animal laws usually specify that the person, corporation or other entity must harbor, have an interest in, or have custody or control of the animal.

Ironically, municipalities that have changed laws to refer to animal caretakers and/or custodians rather than animal owners can make situations more difficult for rescuers, because officials may claim any person involved in rescuing or caring for dumped/feral rabbits is a caretaker and can be held liable for damages caused by the rabbits and responsible for care expenses. These situations can get quite sticky and require an attorney's help. If this is the case in your area, it would be a good idea to search for an animal-loving attorney who might be willing to help (hopefully at a reduced fee) ahead of time.

Private property

The majority of rabbit rescues will be on private property. The survey Debby and I sent out to seventeen rescuers reflected this fact; eleven of the seventeen took place on private property, two in a park, two on public lands, two at businesses, and one at a school. The first rule in rescuing rabbits from private property is never to go onto private property to capture a rabbit without permission from the property resident or owner. It's easy to think that you'll be quick and no one will ever know you pursued and captured a rabbit in someone's yard, but you have put yourself in the wrong, and if a neighbor or the owner sees you and calls authorities you are possibly in the position of having broken the law. If the property is not posted, knock on the door and ask permission to pursue the rabbit if the resident is home, otherwise wait for the rabbit to leave the property.

Rights against trespass can also work for rescuers. If you have a small group of rescued rabbits you keep in your home, and especially if you are keeping a small group of rescued feral/dumped rabbits from a colony in your backyard (see Chapter 11), be sure you post your property with "no trespassing" signs. This will help keep both unauthorized officials and curious passers-by away from your rabbits.

Releases

Sometimes, both in hoarding situations and in situations where a rescuer sees a rabbit is being neglected by an owner, the owner may agree to relinquish the rabbit to the rescuer. **Never** trust to spoken words being enough. People can (and often do) change their minds and claim they never gave permission to take and animal. For this reason, rescuers should have surrender forms printed out and kept at hand.

Local laws may vary, so the precise wording of the surrender form example on the next page may need to be altered. The name of the rescuer or the organization can be added to the top of the form; or the rescuer can substitute a name for the phrase "new owner." This form is very simple and does not ask for information on the personality of the rabbit or why it is being surrendered. It is for a rescue situation, and the person being asked to surrender the rabbit(s) may respond better to a short, uncomplicated form.

Rabbit Surrender Form

I hereby certify that I am the rightful owner or I am the authorized representative of the guardian or owner of the rabbit(s) that is (are) the subject(s) of this Rabbit Surrender Form. I hereby voluntarily surrender any and all property rights to the rabbit(s) to a new owner. I understand that once I relinquish the rabbit(s), the rabbit(s) will not be returned to me. I also understand that any medical services and their fees that are involved in the rabbit(s) care from this point forward are not my financial responsibility. I further certify that I have read and understand the terms of this Rabbit Surrender Form.

Total number of rabbits surrendered:

Date:

Signature:

Printed name:

Address:

Feeding

Whether a person can or cannot feed an abandoned or feral rabbit is another legal issue that may arise. Although this issue comes up most often in dealing with a large colony of dumped/feral rabbits (see Chapter 9), it can also come up if a person provides food to a single rabbit to help it survive until the rescuer is able to capture it. As always, laws vary municipality to municipality. Research local laws, and if any exist that apply have copies at hand. In many areas there are no specific laws that address the issue, and although feeding may be discouraged by authorities they have no actual power to prevent it.

What to do when approached by authorities

In general, authorities from police, sheriff's departments, animal control, health departments, and other governmental entities are not looking for animal rescuers to hassle. However, if such an official thinks the rescuer's behavior looks odd, or a complaint has been called in by someone, or there is a disputed situation over a rabbit dump site, rescuers may be approached by authorities.

Often the initial reaction of the rescuer that is so approached is to assume the official has the right to challenge them and that they must answer all questions put to them. This is not necessarily the case. Most questions do not have to be answered, and it may be better not to answer them since it is unlikely you will know the motivation behind the questions. Sometimes the official that has approached a rescuer may think they knows a law when in fact they do not, they may lie intentionally to intimidate the rescuer in order to be done with what may be seen as a nuisance call, or they may simply be having a bad day and be more forceful or aggressive than the situation warrants. At other times they may actually be helpful! Each situation is different.

So how should a rescuer or volunteer react if they are challenged by an official? Most important is to **always** be polite, even when refusing to give information that is asked for. In some places a person is not even required to give their name to a police officer, although many police officers themselves believe it is required and will arrest someone who does not. Therefore it is probably a good idea to give your name to police officers and sheriff's deputies, but if you are approached by other officials you may choose not to give your name. Be sure you write down the official's name and/or badge number and note the time.

If rescuers are questioned about what they are doing, a possible response is a question. Ask the person – politely – if you are breaking any laws. If they say yes, ask for the specific law you are violating, its number and where it can be found. If it is a law you have researched and you know the wording allows the action you are being challenged about, this would be a good time to present that printed copy. Or simply say, again politely, that you are choosing your right to remain silent or wish to consult an attorney.

A challenged rescuer should be particularly cautious about signing anything. Animal control officers and other officials may try to get rescuers to sign documents that acknowledge ownership of the dumped/feral animals in questions, or give animal control permission to take action, or – if you are challenged about an animal situation on your own property – a relinquishment of rights to all animals on your property. Usually the only document a person is *required* to sign is a court summons. Again, know your local laws and be prepared. Do not sign anything unless you understand all the ramifications of signing.

Should any official become overly aggressive or intimidating, keep your cool and continue to be polite. Don't even threaten to file a complaint. If you believe the official's behavior warrants a complaint, don't tell them you will file one, simply do it afterwards. And always write down an account of what happened within a few hours while you remember and can document the details.

Other legal issues

A variety of other legal issues may arise in rescue, especially issues relating to rescuing large colonies of rabbits and colonies for which trap-neuter-return is being done. Some of those issues will be addressed in the chapters of Part II; the topic of zoonoses is covered in the next

section of this chapter. If you take nothing else away after reading this section, remember how important it is to know your local laws related to animals and have printed copies of any such laws at the ready. If you are involved with a shelter or rescue, make the effort to find a volunteer specifically to do research on these laws – it may be the single most important volunteer position you fill.

Many of the larger animal organizations have excellent Webpages on legal issues related to animals, and especially on trap-neuter-return. I highly recommend that rabbit rescuers and advocates not only read the pages that are on general law and animals, but read those about cats and trap-neuter-return, or TNR. Much of the information on feral and dumped cat colonies applies to rabbits, and several organizations have a wealth of online information. I especially suggest rescuers check out the legal and TNR information available on the websites of Best Friends Animal Society, the Humane Society of the United States, the ASPCA, and Alley Cat Allies. They are all wonderful resources.

Zoonoses

Zoonoses are diseases that humans can catch from other animals. It is a good idea to know about these diseases ahead of time because they may come up in rescue when municipalities use the potential of zoonoses to prevent rabbit rescue efforts or as an excuse to euthanize colonies of rabbits. However, in many cases an excuse is exactly what the threat of zoonoses from feral/dumped rabbits is. In reality, rabbits provide very little threat of zoonotic disease; far less than dogs and cats. Moreover, municipalities will often name diseases as a threat when they are not, even in some cases where their own departments acknowledge they are not. At times this may be intentional, but at other times the employees of a department may simply make assumptions about zoonoses that are contrary to fact. This happened in Las Vegas, where rabies and tularemia were among diseases listed on posters put up by employees of the state of Nevada as zoonotic threats from a dumpsite of rabbits. Yet according to the US Center for Disease Control, there had been no reported cases of tularemia in Nevada since 2009, and in online material on rabbit zoonoses from the website of the Southern Nevada Health District, Updated 8.9.15, the following quote can be found: "---lagomorphs (including rabbits and hares) are rarely infected with rabies and have not been known to transmit rabies to humans."

Overall, rabbits are considered to present little zoonotic threat, especially to immunocompetent adults. Reported cases of zoonotic disease from rabbits are extremely rare, and in a Rabbits for Vets article on zoonoses it is stated that "Rabbits are infrequently associated with disease transmission to people." And in a piece entitled "The zoonotic threat of rabbits and other wild animals," it is stated that "Rabbits also are low on the list of animals that carry bacterial zoonotic disease agents such as *Salmonella* species, *Escherichia coli*, or *Campylobacter* species..."

As with other disease, zoonotic or not, very young children, the elderly, and immunocompromised are at higher risk. It should also be pointed out that some zoonotic diseases are primarily spread by fleas and ticks, and while those fleas and ticks commonly found on rabbits (especially rabbits living outdoors) can occasionally transfer to humans and bite them, they rarely do. In households with dogs and cats, the fleas and ticks usually found on these pets may also be found on household rabbits and may be more likely to transfer to humans.

Wearing gloves and clothing that covers the arms and legs will help protect against bites from vectors when rescuing feral/dumped rabbits. Face nets help protect a person from biting flies and mosquitoes. When rescuing in rural areas a person should avoid contact with fecal material from any wild animal.

The following list contains diseases that are sometimes cited as being potentially zoonotic from rabbits to humans:

Allergies. Technically the allergic reaction some people have to rabbits is *not* a zoonotic disease, although it will sometimes be listed as such.

Baylisascariasis. The larvae of the parasite *Baylisascaris procyonis*, most common in raccoons, can affect rabbits but cannot be transmitted from rabbit to human (although it can be transmitted from raccoon to humans and rabbits through exposure to raccoon feces).

Bordetella bronchiseptica. Most documented pet-to-human cases of *B. bronchiseptica* have been from dogs; at the time of this writing only one has been documented from a rabbit.

Campylobacteriosis. *Campylobacter* spp. can cause diarrheal illness and campylobacteriosis may be listed as a rabbit zoonotic disease, but it is usually contracted by eating rabbit meat. Even then it is not common. In a 2016 study on *Campylobacter* in rabbits the authors stated that "However, our findings showed that no Campylobacter was present in the animals studied." Most human campylobacteriosis is from exposure through dogs, cats, pigs and chickens.

Cheyletiella-caused dermatitis. The fur mite *C. parasitivorax* is sometimes found on rabbits and can cause an itchy red rash on humans. However, the parasite cannot complete its life cycle on humans, which limits its effect. Dermatitis caused by this mite is rare in humans, and most cases that do occur are in children.

Clostridial diseases. Several species of *Clostridium* can be transmitted to humans from many pets, including rabbits, although such transmission is rare. The bacteria are usually food borne, although they can occasionally infect wounds. Proper sanitary procedure, especially hand washing before and after touching rabbits, will usually prevent rabbit to human transmission.

Coccidiosis. Coccidia that occur in rabbits are species-specific and are not known to affect humans.

Cryptosporidiosis. This is caused by intestinal protozoa of the genus *Cryptosporia*. Transmission occurs when oocysts from feces of infected mammals are ingested. It causes diarrhea in humans, and is most severe in the immunocompromised. Transmission from rabbits is rare, and observing proper hygiene when handling rabbits will reduce any risk.

Encephalitozoonosis, aka EC. EC is found in many species, including dogs, cats, horses, rodents, pigs, and rabbits. EC can potentially be transmitted from rabbits to humans, but at the time of this writing no such transmission has been documented, although there have been reported cases of transmission from dogs to humans and from humans *to* rabbits. EC is very rare in immunocompetent persons.

Giardia duodenalis. Rabbits are rarely infected with *G. duodenalis*, and no cases of rabbit-to-human transmission have been reported at the time of this writing.

Hantaviruses. Hantavirsues are from the family Bunyaviridae. They are very ancient, and co-evolved with rodent, insectivore (shrews, moles) and bat hosts. The disease is most often transmitted to humans through exposure to the saliva, urine, or feces of wild rodents. Antibodies to hantaviruses have been found in many animals, including cats, dogs, horses, cattle, and rabbits, but there have been no reported cases of hantaviruses being transmitted from rabbits to humans at the time of this writing.

Mycobacteriosis. As of this writing there have been no documented cases of infections from rabbits to humans.

Pasteurelliosis. *Pasteurella multocida* is common in several species of pets, including dogs and rabbits, but more cases are reported of transmission from dogs to humans than rabbits to humans. The disease can be transmitted through bites and scratches, so any wounds received while handling rabbits should be properly cleansed and bandaged. Pasteurelliosis may produce local inflammation, flu-like symptoms or respiratory infections in humans.

Plague. The bacterium *Yersinia pestis* causes the disease known as plague. First brought to the US around 1900, the disease is now endemic in the southwestern US. It is primarily transmitted by rodent fleas. There has been an average of about seven cases of plague in humans per year in the US (most in northern Arizona and New

Mexico), but as of this writing there have been no documented cases of transmission from rabbits to humans. In New Mexico (New Mexico and Arizona have the highest prevalence of plague) there were 28 animal cases of plague that were verified in 2017; found in nineteen dogs, seven cats, one mouse and one wood rat. Although the disease was considered a death sentence in the past, it can be treated with antibiotics if diagnosed early. Flea control is the best detriment to spread of the plague.

Rabies. Rabies is extremely rare in lagomorphs, possibly because the rabbits are usually killed by the attack that might transmit the disease to them. According to the Center for Disease Control, "Small mammals such as rabbits and hares are almost never found to be infected with rabies…"

Ringworm. This fungal skin disease is transmitted by direct contact with the animal or through fungal spores on grooming equipment or bedding. Ringworm can occur in many species of pets, including rabbits.

Salmonellosis. Species of *Salmonella* bacteria are ubiquitous in the environment. *Salmonella* can potentially be transmitted from many pets to humans, including rabbits, but most cases of such transmission have been from reptiles. Proper sanitary procedure will usually prevent rabbit to human transmission, which is most often through the fecal-oral route. Any materials contaminated by feces (feed, bedding, other surfaces) are a potential source of infection.

Scabies. Varieties (forms) of *Sarcoptes scabiei* are species-specific. Therefore, while mange mites on rabbits can infest humans – and human scabies infest rabbits – they cannot breed and complete their life cycle, which limits the infestation (usually the mites will die within 10-14 days). Scabies mites from a different species can cause an itchy rash on an immunocompetent human, but the person is not usually treated for scabies, only the rash is treated (often with a topical steroid cream).

Tularemia (rabbit fever). Found in wild cottontail rabbits in some areas of the United States, especially south-central states, tularemia may be subclinical or can cause diarrhea, flu-like symptoms, and pneumonia in humans. Tularemia is a bacterial infection caused by *Francisella tularensis*, and is normally transmitted through tick, fly, or flea bites, and most human cases (cats and dogs can also become infected with tularemia) arise from handling wildlife, especially dead animals. Tularemia can be treated by antibiotics.

Toxoplamosis gondii, a protozoal parasite, may infect rabbits, but humans do not contract the disease from live rabbits (although a person could contract the disease by eating undercooked infected rabbit meat). Cats are the only species of mammal known to spread the disease when alive (usually through their feces).

PART II
RESCUING LARGE GROUPS
AND COLONIES OF RABBITS

CHAPTER 6: INITIAL ACTIONS TO TAKE WHEN A COLONY IS DISCOVERED

A person or rescue may become involved in a large rabbit rescue in a multitude of ways: You or someone you know may notice domestic rabbits living on their own in a park, empty lot or a person's backyard. Animal control or another governmental office or department might ask for help with a large group of rabbits, a hoarder could call and voluntarily ask for help, a business might report a colony that has appeared on business property. Brett and Jacqui Steele, the founders of Big Ears Animal Sanctuary in Tasmania, Australia, became involved in rescuing and caring for a large number of rabbits in yet another way:

Big Ears Animal Sanctuary
by Brett and Jacqui Steele

Big Ears Animal Sanctuary idea was conceived after a trip to Egypt in 2003/04 by the co-founders Brett and Jacqui Steele. The cruelty they saw there made them want to make changes when they returned home. They both committed to a vegan lifestyle and used their land to start accepting animals that needed rescuing – mainly farm animals, as they had nowhere to go. In 2009, Big Ears Animal Sanctuary became a registered charity (the second one in Australia after the RSPCA). Since that time the Sanctuary has grown to be a home for approximately 500 animals, 220 of which are rabbits, the rest being poultry, cows, sheep, goats, pigs, donkeys, ponies, cockatoos, dogs, and cats (feral cats we capture on our property, tame and then live in enclosures). Big Ears Animal Sanctuary is a Sanctuary in the true sense of the word and we don't focus on re-homing rates for our animals; more about providing a safe forever home.

Jacqui's passion is for rabbits. In 2012 we were contacted about a rabbit meat farm for sale. Brett and Jacqui purchased the farm outright, using their own personal savings and donations from other likeminded rabbit people. At first the deal was for 150 rabbits but on the day of collection it turned into 300 rabbits when the owners decided that the ones due to go to the slaughterhouse that week could also go to Big Ears. So the rabbits travelled home, a 250 kilometre drive in a semi-trailer. They arrived late afternoon and we were against the clock to get them out into pens and sorted before dark, with only four people, including a vet. We were able to separate them into males and females and the vet was due the next day to look at triage and starting a vaccination program. The pregnant females and new mums moved into our house. There were literally bunnies everywhere. We did not re-home many of the buns, they have lived out their lives here with us and many have passed away due to illnesses to do with abscesses in lungs, organs, hocks, heads, backs, necks, you name it there was an abscess there. We also had pastuerella, which we treated *en masse* and saved many bunnies. Jacqui is still fighting for the remaining rabbits' lives as they continue to have abscesses, head tilt and cancer. All the rabbits

were de-sexed, vaccinated and lived in a small group or in pairs.

Wiseman, who was in the original group from the meat farm, is our spokes-bunny for factory farmed rabbits and he lives with the ravages of head tilt from the parasite *E. cuniculi*. Wiseman is famous world-wide, as many people have taken an interest in his story and the story of the only known rabbit buy-out/rescue of this size and nature.

However a person becomes involved in a large rescue of rabbits, once the initial commitment to save the rabbits is made there is a myriad of tasks that must be attended to, from providing medical care for the rabbits to soliciting donations. Colonies of dumped/feral rabbits present special challenges. This is a relatively new area of rabbit rescue in North America. One of the first large rescues to hit the news was the Reno Rescue of 2006 (see Chapter 9), but the first one that got much international attention was that at the University of Victoria in British Columbia in 2010.

Rabbits had been noticed on the grounds of the University of Victoria since at least the early 1990s, but of course with time both the number of rabbits and the university itself expanded. At first the rabbits were tolerated on the grounds and – ironically – even used as a marketing tool to attract potential students. Then more expensive landscaping was put in and more voices against the rabbits were heard. I happened to have a relative who was a professor at the university during this time, and from what I was told most people on campus thought it was acceptable for the rabbits to be there, and many enjoyed their presence. Early articles on the situation in 2010, such as the April 1 article "Rabbits causing headaches at UVic" by CBC News, included claims about problems the rabbits – estimated at the time to be from 1400-1600 in number – were causing, but getting rid of all the rabbits was not yet considered much of a possibility.

However, the tone of articles quickly changed, with more and more problems attributed to the rabbits, and more calls to remove them by euthanization. In a July 8, 2010 article on Vancouver Media Co-op entitled "Killing the campus rabbits – debunking the misinformation of the University of Victoria," the author claimed the university was fear-mongering through assertions disease was being spread by rabbit feces (see section on zoonoses in Chapter 4 for information on rabbits and disease), that catastrophic injuries had occurred to athletes as a result of the rabbits' presence (although there was no documentation to support the claim), and that the efforts of rabbit rescuers were being deliberately sabotaged.

It was primarily through the efforts of Susan Vickery, founder and director of Earth Animal Humane Education and Rescue Society (EARS), who raised awareness and funds and worked with the university, that most of the UVic rabbits were removed to sanctuaries. Animal activist Laura-Leah Shaw was also instrumental in saving UVic rabbits, as was Sorelle Saidman, who first worked under Laura-Leah before getting her own permit to take on 100 of the Uvic rabbits.

In the decade since the Reno rescue and UVic rescue there have been many other large rescues. While this area of rabbit rescue is still rather specialized, the sheer number of feral domestic rabbit colonies that need to be rescued is slowly but steadily involving more rescuers. As part of our preparation for writing this book, Debby and I – at Sorelle Saidman's suggestion – collected information through a survey. The questionnaire we designed and distributed, the "Domestic Rabbit Colony Rescue Survey," can be found on the dontdumprabbits.org website, and we will share some of the information we gathered in these chapters.

There is no question that rescuers are being called upon to tackle rescuing large colonies more frequently than in years past. When that call comes in asking for help with a large-scale rabbit rescue, hopefully the pre-planning suggestions Debby and I made in Chapter 5 will have already been accomplished. Now those plans will need to be put into action. Debby offers the following advice:

> Each rescue inquiry and situation is unique. There is no protocol and agenda that won't have to be adjusted, compromised, re-considered, or be without conflicts, without mistakes made, and without trying something new and outside the conventional. Despite that, and expecting it, never go in without a plan, without the opinions of the experienced (even if those opinions are not your own), without the willingness to work with other groups/organizations, and without realistic expectations of the time, energy and money it will take.

The first task after making the decision to consider taking on a rescue is to make multiple phone calls. Call volunteers who might help, alert the veterinarian(s) you will be using for any emergency medical care, obtain permission to enter the property where the rabbits are located for your evaluation visit (see next section), and call upon any persons in rescue you know that might be able to advise you. Once you have a good estimate of the number of rabbits to be rescued and how feral they are, call the owners of properties and/or shelters you have lined up as possibilities to provide temporary housing for the rabbits. A place to house the rabbits during the initial quarantine, medical treatment and sorting period is one of the most pressing tasks you will have. Debby Widolf:

> Locating temporary shelter for the rescued or surrendered rabbits will depend on current budget, and realistic estimated costs. Finding an appropriate space can be one of the biggest obstacles and requires thinking outside the box. Here are just a few suggestions: ask and ask again through word of mouth and use all the social media tools available. Check with fairgrounds, they sometimes have large rooms, extra out buildings. Contact local racetracks and ask if there are available stalls that might work with a little adaptation for rabbits. Organic farmers,

community gardens may have space if rescuers can construct a habitat if one is not available. Cover your basics and answer the following: is the space safe, do you need to make adaptations, is a contract agreement needed? Do not discard the possibility of other groups that might help – this includes 4-H groups and those that show and breed rabbits – and ask other species rescues, such as cat rescues, for temporary space. When the lives of rabbits are at stake and space is critical, reach out! We never do know where the help we need may come from.

Site Evaluation

Once the call about a colony or other large rabbit rescue situation comes in, a potential rescuer will need to make a personal visit to assess the situation and decide what type of holding area will best serve the rabbits. Until a person has seen the situation first-hand, it is not possible to make good estimates of the resources that will be needed to rescue the rabbits. Calls can be misleading; for example it is common for the actual number of rabbits needing rescue to have been greatly over- or under-estimated.

Don't go unprepared; even for this initial visit it is a good idea to take blank Rabbit Surrender Forms (see Chapter 4) and carriers. And be sure to obtain permission in advance to enter the property; don't put yourself in the wrong by trespassing. Finally, while speaking to the property owner(s), be sure to ask what type of help is wanted. Debby Widolf:

Do they want all the rabbits gone with no further responsibility or are they willing to keep the rabbits, some or all, if given help to care for them? Sometimes people do care for the well-being of their rabbits and are grateful for resources, volunteers, and education. On the other side, there will be rescue situations that very clearly indicate that immediate removal of the rabbits is paramount, such as physical abuse, starvation, court-ordered confiscation cases, or impending euthanasia.

The following piece by Debby describes her method for

categorizing the colony of rabbits during the evaluation visit to the site:

Using Tiers for Categorizing Groups of Rabbits
by Debby Widolf

Each rescue of abandoned rabbits living on their own resources will vary according to the size of the colony, how long the colony has been established and the environment. All three considerations must be taken into account when evaluating the rabbits. Always get permission to search and/or remove abandoned rabbits from private or government property before making your initial visit to the site of the colony.

Tier 1

Tier 1 abandoned rabbits includes single rabbits or small groups of

rabbits that were dumped in a neighborhood or on private property. This is the grouping that most rescues are called about and respond to. One or two rabbits are spotted and often additional rabbits are seen within a small but scattered range. Often these small groups are not well bonded to the others and have been recently dumped. The rabbits have developed few survival skills (digging burrows, finding food/water) at this point and are especially vulnerable to illness, injury, starvation, stress and predators. After capture and settling into foster or placement the rabbits are fairly quick to build a relationship with their new home. Rescue for Tier 1 rabbits needs to proceed quickly to save the rabbits and prevent the initially small numbers from expanding if the environment is favorable.

Tier 2

Rabbits in this grouping are a more mixed population; some rabbits may have resided all their lives in a colony of abandoned rabbits, some may have had a past as hutch, breeding or companion rabbits and have found companionship, social interaction and acceptance within the group, and some are recently abandoned rabbits existing with minimal support and skills within a colony or group. Tier 2 rabbits are exposed to humans and may be co-existing with the inhabitants of nearby homes or the working public. They may be tame, taking food from the hands of passers-by and be curious about novelties involving human activities. They will often roam beyond safe boundaries and be in danger from roads, traffic, dogs and human harassment. More than one type of rescue, holding and placement will be needed for Tier 2 rabbits. Some will be comfortable living in a group setting without a lot of human interaction while many will become more trusting and be happy companions in a home. The recommendation is to keep them with at least one other companion that they get along with and adopted as a pair.

Tier 3

This group consists of established colonies of rabbits, plus occasional newly dumped rabbits. The length the colony has been in existence will determine the rabbits' behavior toward humans and subsequent life in a rescued environment. Psychologically, factors such as fear, stress, warrior/protector behavior, curiosity, dominant males and females are more defined in a long-term colony. Newly dumped rabbits will be at greater risk of rejection by the established colony, especially lone males.

These rabbits will be the most "feral" or the least adaptable to life with people. Being captured, separated from their companions, moved to new locations will be very stressful for this tier of abandoned rabbits. It is recommended that they are rounded up in small groups, optimally those that they are seen interacting with each other. Even if a rabbit is obviously ill or injured, another companion rabbit should be rescued with them for physical and psychological comfort.

When the rabbits are removed from their current area they will need each other, places to hide, quiet, and a slow introduction to human interaction. Eating is usually the first physical habit to adapt positively to rescue, especially if food has been scarce. Adoption as house companions can be a difficult transition and may never be comfortable for rabbits coming from an established colony that has existed for many generations, including the adults and young. It is my opinion that group living in an outdoor or indoor/outdoor shelter that is totally predator proof and is managed by a knowledgeable, patient caregiver may be the preference of Tier 3 rabbits that have little experience with humans. A managed Trap-Neuter-Release (see Chapter 8) program has possibilities for such a colony if carefully monitored and maintained with community support.

Working with State or Municipal Government

Unless you already have an established relationship with a state or municipal animal control or humane society, caution is recommended, especially when dealing with large rescues of rabbits. While many of the rescuers who have contributed pieces to this book report having good or even excellent working relationships with these governmental entities, not all do. In many municipalities employees of humane societies and animal control departments have little experience catching and caring for rabbits and their policies and actions will reflect this. Be particularly careful about signing any agreements to help such organizations. In one municipality stray rabbits are given to research labs and restaurants after they are rounded up. In another state, a backyard breeding situation had gotten out of control and complaints were made by neighbors. Initially the governmental humane organization encouraged the breeder to capture and kill (the owner was breaking their necks to kill the rabbits) what rabbits he could to reduce the population. A rescuer was called and agreed to help animal control with the understanding she would be able to take the rabbits; she later learned that any rabbits with medical problems – even those with treatable medical problems – were to be euthanized, and she was not allowed to save those rabbits. Furthermore, although the rescuer was called once animal control had a group of healthy rabbits ready to release to her, if she was unable to go and pick them up within a short time the rabbits were euthanized. Out of 100 rabbits, only thirty ended up being released to the rescuer.

It is not only animal control and municipal humane societies that can be difficult to work with; rescuers who wished to remove rabbits from an island in a park where domestic rabbits had become established found the Park Service was often unhelpful and almost obstructive. One rescuer speculated this was due to Park Service concerns about water birds on the island, but employees appeared unwilling to work with rescuers in a manner that would address the concerns of both sides.

If you do decide to work in conjunction with a governmental entity you have not worked with before, whether state or municipal, it is a good idea to have the key points of the agreement written out and agreed to in either an email or a signed document. Do not trust to spoken words.

The other side of the coin

Occasionally it happens that municipal officials try their best to come up with a humane solution for rabbits that have become a problem in a city or county. Whether their motivation is genuine concern about the rabbits or fear of being labeled "bunny killers," or both, rescue groups and rabbit organization need to **respond in a positive manner** to such efforts on the part of municipalities. *Not to do so fails the rabbits.* If you don't feel the municipality's plan is a good one, don't just criticize and tell them they are harming rabbits. **Offer concrete help**. Present a plan for a structure or a managed trap-neuter-return program, complete with an estimate of the costs of your plan. Tell the officials you have X number of volunteers that will show up on a particular day to help with the rabbits and be sure your volunteers understand the importance of following through as promised. Listen to what the officials have to say about their time and financial constraints. Remember that it is relatively rare for a governmental entity to wish to work with rescuers and appreciate your good fortune. Work *with* them for the rabbits' sake.

Funding a Large Rescue

The expenses involved in a large rescue of rabbits will most likely put a strain upon the financial resources of any shelter or rabbit organization. One of the ways to help alleviate this is to make a special appeal for the particular rescue. First publicize the rescue. Have your social media volunteer post about the rescue with pictures of the rabbits. Television news media may be interested in unusually large rescues, and a story that makes it to the local news will help considerably in fund-raising efforts. However, most rescues will not end up as television news stories, and other fundraising techniques must be used to generate the donations necessary to pay for the rescue and care of the rabbits. Kim Dezelon of Brambley Hedge Rabbit Rescue offers these suggestions:

BHRR has a GoFundMe page, https://www.gofundme .com/brambleyhedgerabbitrescue, and we have found this helps bring in donations. We use all platforms of social media to help spread the word: Facebook, Instagram, email and we also have an Etsy store – The Stylish Bunny! None of these cost any money so it's an easy way to go.

We still do a holiday letter as well, which reaches those donors who are not online frequently or who prefer to donate by mail. In addition, if we have a bunny who has had a very expensive surgery (we had three amputations last year) we do a fundraiser on Facebook. This has worked well for us as we can detail exactly what is taking place. We will post x rays, vet protocol, and follow up, so people can see how procedures their donations are helping to pay for are helping the rabbits.

Debby Widolf suggests another way to generate donations:

One of my favorite fundraising events is a celebrity meet and greet event. We don't all know someone in Hollywood, so think statewide or consider local celebrities who have a love of animals. A short talk, some wine, snacks and a silent auction might be a great fundraiser! You may know of an artist or crafter that will offer a painting or crafting party to benefit rabbits. Please remember that artists need to make a living too, but many who love animals may be willing to donate an item or teach for a reduced fee for a great cause such as your rabbit rescue! Regional or local bands might be willing to help by giving a concert or playing for a dance. Sports figures and events can also be good draws for fundraising. Remember, to help save the lives of rabbits we should accept any contributor who has a genuine desire to help and a heartfelt belief in our work; we should not make judgments on lifestyles that may not be of our choosing.

Responding to Offers of Help

Once a rescue is publicized and fundraising efforts in place, offers of both help and money will begin to come in. Once again, here is where that retired or homebound volunteer whose only job is to send out thank-you emails is invaluable. Such a volunteer can respond immediately to each person, thanking them for their donation or offer of help and then notify you of any that will need your personal attention or that of another person in your organization.

Even those offers of help you may not choose to accept should be recognized and your appreciation made known at the time they are received. The world of rabbits and rabbit rescue is not that large. If a rescue fails to acknowledge offers of help it will eventually get around, and fewer offers may come in the next time you need them. Your email-answering volunteer respond politely to each and every offer of help that comes in during a rescue, whether it is accepted or not. Rescuers themselves often get so overwhelmed by the multitude of tasks during a rescue that saying thank you is ignored. It shouldn't be.

Capturing Rabbits and Transporting Them to Temporary Quarters

Abandoned and feral domestic rabbits are often very wary of people. Almost half of the respondents to our survey checked "extremely wary," a fourth of the respondents considered the rabbits "wary," and another fourth responded that they rabbits allowed limited interaction with humans. One rescuer who filled out the survey elaborated, writing that the rabbits were "…all very scared and difficult to catch, especially in the woods and brush…" Hopefully some of your volunteers will have experience in capturing rabbits and you can pair those volunteers who do not have experience with those who do. The majority of the respondents to our survey used exercise pens to capture rabbits, although live traps, nets, drop-down traps were also used. Some even captured rabbits with their hands. Depending upon the situation, more than one method may need to be tried. Capturing rabbits is rarely easy!

The first thing to remember when trying to catch dumped rabbits is that speed is necessary. Dumped rabbits are rarely altered, and there is a reason rabbits have been associated with fertility for centuries. One respondent to our questionnaire told of a situation in which people moved out of a home leaving an 18-year old cat and a pair of intact rabbits. In a very short time the number of rabbits was about fifty, and they were branching out into other areas of the neighborhood.

Erin Urano, founder of "Rusty and Furriends, Vegas Dumpsite Bunnies" in Las Vegas has had a great deal of experience capturing rabbits. She offers these tips:

Catching Feral Bunnies

by Erin Urano

I feel the optimum way to catch a single feral bunny or a group is to observe them first. Familiarize yourself and your catching crew (small experienced group of 2-4 people) with not only the bunnies but the terrain.

Secondly, be prepared. Pack and load more gear than you feel you will need. Bring more carriers than you plan to use. Bring four to six 24-30" tall x-pens. Bring bunny-safe nets, blankets, and small dog crates. Also bring assorted food and greens as lures. Use strong-smelling greens like cilantro, mint, basil, and dill.

Set up pens and use stakes if needed. The most important things are having a plan and communication. Define the role of each team member before approaching the bunn(ies) you want to catch. Do not go off half-cocked with no plan. Designate a role for each catcher: who will close the pen the bunnies go in, who will jump inside and press the bunnies to the ground before lifting up, who will run and bring the carriers, who will push the pen down to make sure when bunnies hit the sides they don't escape.

Success means:

1. Observation
2. Gaining the bunnies' trust
3. Packing supplies well
4. Teamwork and a solid plan
5. Trying not to miss. The best rescue is a swift one. Most times you don't get a second chance in an outing (once you spook the bunny).

The geographical region and time of year should also be taken into consideration (if possible – in some situations rescuers will not have that option). It is easier to trap rabbits when native vegetation is sparse, and it is better to trap at a time of year few of the does are pregnant.

Debby Widolf makes the following additional suggestions for capturing rabbits (and Chapter 10 has basic information for those with less experience):

Refer to people that are experienced with catching or rounding up rabbits if they are to be removed from their home for spaying/neutering, re-homing or medical care. Wear gloves and long-sleeved clothing and remember, the least possible handling, the less stress for the rabbit and for you. One often-successful method is to surround the rabbit/s with an exercise pen and place open carriers inside the pen with greens or food in them. Encourage the rabbits to enter the carriers, close the door and cover the carriers with a sheet or light blanket. Long handled, soft rimmed bird nets are sometimes used, but the net needs to be closed over the rabbit quickly, their movement restricted, and hindquarters supported to prevent injury. Never chase a rabbit. You can slowly and quietly walk after them, but be patient and look for signs of undue stress.

Feral rabbits and rabbits that have been dumped can be difficult to handle once they are caught. Debby shares some tips for dealing with skittish, scared rabbits:

Frightened and stressed rabbits do not like to be held. This is especially true of community or feral rabbits. You will be perceived as a predator. Keeping the handling of these newly caught rabbits to a minimum is essential to prevent possible shock. One strategy for removing a rabbit to a safe place is to surround them with an exercise pen or barrier and quietly, gently guide them into an opened carrier. If another rabbits is rescued, place the rabbits together if the carrier can accommodate them both. Cover the carrier with a sheet or towel.

When a frightened rabbit must be held and carried, the following methods can be used to keep you and the rabbit safe.

Wear long sleeved clothing and gloves that will provide protection from scratches and possible biting. Never chase the rabbits. Occluding the rabbit's vision by placing a hand or blanket over their eyes may calm the rabbit, but do not cover their nose! Using a "football hold;" tucking the rabbits head in the crook of your elbow, having one hand and arm underneath the rabbit and one on top of the body is a good holding technique. Other safe and useful holds include placing the rabbit with their back against your chest, feet facing out, securing the rabbit with one arm under the forelegs and the other cupping the hips and rear legs. Rabbits feel more secure if all four feet are against a surface; another way to hold them is with their feet against your chest and a hand on their head and the other on the lower back.

The rabbit will be easier to put in a front loading carrier if they are backed in rump first or if available use top loading door carriers. Never force or pull a frightened rabbit out of the door of the carrier, it is safer to resort to taking the carrier apart.

Rescued rabbits should be kept with each other when they are moved to their temporary quarters, if possible. Debby Widolf explains why this is:

Do not underestimate the need and comfort that the rabbits in these large rescues or colonies provide each other. Whenever possible keep rescued rabbits with another one or in small groups. The rabbits will be less stressed. When a rabbit needs medical attention, take a rabbit friend along to comfort the ill bunny. It has been my experience that an ill rabbit will recover more quickly if kept with a friend for the duration of any confined treatment.

Feral or dumped rabbits that have lived their lives – part or all of their lives – in colonies are most secure in the presence of other rabbits they are familiar with. It is my experience that the rabbits are calmer, easier to care for, and in the case of illness, recover faster, if kept with another rabbit. With newly dumped domestic pet rabbits this does not seem as critical as they are usually more accustomed to human contact. In any case, living alone is not natural for a rabbit.

Of course in some circumstances rescuers may not be able to keep rescued rabbits together due to the type of housing that is available for the rabbits as they are caught. One of the respondents to the questionnaire Debby and I sent out told of a rescue in which the rabbits had to be kept singly in shelter kennels. This led to the breaking of bonds and rescuers were unable to re-establish the rabbits as a colony or even pair the rabbits after they were altered. The rabbits were ultimately adopted out singly.

Initial Medical Intervention

Although some rescued rabbits will be in relatively good health, many will have various illnesses and medical conditions that will require treatment. Respondents to the survey Debby and I sent out reported that the most common injury by far was bite wounds. Some of these were the result of the rabbits fighting amongst themselves, others from predators such as foxes, and one rescue reported a puncture wound that had apparently been inflicted by a water bird on the island where the rabbits were found. Many other conditions requiring medical treatment were reported as well, including parasites, bone breaks, and abscesses. One respondent listed the following as being present in the rabbits of one rescue: bite wounds, torn ears/tails, eye  infections, ticks, fleas, abscesses, and urine scald.

Given the wide variety of medical issues that are likely to found in rescued rabbits, some form of triage will be necessary once the rabbits are captured, especially if the rescue is a large one. Debby explains how to triage in a large rabbit rescue situation:

Triage for Domestic Rabbits
by Debby Widolf

The word "triage" comes from the French verb *trier*, to separate, sift or select. During triage operations, victims, rabbits for this piece, are involved in a process of sorting and assigning the allocation of treatment according to priorities to maximize the numbers that will survive an emergency situation. Primary triage is done at the scene, secondary triage happens at the clearing center or temporary rescue housing. Rabbits being triaged would be given a quick examination to determine which are to be treated first according to the seriousness of wounds and illnesses.

You may be required to triage rabbits in a wide variety of situations: emergency rescue from fire, floods, other natural or manmade disasters. Triage may be required in confiscation cases, other scenarios could be an extended operation to rescue large numbers of rabbits that have been abandoned on public or private property.

Knowing which types of rabbit injuries require the first priority of treatment is necessary to your triage effort to save lives. The following is a general list of first and secondary treatment priorities during triage of rabbits. Remember S.A.L.T.: Sort, Assess, Life Saving Interventions, Treatment or Transport. This four step process will help to prevent chaos and maintain order during triage.

Triage Priority 1

- Respiratory: whether the rabbit is breathing or having difficulty breathing, or has a heartbeat.
- Circulatory: actively bleeding from orifices or wounds.
- Burns: second and third degree.
- Gunshot, serious puncture, bite or impalement wounds.
- Compound fractures.
- Signs of shock.
- Head trauma, compression
- Known to be poisoned.
- Crushing injuries, hit by vehicle.
- Deep flesh wounds or amputations.
- Fly strike (can lead to shock when severe)

Triage Priority 2

- Evidence of infection: runny nose/eyes.
- Simple or possible fracture/dislocation.
- Head tilt.
- Abscesses.
- General weakness not related to injuries.
- Wounds that have clotted and appear stable.
- Starvation: rabbit looks emaciated but stable.
- Dehydration, (not related to serious illness, injury or evidence of shock.
- Fear not due to illness or injury.

Basic Triage Supplies

- Compression wrap, vet wrap
- Betadine solution
- Gauze
- Syringe, needles
- Pressure pads
- Medical tape, butterfly closures
- Sub-Q fluids and supplies
- Towels, blankets
- Medications
- Disposable gloves
- Wire cutters, scissors
- Rabbit food/water
- Evacsak, carriers
- Quik-Stop or cornstarch
- Flashlight
- Colored markers, pen, notepad
- Camera, laptop for intake
- Phone

If possible, have a triage coordinator to arrange transports, contacts vets and to provide direction to volunteers and/or staff.

Spaying and Neutering

Unless a rescue organization has a vet willing to perform spays and neuters for a discount, this can be a major medical expense. For the majority of the respondents to the survey Debby and I sent out to rescuers, the cost was between $100-300 per rabbit. These costs can rise higher if any of the spays are not routine; one rescue had their costs increase significantly because some of the female rabbits had decomposing fetuses and others had uteruses filled with lesions and pus.

Getting captured rabbits spayed and neutered as quickly as possible is almost always a priority to rescuers because they wish to stop the rabbits from breeding and making the problem worse. This is understandable, but in the rush to alter the rabbits, many pediatric spays and neuters (those done before the rabbit is six months old) are performed. Pediatric spays and neuters can be done safely provided females are sexually mature and the testicles have descended in males. The problem is that the age at which this happens varies by the size of the rabbit. Small rabbits may be sexually mature at four to five months old, but medium-sized rabbits often do not reach sexual maturity until six or seven months and large rabbits until eight to ten months. Some giant breeds do not reach sexual maturity until 12 months. Mixed breeds are a special problem because it may be impossible to guess how large the rabbit will be at maturity.

In general, spay and neuter operations are riskier for very young rabbits, and the sexual organs not fully developed. In males the testicles may not have descended and in females the ovaries are threadlike and hard to locate. If any tissue is missed during an operation it results in what is termed an incomplete gonadectomy. These are rare in rabbits spayed or neutered after they have reached sexual maturity, but are not uncommon if the procedures are done earlier, and some veterinarians in the US are reporting increasing numbers of incomplete gonadectomies. If the tissue remnant redevelops, it can again produce sex hormones. In ferrets that are neutered early it is not uncommon for the adrenal glands – which normally produce low amounts of sexual hormones – to begin producing abnormally high amounts, which can lead to serious disease. Several veterinarians have pointed out it is not yet known whether early spays and neuters can have a similar effect on rabbits.

Unfortunately, many rabbit rescuers and shelter operators are so focused on preventing further breeding of the rabbits that many are not much concerned about too-early spays and neuters. Rescuers usually do not have to deal with the consequences, but the rabbits do, and so do the people who adopt them. Rabbits that receive incomplete gonadectomies will engage in the behaviors of unaltered rabbits, including aggression and spraying urine. Females will be at risk for the cancers and other diseases from which a complete spay would grant some protection.

I know it is more difficult to correctly sex and separate young rabbits until they are sexually mature. But in fairness to both the rabbits and the people who adopt them, I believe it is the ethical thing to do. Being rescuers and believing we are acting for a greater good does not give us a pass to engage in practices that could harm an individual rabbit down the road.

Finding Placement for Rescued Rabbits

After the initial emergency actions are taken and buildings found to hold rescued rabbits for a quarantine period, it is necessary to start searching for shelters and rescues that will take the feral rabbits permanently, or until they can be adopted out. Most rescuers already know of some shelters and organizations that will either help with this process or take rabbits themselves. Other offers to take rabbits will come in as the rescue is publicized and word spreads through the rabbit world. For the most part this network of rescuers and "rabbit people" works fairly well. However, there is a disadvantage to using this network: rumor.

During one large rescue I happened to become aware of an offer by a rescue to take 200 rabbits. The rescue was a good one and had been used by people in other large rescues of rabbits. Furthermore, the rescue had recently had a large donation and caring for the rabbits long-term would not be a financial problem. This offer was not accepted. Why? One of the people involved with the rescue did not want rabbits going there, perhaps because that person had listened to rumor or perhaps because that person had a dislike of someone at the rescue which had made the offer. I knew people involved on both sides of this situation, and I know the purported reason for not accepting the rabbits

– not having enough shelter – was not accurate since the rabbits had buildings for shelter as well as a yard for exercise. Other rescuers who had placed rabbits there had been satisfied. Worst, the offering rescue did not receive an acknowledgement of their offer for some time. Ironically, in this particular situation some of the rescued feral rabbits ended up in small shelters that, excellent as they were, had to keep the rabbits in separate cages. Try to think from a feral rabbit's POV. If you had been free and feral, associating with others of your kind, would you be more comfortable confined in a cage or at liberty to run from building to yard with other rabbits from your colony?

I myself have been both slandered and libeled, and I know how very frustrating it is when you cannot defend yourself against falsehoods because you are never given the chance. Rumor is often wrong, and frequently started by people with personal grudges or who themselves have believed stories without facts to support them. When placement for large numbers of rabbits is so difficult to find, it is critical that rumor not be accepted. If you yourself or a person you know well has not seen a shelter, do not trust someone else's word. Check it out personally if possible, and if that is not possible, have someone you trust to give an unbiased judgment check it out. If there is a small problem with the shelter, ask if it can be remedied. If you still decide not to accept a particular offer to take rabbits; at a minimum thank the people for that offer. Not to do so is inexcusable in my opinion, and word soon gets around – the rabbit advocate and rescuer community is not that large. Again, that often-forgotten courtesy is critical.

Housing standards

While rescuers should have high standards for any potential feral colony rabbit placements, these standards cannot be the same as those we use when checking out potential adopters for companion rabbits. For one thing, in most cases one is seeking housing for a fairly large number of rabbits. For another, dumped rabbits have been living a very different life than house rabbits and therefore have different needs. One issue is whether the rabbits will be living outside or not. For feral rabbits, this is not necessarily a negative if the enclosure is adequately predator-proofed and structures provided for protection from the elements. Furthermore, rabbits that have been living feral lives will often be more comfortable in outdoor environments and therefore easier to work with and socialize.

Tony and Greg, founders of Broome Animal Sanctuary (BAS), a sanctuary for farm animals in Middleburgh, New York, try to be very sensitive to the preferences of their rescues. When a big beautiful white  rabbit came to live at BAS, Tony and Greg noticed that the bunny, Snowball, liked to follow them around and had a very puppy-like personality: "He loves to be held and cuddled. He insists on being the center of attention." Tony went on to explain the sanctuary has enclosures for the rabbits and assured me Snowball is secured nights and when no one is in the yard, but that when he or Greg are in the yard during the day Snowball wants to be out with them. When they left Snowball secured during the day he became very depressed and chewed and dug out of several enclosures. "It's like he was letting us know this is what he wanted," Tony wrote, "I guess we came to the conclusion we couldn't steal his happiness."

Nor is it always necessary that the rabbits go to an established shelter. An individual with a farm or a large property and who likes rabbits and is financially able to take on such a project may be willing to provide space and housing for a colony of rabbits. And in some situations a business may be willing to house the rabbits as an attraction (one overseen by competent volunteers associated with an established rabbit shelter or organization, of course). As Debby Widolf often comments to me, "It is necessary to think outside the box" when considering ways to contend with the huge number of abandoned rabbits.

In general I have found rabbit rescuers and advocates in the United States less willing than those in some other countries to look at placing colonies of feral/dumped rabbits at farms or businesses, but I believe that this will have to change if we are to continue to find placement for the increasing numbers of feral/dumped rabbit colonies.

Sorelle Saidman is a founder of Rabbitats Rescue Society, which is "...a non-profit that promotes sanctuary rescue for their abandoned pet rabbits and their feral offspring by developing predator-proof, sustainable, visually appealing and gently interactive colony environments for the rabbits focusing on low maintenance and sustainable care." I strongly recommend that anyone willing to consider non-traditional but rabbit-safe placements investigate the many options suggested on the website rabbitats.org, including farm markets, hobby farms, garden centers, care homes, and city parks.

Niki Chapman, who comes from a farm family, took a group of feral rabbits from a colony that was being relocated:

> We were pretty well set up from the get go. My family has a farm and were set up for pigs. They now only have a few horses and got out of pigs quite a number of years ago. We used the ex-manure pit which was filled with dirt, fenced it with wire and then put I canopy of fabric mesh so no predators could get in. We also used a low barn and wired any openings so nothing could get in or out. We made a simple wire tunnel so the rabbits could go back and forth from inside to out. The "bones" were there already so it was just a lot of prep, clean up and hours spent making it work for the rabbits and us.
>
> We started with fifty rabbits because that is what we (my husband and I) felt we could manage on our own. We didn't do any other fundraising et cetera. Everything since has just been out of our pocket. The rabbits live on hay and pellets, which isn't a huge expense: $12 for a bag of pellets and $7 for a bale of hay.
>
> At present the number has come down from the original fifty. The main problem we have had is rabbits having EC. Other than that, they have been healthy and lived a fairly natural and happy life. They have sorted out any territorial issues, although that was a process in the beginning.
>
> I wouldn't have wanted to take on any more, although the number we have is quite manageable. We both have jobs, kids etc. and they take time. I personally just couldn't let the rabbits be killed and so I joined the fight. I had the space to do something so we did.
>
> Simplicity is pretty key, and having the right set up to make it all work for you is essential, as it not taking on more than one can handle. It's very handy having someone who is skilled at building and the grunt work involved with setting up. That will

cut down on work in the future and protects everyone. Our rabbits don't require a lot of maintenance, just clean out the barn weekly, etc. The rabbits are essentially contained with a concrete bottom and sides so they can dig down but not out. We have never had a loose rabbit or any complaints.

It's been five years and we have about thirty now. Most were young when we got them. No babies, but within their first year. All in all, I am very glad we got involved and were able to provide the rabbits with the life they needed.

Sorelle Saidman and Rabbitats.org are promoting adoptions of small colonies, which they term micro-colonies, as one way to help increase adoption of rescued abandoned colony rabbits. (See Chapter 11 for an in-depth look at this type of adoption.) While these adoptions are still fairly unusual in the US, they are not entirely unknown. One of the respondents to the survey Debby and I sent out told of a rescue that ended in what was essentially the adoption of a micro-colony. Several abandoned domestic rabbits moved into a woman's backyard. The woman was concerned about them and provided them food and water.

But, of course, being rabbits and being unaltered, they multiplied. Before long the woman had between thirty and fifty rabbits in her backyard and she contacted the rescuing organization. Although the rabbits were in generally good health, they were extremely wary. After the rabbits were spayed and neutered a few were adopted out, but the majority were too unsocial for adoption. Fortunately, the woman on whose property they were living was willing for the rabbits to remain in her backyard once they had been altered and the yard adapted for them. More such people willing to take on small colonies are needed.

Debby Widolf also believes we must look at new options for housing colonies of rescued rabbits:

> There is an ever growing need to rescue and find placement for abandoned rabbits. Shelters and rescue groups work tremendously hard and are most often stretched to their limits for space, volunteers and finances. I am a proponent for colony/group living for large rescues of community, unsocialized, bonded groups. I also believe it is an option for

those rabbits that have lived for years in confined sanctuary care and have been continuously passed by for adoption. Set-ups for colony living have had success in giving rabbits a good quality of life. Colony sanctuaries are not a panacea; there are challenges, but some rescues are making them work. Please see "rabbitats.org" in Vancouver as an example and leader in developing colony rescue living.

We are learning more about caring for and providing an enriching, safe environment for group living. I believe one of the advantages for this type of placement are a decrease in the amount of labor needed to care for the rabbits verses individual pen or cage cleaning for one or two rabbits at a time. It allows unsocialized rabbits and rabbits that are bonded to their group to continue their natural lifestyle but within a caring and safe "home" or sanctuary. This model also allows those rabbits that enjoy human company to be featured as house rabbits. Groups within the managed colony can also be adopted to homes that would love to share their lives with a spayed and neutered "family" of rabbits. We must widen our national and international view of how to care for, stop the suffering and save the increasing numbers of discarded domestic rabbits.

Transporting Rabbits to their Permanent Location

Once all the rabbits have been captured, placed in temporary housing for a quarantine period, and their initial medical needs have been taken care of, they will need to be moved to their final destinations, whether foster homes, shelters, or specially-built enclosures. Sometimes, particularly in the case of foster homes, the new home may be not be far away. But shelters willing and able to take in large numbers of rabbits may be located several states away, or even in another country. Finding transportation for large numbers of rabbits for large distances can be challenging, to say the least!

Lisa White tells the story of a unique organization that helps with transporting rabbits:

The Bunderground Railroad
by Lisa White

The Bunderground Railroad was founded in 2003 as a part of Rabbitwise by Lana Lehr. Sadly Lana passed away in 2016, but her legacy of rabbit advocacy lives on in the Bunderground. The Bunderground functions as a volunteer-based group of drivers that transport rescued rabbits from overcrowded areas where rabbits may be facing euthanasia due to lack of space to less stressed areas where the rabbits have a chance at finding a home. We also transport rabbits to their adoptive homes for rescues. Bundergounds drivers are strictly volunteers and accept no payment for their services.

A Bunderground starts with a request from a rescue group or shelter. The starting point and destination are determined, as well as dates and how many buns and carriers will be on board. The transport request is posted and volunteers sign up for legs that are anywhere from 70 miles long to 200-300 miles long. Once the transport legs are all filled a run sheet is completed that includes drivers vehicle and contact information, meet times and locations, any special instructions needed for the buns on board, and then the buns are their way!

We request, whenever possible, that the sending rescue or shelter provide carriers for the trip. If the buns can stay in one carrier their whole trip it minimizes the stress of being handled that is necessary to switch carriers, and saves the time of switching carriers as well. If this isn't possible the buns are switched to new carriers at each stop, which is done inside the vehicle with the doors and windows closed.

We like to use hard side carriers with newspaper or Carefresh type litter on the bottom with a generous layer of hay on top to keep the buns clean and dry while traveling. All carriers must have a water source – either a water bottle or a bowl that attaches to the front of the carrier

– and greens are provided for the buns to snack on throughout the trip. We ask everyone to bring along bottled water to refill bottles and bowls. Most buns don't want to eat or drink much while the car is in motion, so we stop every 2-4 hours to let the buns have a break and eat and drink.

We do roughly forty to fifty transports a year, sometimes more. Some of these runs are posted on the Bunderground Facebook page; others are along routes where we have regular drivers and are arranged by private message

The Bunderground is also active after natural disasters like Hurricane Irma. We helped transport bunnies from the Key West SPCA after their bunny house was destroyed in the storm. All bunnies were moved from the bunny house before the storm, so thankfully no one was injured, but they needed to be moved to other rescues as soon as the roads into the Keys were open. A group of dedicated bunny advocates mobilized to move the bunnies all the way from Key West to Triangle Rabbits in Raleigh North Carolina.

Health certificates are generally a good idea for travel within the US, but are not required by all states and there are exemptions for states you are only traveling through or where you are only spending a short time. Crossing the border into Canada we always recommend checking

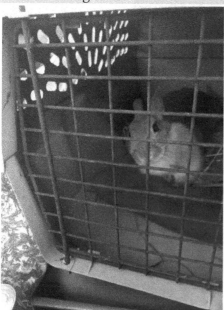

with the appropriate Canadian authority regarding importation of pet rabbits. Each province may handle it differently and requirements and laws can be changed and updated, so having the most current information is crucial.

In many cases Bunderground drivers are asked to pick up bunnies from situations where they have been abused, neglected, or have illnesses and injuries allowed to go untreated, and we transport them to rescue or veterinary clinics where they can receive medical care. In some cases the nearest place where they can receive care is several hours away. In one case a little bunny later named Chocolate was thrown from his hutch in West Virginia (at the time it was believed his back was broken). A neighbor saw this happen and was able to get Chocolate from the yard and bring him into her house, but she couldn't keep him or get him medical care. She reached out for help and sent a video of Chocolate struggling to move. This was a critical

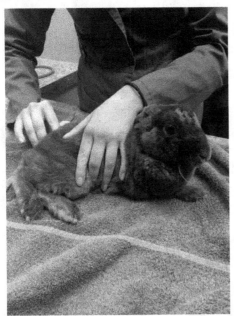

situation; a volunteer in WV about one and a half hours from Chocolate's location was contacted, and a rescue in VA Friends of Rabbits agreed to take Chocolate in and get him the medical care he needed. The nearest truly rabbit-savvy vet was 3-4 hours away in Fairfax, VA but Chocolate was not going to be able to travel there without assessment and pain meds to stabilize him. A vet clinic in WV about an hour from Chocolate and was willing to see him was found. At the clinic he got x-rays which determined his injury was not a spinal fracture but a disc injury. He received medications for pain management and sub-q fluids, which enabled him to safely make the trip to the vet clinic in Fairfax where he spent a week recovering from his injuries. Chocolate is still unable to hop normally, but he is a happy boy and get around very well.

In cases where we are asked to transport highly at-risk buns we do everything in our power to assure the bunny is stabilized before traveling. So far we have been very lucky in that everybun has made it to their destination, but we realize this may not always be the case, for bunnies are such a combination of strength and frailty. Most of the transports the Bundergound does are done by relay drivers, but occasionally our trip coordinators act in an advisory capacity to larger transports of buns.

We help with planning, mapping out overnight stops for the drivers and buns, and advise on how best to prepare carriers for a long trip and what emergency supplies should be on board. We also locate vet clinics and emergency clinics along the route just in case they are needed, and sometimes find rescue placements. While Bunderground drivers accept no payment for their time and effort, on longer transports with a lot of bunnies on board a van is needed as well as hotels for the drivers. In these cases we will help estimate the cost for van, gas and hotels. We helped with transporting bunnies from the Humane Society of the Treasure Coast, the Key West SPCA after Hurricane Irma, and assisted with the rabbit crisis in Las Vegas.

Finding overnights along the route so drivers can go sleep and the buns can be out of carriers and rest is an important part of any long transport and it's an incredible amount of work for the overnighters. All bunnies must come out of their carriers and the carriers cleaned after noting whether there is an  appropriate amount of elimination in the carrier for each bunny. Any bun who doesn't have enough poop or pee in their carrier is tagged for observation and potentially a vet visit. On long transports drivers will stop every four hours to check each bunny and make sure all have water and greens and hay and that all buns look alert and in good condition. To date we have not worked with a transport that went straight through without overnight stops, but would certainly be open to it if there was no other way, and would make it as safe as possible for both drivers and buns. Rabbits always travel with their bonded mates in the same carrier.

Releasing colony rabbits in a new location

Letting captured colony rabbits loose in their new location can be a worrisome time. Sorelle Saidman, who worked under Laura-Leah Shaw during the UVic rescue, went on to be involved in many more large rabbit rescues, and founded the non-profit Rabbitats Rescue Society. On the Rabbitats.org website there are several suggestions for making the release of rescued colony rabbits easier, including releasing the colonies of rabbits at the same time to avoid territorial fighting, and having two or three smaller colonies in the new area instead of a single large one. This allows the rescuers to rotate rabbits among the colonies and separate any that fight constantly. See the rabbitats.org website for more information.

After the move

If life were 'fair' one would expect that after colony rabbits survive the trauma of being trapped, moved and relocated, they might have a relatively peaceful and stress-free life. Sometimes this does happen. But other times it does not. Feelings can run high over colony rabbits, especially if the rescue was a high-profile one. And not everyone shares the rescuers' view that these rabbits are much sinned-against and deserve a chance for a good life.

In a July 2011 piece by Andrew Weichel entitled "Intruder stomps 20 rabbits at BC sanctuary," it was reported that at a sanctuary housing many of the UVic rabbits a human intruder literally stomped twenty of the rabbits to death. Less than a year earlier, several rabbits that had escaped the same sanctuary had been shot by neighbors before the rabbits could be recaptured and returned to the sanctuary.

To help prevent vandalism it is recommended that sanctuaries taking large numbers of rescued colony rabbits have some kind of security system that includes cameras. An expensive monitored system is not necessary; good coverage can be provided using hidden trail cameras.

Examples of Rabbit Rescues

It is heartening to see that many, if not most, rabbit rescues that are attempted result in saving the majority of the rabbits. That does not mean that success comes easily! Every rescue is different, and no matter how experienced a person may be, new problems a rescuer has never faced before have a tendency to crop up. In this section we have stories about a variety of rabbit rescues, from small to large, each of which arose in a very different manner. The first of these was a very small rescue of a different kind by a person who, although she had worked in animal welfare for nearly thirty years, was NOT a bunny person:

Ginger and Cinnamon
by Shari Olson

I have worked and volunteered in animal welfare for going on thirty years. I have done everything from intake to adoptions to investigations. During that entire time, I always had the same question: "Why on earth would people want a pet rabbit?" Don't get me wrong, bunnies are cute, but seeing many times their more snarky side when surrendered to animal shelters, I just didn't see the appeal.

My partner and I have moved around the country and are currently residing in New York, where I became a volunteer wildlife rehabilitator. When I first started out, I helped on the hotline that our organization has for the public to call when in need of help regarding wildlife matters. One of the first things I learned was that I could find someone to take a rabid grizzly bear before they would take an orphaned bunny. Baby wild bunnies have a high mortality rate, which is how I got into specializing in them. I learned that it is extremely helpful to have access to adult rabbits when raising eyes-closed baby bunnies. The reason is that once their eyes open, they need to have access to cecotropes from an adult rabbit. This helps their digestive tract be able to process grass.

I was working one day when a customer and I got to talking. I mentioned that I was a wildlife rehabber and specialized in orphaned baby bunnies. Come to find out he was a "rabbit guy" who had a couple of Flemish giants, Ginger and Cinnamon. I asked if I could go by and see if I could find some cecotropes, and then had to explain what they were. He laughed and said, "Sure, knock yourself out." So I went to his house when I got off work. He took me out to a shed where the rabbits were housed in wire cages. It was sad to see. I pulled grass and weeds from the yard to give them a treat. I was able to find some cecotropes, which helped with my batch of orphaned bunnies that had just opened their eyes.

I eventually found out the reason he had the rabbits. It was for meat. He would breed them and raise the offspring for food. I was shocked. I try not to judge people. I asked him why he ate rabbit. He said he was raised on it, along with squirrel and opossum and whatever else his family would be able to get. Over the course of the next couple of years, I would go over and see the girls and make sure they had food and water. During that time he must have stopped breeding them, as I never saw any babies. I would go over even when I didn't have any orphaned bunnies that needed cecotropes.

The gentleman who owned Ginger and Cinnamon was an older man, and he started to have health problems. One day I got a call from him. It was late winter, early spring. "Shari, I wanted to see if you would like the girls, I can't take care of them anymore. It's getting to be too much. I know how much you like them, so I thought I would ask you first." I told him I would talk it over with my partner and give him a call back in the next day. My first thought was, she is going to kill me. I needed another pet like I needed a hole in my head. But I could not bear to think what would happen to them if I didn't take them. My partner, being compassionate like me, caved. We made space for them in a little room we were using as a work space in the house. Now it became "the bunny room."

We put a divider up through the middle of the room, as they had obviously not been spayed yet. We had a lot of guidance from my friend Meg, aka "the crazy bunny lady." We got them spayed and about a month after the surgery we introduced them. They bonded instantly. It was like they had

been waiting their whole lives to be able to snuggle with each other. It made my heart melt.

Their personalities have really come out since I brought them home. Ginger, who is actually the mother of Cinnamon, acts younger. She loves running around and tossing toys. Cinnamon, the daughter, is much more laid-back and enjoys lounging around nibbling on hay. They no longer had to be on wire flooring, no longer had to be separated from each other in wire cages, no longer had to stuck out in a shed in a backyard. Seeing them run, play, and snuggle with each other and me, I finally realized why people have bunnies as pets. They are the sweetest, most loving, and affectionate pets you could ever have. I am so glad they came into my life. I am now officially a crazy bunny lady…and proud of it!

Caroline Charland, the founder of Bunny Bunch, has been involved in large rabbit rescues at several dumpsites. She describes two of those rescues:

Garden Grove, California, Park Abandonment

Rabbits were being dumped at a large park in Garden Grove, California; a park that was not open to the public anymore, although at one time it was a place where people fished and camped. It had a large pond in the middle surrounded by trees and brush, and was fenced in by tall chain link fences. Over the years people started dumping their rabbits there. We got a call from the city asking if we could catch and take the rabbits, as the local businesses were complaining about the burrows the rabbits were making under their buildings. The burrows were affecting the foundations of the buildings, and if we didn't take this on and rescue all the rabbits they would have been killed. We were told there were about two hundred rabbits but when we had finished the rescue it ended up being over five hundred.

Ontario, California Business Rescue

We were told rabbits had been living loose on the property of an equipment rental business for over twenty years. The rabbits had been there so long they had formed multiple colonies, and the colonies had spread to over eight more properties. There were many hawks in the area getting the rabbits and squirrels were eating newborn rabbits. The property next door was a car rental, and one of the employees there was caught on tape killing the rabbits. The authorities got involved and the employee was changed with animal cruelty. All the rabbits were rescued, and several people got involved in re-homing the rabbits. Right in the middle of this rescue a breeder dumped about thirty more rabbits on the property; they were all caught and taken in at Bunny Bunch.

Our History with Rabbits and Rabbit Rescue
by Bob Sherman

Our history with rabbits began in 2006 when we adopted Penny Ann, a Holland Lop. She had lived in a neighbor's backyard hutch and we gave her a forever indoor home. We didn't know a lot about house rabbits, but learned quickly with the help of Portland Rabbit Advocates (rabbitadvocates.org). At the time, they were closely connected to the Oregon Humane Society. After retirement from Portland Police in 2007, I began volunteering at OHS. I would work two shifts per week, Tuesday through Thursday, 10 a.m. to 2 p.m., in the small animal room. I would care for the rabbits and meet people who were interested in adopting.

We moved to Kelowna, B.C. in 2009. Here we connected with a group that had conducted a rescue operation that involved hundreds of rabbits that had been abandoned in an industrial area along a main road. The City of Kelowna was pressured to "do something." They did. They hired a "contractor" to "cull" the rabbits. Although humane methods were to have been used, this was not the case. All came to a head when a security guard witnessed the daughter of this contractor stomping rabbits to death. After the guard reported this incident, the City dumped the contractor and the rescue group stepped in to do an urgent rescue. *(Note: The City then enacted a by-law that prohibited the sale or give-away of rabbits not spayed or neutered. This helped a lot to prevent future problems. Of course, there are still dishonest people, and people who are outside the city.)*

We volunteered and helped build well planned, safe outdoor

enclosures that housed about 50-100 rabbits each. With the rescue group's support we began an adoption program. We figured that the volunteers had been so busy with the rescue and on-going care that no one had time to do this. But as we began this program, we were met with resistance by a group of recalcitrant volunteers, who seemed to think that the rabbits were "their rabbits." We were successful in finding forever homes for about twenty rabbits (out of about 600) before that group of volunteers became so annoying that several of us said "enough" and left the organization.

My bride Marie and I then began volunteering at the Kelowna SPCA, caring for the rabbits. There were generally two to five at any given time. We helped with adoption counseling, and tactfully offered suggestions to staff. We presented this in such a way that our ideas were implemented when possible. We also developed good relations with the manager and staff. We even made ourselves available to go out and respond to reports of loose rabbits. We successfully rescued all that we encountered; which were lone rabbits in neighborhoods. We would use x-pens and were able to corral them for transport to the shelter.

As we continued to volunteer at the Kelowna SPCA, we had the opportunity to make presentations about rabbits to the Summer Kid's Camp attendees. Each summer for about five years, we have reached 150-200 children. We have a power point presentation, have a real rabbit or rabbits at the session, and engage the children with various methods. Our efforts are well received. We firmly believe that the best way to improve the future of rabbits as house pets is to educate the youth. We have also annually offered a "Bunny 101" Session at the shelter for adults who want to learn about rabbits. Kelowna is a small town, so even if only a few people show up, we feel that it is successful.

The Kelowna SPCA has, in my opinion, become a model for rabbit care. Staff have become familiar with nutritional requirements, need for space, medical care, and adoption criteria for rabbits. The past and current managers have been very supportive.

Marie and I plan to move to the Roseburg, Oregon area when our house in Kelowna sells. We still have our one house rabbit, Mr. Lucky. We plan to continue wherever we are in working for rabbits. We are also considering starting a Bunny Boarding service to help people who need care for their pets while on vacation.

Not all rabbits that end up needing rescuing were intentionally and callously cast off. A respondent to our questionnaire told of a gentleman who genuinely loved and cared for rabbits. He took in many rabbits that others no longer wanted and gave them a home. At the time he died, it is estimated he had about 200 rabbits. But unfortunately he had not made provision for his rabbits in the event of his death. Although neighbors and others gave the rabbits food, it was often not rabbit-appropriate and over time the population dwindled. Finally a Good Samaritan contacted the local HRS and the remaining rabbits – about fifty – were rescued. But by this time the rabbits were thin and wary. Many had bite wounds and torn ears/tails and a large proportion of them needed immediate veterinary attention. Of those rabbits found dead, most had been victims of predators or had been struck by vehicles.

This story illustrates the necessity of making provision for one's rabbits in one's will. It is easy to put this task off if one is busy, but a person's much-loved rabbits may suffer and die if it is not attended to in time. Whether you have one rabbit or run a shelter with hundreds, if you have not already made provision for them, please do so without delay! They depend on you for their care; now and after you are gone.

CHAPTER 7: MANAGING CARE FOR LARGE NUMBERS OF RABBITS

Taking care of many rabbits is not an easy task, whether they are large numbers of individually rescued rabbits or a group of rabbits from an established colony. Most rescued colony rabbits do best if their placement after rescue allows them to continue to live in a colony, even if it is a smaller one. Large feral colonies tend to be composed of smaller sub-colonies, and this makes a natural way to divide the colony for their final placements. Individually rescued rabbits may be more difficult to integrate into small groups or pairs, but it can be done.

Although rescuers may occasionally be fortunate enough to find a place that is already set up to care for such a group it is more likely that some structures will need to be built. Nor is housing the only factor that will need to be considered when planning to establish a sheltered rabbit colony; feeding, sanitation, medical care, and many other aspects of colony care will need to be carefully thought through in advance.

Housing

Housing for a colony of rabbits that is going to remain at the site for the lifetime of the colony is the first, and perhaps most important concern. One of the determiners of the kind of housing will be the geographical location. What works for the rabbits in a temperate coastal situation will not be the same as successful housing for a desert location. The kind of predators in an area may also influence the style of housing, as will the origin of the rabbits to be housed, *i.e.*, whether the rabbits are individual dumped rabbits that have been rescued or are from a colony of dumped/feral rabbits. Debby offers these general guidelines:

Invest in quality construction that will provide the safest environment, whether the rabbits are to live in outdoor colonies, indoor-outdoor housing or an inside sanctuary. Speaking mainly to outdoor spaces, never underestimate the power and intelligence of predators. Keep in mind how adept dogs and coyotes are at digging under fencing, how a raccoon can use their "hands" to open latches, and the ability of a mountain lion to jump over an electric fence from a nearby tree or rocks. Overhead protection – netting or a roof- is essential, as is predator-proof flooring, visual barriers and places for a rabbit to hide. Climate and common weather conditions will dictate adaptations that may have to be made. A good rule of thumb is to make the rabbits' environment predator-proof enough to keep them safe from a strong, large predator as well as being constructed to keep that predator inside if the situation was reversed.

Predators are not the only life forms from which it will be necessary to protect the rabbits. Please see the story on botfly larvae and fly prevention later in this chapter to help keep rabbits safer when exposed to flies. Also be extremely careful that your rabbits are never in contact with raccoon excrement via hay, grasses, or other food as serious disease or death can result from raccoon roundworm (*Baylisascaris*).

We present three different types of housing for rabbits. One for housing large numbers of non-colony rabbits (but which could easily be adapted for colony rabbits as well), one designed for colony rabbits in the northwestern US, and one that was used for colony rabbits (but which will also work for non-colony rabbits) in a high desert landscape.

South Carolina

One of the pioneers in rabbit rescue in the United States is Caroline Gilbert of The Rabbit Sanctuary, Incorporated, located near Simpsonville, South Carolina. I have great respect for Caroline Gilbert and her contributions to rabbit rescue over the years and felt very honored when she agreed to contribute to this book project on discarded rabbits.

Caroline began rescuing rabbits in the mid 1960s and before long started a sanctuary specifically for domestic rabbits on her 30-acre farm, a project which grew with guidance from Cleveland Amory of the Fund for Animals. Rabbits at the sanctuary are not adopted out, but given a "Home for Life." They live as natural a life as possible in a predator-proof safe environment. Many of the rabbits have been rescued from laboratories, meat farms, or situations where they were treated with neglect and cruelty. The Rabbit Sanctuary, Incorporated, is the first lifetime care rabbit sanctuary to receive verification from the Global Federation of Animal Sanctuaries.

Caroline designed the living quarters for the rabbits, which she termed "rabbitats." To my knowledge, she was the first person to use this term for rabbit housing, although many rescues and sanctuaries now also use the term.

The Design and Construction of Rabbitats
by Caroline Gilbert

Rabbitats provide rabbits with as nearly a natural rabbit life a possible and still allow caretakers to provide individual care.The ability to make daily observations for potential and visible problems (e.g. abscesses, parasites, injuries, infections, ear scratching, weepy eye, growths, nasal discharge, needed nail trimming, etc.) is critical.

The rabbitats described herein provide adequate protection for an Upstate South Carolina climate: winter lows in the mid-30's and summer highs in the mid-90's. Modifications would be required for climates less temperate.

The rabbitats are completely predator proof against indigenous Upstate South Carolina wildlife (except bears) and stray dogs and cats. There are no black bears in this immediate area. Rather, they are located further north in the mountains. Here again, modifications would be required to ensure the rabbits' safety against predators in the immediate area of the build.

Location

Wooded areas provide an adequate mix of sun and shade as well as wind breaks. Trees should be cleared back about 30 feet so they pose no threat to the structure. The area should not be prone to flooding and should drain thoroughly.

Main Structure

The structure measures 100 feet long by 20 feet deep and is constructed of ¼-inch hardware cloth framed at the bottom. There is a 1-foot deep cement perimeter (walkway) around the outside of the structure which prevents predators from digging into the structure. The roof is galvanized metal. The floor is 1-inch stainless steel wire set at a depth of about two feet. This wire is covered with about two feet of soil. (In South Carolina, this would be hard red clay.)

There is one main door measuring about 4 feet for general access. A large double door should be built at one end of the structure to allow access for machinery such as a bobcat.

Outside the main door is a lamp on a post with an electrical outlet and a water hydrant (to ensure water availability in below freezing temperatures).

Territories

The rabbitat contains nine ten-foot-square individual territories (i.e. yards) located in a row down the center of the structure. Each territory has its own three-foot wide gate access, is framed out in one-inch wire on metal posts, and is four feet high. This configuration provides added  safety for the rabbits. Should one escape an individual territory, he/she is still safely confined in the main rabbitat structure.

This row of individual territories is surrounded by an 8-foot walkway in front, allowing for easy gate access. The back walkway  measures two feet with five-foot walkways on each end. These walkways provide a buffer against any animal that may wander onto the property. Without these buffers, nose-to-nose contact (or near contact) would incite panic causing the rabbits to injure themselves.

Plastic lumber boards are set around the base of each territory to prevent rabbits from digging next door into their neighbors' territories. Further protection is provided by the stainless steel wire floor covered with approximately two feet of dirt. This supports the rabbits' natural instinct to dig but doesn't allow them to dig out or anything to dig in.

The end result of this rabbitat model is that the rabbits are completely wrapped in wire and are safe. More importantly, the rabbits know they are safe.

Burrows

The simulated burrows set into the ground in the center of each territory are made of linear polyethylene, a material not desirable chewing for rabbits. The design was created by the Rabbit Sanctuary Inc. and molded by Moeller Marine Products of Chattanooga, TN. [The design could  not be replicated due to copyright; contact the Sanctuary if interested.]

 The design of the burrow provides warmth in the winter and is cool in the summer. In addition, the burrow offers a hiding place which a rabbit can dive into when alarmed, affording safety and a place to hole up, which is a rabbit's natural instinct. Straw should be kept in the burrow for comfort and nesting.

Food and Water

A bottomless wooden frame lined with straw is set at the front of each territory. Clean hay is placed into the tray daily. Some rabbits will use a corner of the tray as a bathroom. Others think the tray is a great place to hang out!

Of course, each territory contains a dish for chow and a large heavy crock for water.

Enrichment

Some territories have terra cotta flue pipes which the rabbits rest in, hop through, or sit on. These pipes may be difficult to find, but they are a rabbit favorite.

Toys are not recommended or required. Rabbitat rabbits have companions, rabbit neighbors, and space for digging and tunneling. The straw provides nesting material for does, pregnant or not. (All Rabbit

Sanctuary Inc. does are spayed.) In addition, the rabbitats allow for sunbathing, dirt bathing, grazing in full hay trays, grooming, napping, and exploring.

Caution: Whenever placing **anything** in a rabbit's territory, it MUST be placed directly on the wire floor. This will prevent a rabbit from digging under the item, resulting in the item falling on the rabbit, trapping or injuring it.

Roomies

No more than 3 rabbits per territory, please. All spayed or neutered, of course! The ideal roommate situation is two females and one male per territory.

"Bunny" Building

The Rabbit Sanctuary Inc. has an on-site health building where rabbits recovering from surgery and those ailing are housed until recovered and can be returned to their territories. Elderly rabbits who can no longer tolerate outdoor temperatures are housed in the "Bunny" Building to live out their lives.

Washington State

Precious Life Animal Sanctuary

by Debby Widolf

Ralph Turner and his wife Caryl co-founded Precious Life Animal Sanctuary (501C 3), which is located on 85 acres on the Olympic Peninsula in Washington State. Precious Life Sanctuary gives wildlife, farm animals, dogs, cats and rabbits that have had a rough start to life a second chance; to be who they are and know they are protected and valued.

I had many questions for Ralph about the domestic rabbits at the sanctuary. Ralph is adamant about giving the rabbits – which number about 100 – total freedom to be who they are. He lovingly describes his own joy at watching the rabbits burrowing, socializing, establishing territories, running, chasing and exploring their natural environment with curiosity.

The hilly rabbit enclosure, located on two-thirds of an acre, is surrounded by 8-foot cyclone fencing that is buried two feet into the ground and filled with concrete to keep the rabbits safe from predators. In addition, another 6-foot strip of cyclone fencing was

laid down inside and along the entire perimeter fence, kept down with u-shaped rebar. This eliminates any deep burrowing next to the perimeter fencing and is an added safety measure that insures that no rabbit can ever escape and be put in harm's way.

Attached on top of the cyclone fencing is strong netting supported by pipe beams. A variety of structures were built to provide the rabbits proper shelter from the weather and keep the hay and pellet feeders dry. Ralph adds that, even though the rabbits' homes are comfortable, many still prefer to burrow through the hard ground to make their own elaborate abodes.

Ralph found that the enclosure withstood most weather although the 1.5 inch square netting had to be replaced after an especially severe winter. The heavier snowfall caused snow and ice to build up on the netting, collapsing the entire net. New netting with 3.5 inch squares was used to replace it. The larger openings in the netting did not allow as much snow and ice to build up but were still small enough to keep predatory birds from getting inside.

The use of heavy equipment to clear much of the site, installing the perimeter fencing plus inside fencing, and the extensive burrowing by the rabbits severely disturbed the soil. In a short time, thistles and

nettles took over the entire enclosure and eliminated all the native grasses. It took a number of years of grueling work by dedicated volunteers to literally dig out the weeds by the roots and re-seed with native grasses. Now the rabbits enjoy a lush carpet of green grass under their feet and can munch on it throughout the year. I was impressed by the tenacity of the Precious Life team digging out all noxious weeds by hand month after month.

Feeding 100 rabbits can be an expensive and daunting task. Fortunately, a local grocer donates greens for the rabbits twice a week during the winter months and three times weekly in the summer, usually around six boxes of produce at a time. Ralph stated that in addition to the greens the rabbits consume four to five fifty-pound bags of pellets a month and hay is provided year-round. Though different systems were considered to provide water for the rabbits, Ralph found the most realistic and reliable solution was simply to bring large containers of water using his trusty ATV.

Precious Life Sanctuary is not situated close to town or to a rabbit vet so many minor problems are treated at the sanctuary. Ralph states that rabbits do get vet care when problems are too serious to treat on site. Common ailments include eye problems and occasional fight wounds. Their Rabbit Coordinator monitors the rabbit area several times a week and keeps an eye on the health and well-being of the rabbits. Ralph noted that fighting among the rabbits usually occurs when new rabbits are introduced or when a rabbit(s) crosses over into an established colony. With time, most rabbits establish themselves into colonies, but Ralph has found that about five percent do not adapt well into colony living and these timid rabbits are removed from the colony and found new homes.

Precious Life Sanctuary works with the Tacoma Humane Society in Tacoma, Washington. Two or three times a year the Humane Society brings rabbits that have not been successfully adopted for reasons such as aggression, biting, or poor litter box behavior. These rabbits often adapt better to sanctuary living. Ralph and the Precious Life Sanctuary team have also taken large groups of feral/community rabbits that had been abandoned.

In 2006 fifty of the abandoned domestic rabbits living on the University of Victoria campus found sanctuary at Precious Life. These rabbits started life in the sanctuary barn and were then introduced into their protected outside area in groups of five at a time to ease the stress on the rabbits. Although initially the 50 rabbits had an area of the rabbit enclosure to themselves, over the years they joined in with the other

groups. Precious Life Sanctuary also took on 102 rabbits from Woodland Park in Seattle, Washington, in 2007. Several of these rabbits are still alive at age 12! Most recently a group of rabbits from a hoarding situation in Los Angeles joined the Precious Life family.

Ralph finds that the majority of the rabbits live a normal life span, between seven to ten years or more, have stable health and utilize their above ground housing as well as their underground burrows. He is adamant that building the proper enclosure for the geographic areais most important to establishing successful sanctuary living. He added that sometimes people who have house rabbit(s) in the city can be unrealistic or critical of the lives of the rabbits in their large enclosure where they experience all kinds of weather. He says he only has to watch them exploring, digging, chasing, playing and exhibiting their natural behavior to know they are happy and content in their own world.

Kanab, Utah

Housing Option for Domestic Community Rabbits

by Debby Widolf

A yurt is a very old type of shelter that can be traced back to Genghis Khan. Nomadic people of Mongolia were observed by Marco Polo using their sturdy round "tents" made of rods and thick layers of felt. Yurts have been used in some of the most inhospitable climates in the world, from the Sahara to the polar tundra.

Modern yurts are moveable circular dwellings made of lattice and flexible wood. Some yurts are set on a wood platform floor, while others are set up on a concrete slab. They come in different sizes, from about sixteen to thirty feet across.

It is not surprising is that yurts are used as a shelter for animals, including sanctuary rabbits. The versatile yurt may be a cost effective structure for domestic colony rabbits, a rescue/adoption building, and/or a medical unit. A total of five thirty-foot yurts housed three hundred feral/community rabbits at Best Friends Animal Sanctuary in Utah. The yurts were set up on wood platform floors that were covered initially with tarps. The tarps were replaced with vinyl floors in some of the yurts due to breakdown of the tarps from hard use. The floors were easy to sweep and mop. All yurts were cooled in the summer with swamp coolers and ventilated using the up-lift in the center of the dome. Electric heaters were used for heat in the winter months. Double laundry sinks and running hot and cold water were installed in each yurt. Solar panels can be installed in appropriate climates, dramatically cutting the cost of electricity

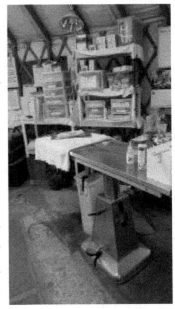

particularly if you put up the yurt as long term housing. A basic yurt can be put up by four people in around four to five days; more time is needed for plumbing, electricity, and the construction of inside and outside connecting areas for the rabbits.

A portion of one yurt can be set up as the medical area using a stainless steel vet examination table or table/s that allow for easy cleaning and disinfecting. Stacked shelving, sealed containers for medications, supplies, a refrigerator for medicines needing refrigeration, special rabbit diets, and produce will be needed. A sharps container, lock box for medications considered narcotics, a log for controlled medications, and responsible person/s appointed as keepers of the keys to the box are also needed. If there are a number of quarantined or ill rabbits, they can be housed in the medical yurt.

Depending on the floor area of the yurt you choose, the inside can be converted into angular shaped runs for the rabbits. Use the center of the yurt for supplies. Plan on a 4×5 or 5×5 feet space for 2-3 rabbits; multiply this out according to the square footage of each run in the yurt. Gates and runs can be constructed from inexpensive PVC pipe and ½" hardware cloth. Other supplies for runs include: blankets, rugs, towels, rabbit-safe toys, large feeding bowls, (round metal pans are good), and large water bowls. Tunnels made from large cardboard tubes or pvc pipes, "hidey houses," made from cardboard boxes, tops of pet carriers or other safe materials will be appreciated  by the rabbits. These will give the rabbits a place to get away from each other if they want. Large black plastic litter pans, (mortar pans from places such as Home Depot), filled with wood stove pellets, and fresh hay need to be placed in each run. A general rule would be 2-3 rabbits per large litter box. Newspaper makes a good litter for the bottom of the pans, is easily disposed of, and very economical if finances are a concern.

Large plastic garbage cans with tight-fitting lids are good storage containers for rabbit pellets and litter material. The cans with wheels are worth the extra money. If your rabbit food is stored outside, metal cans with locks will keep out wildlife and protect the food from weather. If the numbers of rabbits housed requires the storage of many bales of hay that can't all be stored in the yurt, a wood or metal shed makes good storage, or cover the hay bales tightly with tarps and place them inside a fenced area.

If the property is large enough, outdoor runs can be built out from the yurt, connected to runs inside by a small rabbit or doggie type of door with a slide in door to keep rabbits in at night if needed is best and safest. These spaces will allow you to double the numbers of rabbits the yurt can accommodate comfortably. The outdoor runs can be built on a wood platform or with an earth floor. If using the earth floor, either dig down a minimum of two feet to imbed the fencing or connect a floor of hardware cloth onto the vertical fencing of chain link and cover it with earth or sand. A snake and small animal barrier can be placed along the bottom 20-25 inches of fencing using ¼" hardware cloth. It is recommended that the entire yurt area be fenced and electrified if you are in a high predator area. There are multiple types of roofing material available for the outdoor runs: metal, wood, heavy netting (consider snow loads in areas with harder winters). Sun screen cloth can provide outdoor shade areas. One or two outside doors are needed for access to the outside runs and gates between the runs will give better access for caregivers and volunteers. Locks, combination or padlocks are necessary for outside doors. Be aware that some predators are very adept at opening slide or hook types of locks.

There are multiple resources and companies that sell yurts online. Used yurts can be purchased on E-bay and online lists. Yurts are subject to some zoning regulations. Be sure they are allowed on the site you choose and what the requirements are. Yurts are a great option for housing colony/community rabbits or other type of rabbit rescue. They are approximately half the overall cost of a metal or wood building.

Introducing New Rabbits to an Established Group

When rabbits live in colonies they develop a hierarchical society and may not be welcoming to new rabbits. For this reason, care must be taken in introducing rabbits to an established group. Debby Widolf describes how to maximize the chances of a positive outcome:

> Collective experience has shown that if a small group of four or more rabbits are introduced to an established colony at the same time, the outcome can be more successful and less stressful for the entering rabbits. The new rabbits will have allies

and the established colony will usually accept a new group more easily than a single rabbit or pair of rabbits.

New introductions need to be observed carefully. Give yourself ample time to allow observation. It is recommended that a volunteer sleep over at the colony if possible, for one or two nights, as well as daytime supervision. Some hair pulling, chasing and mounting behaviors can be expected. Colony rabbits will most often work out their differences in time, although serious fighting, biting, rolling fights, aggressive circling behaviors need quick intervention. Concurrently with new introductions, provide new items of interest, rearrange old houses and add new ones (remember to build hidey spaces vertically as well). Also add more litter boxes, food dishes and hay to the area. This will somewhat break up the territory and give the new rabbits a chance to establish themselves.

When first building a colony site, make more than one area within the colony using moveable fences and barriers that can be set up quickly. Having several areas will give you the option of moving rabbits to a group they are better suited for. Examples are older rabbits, disabled rabbits, timid or "bully" rabbits to another grouping.

Feeding and Nutrition for Colony Rabbits

Feeding a colony of abandoned/feral rabbits is a little more difficult – at the outset – than feeding small groups of rabbits in a shelter. But once it is figured out and a routine established, feeding a colony often takes less time than feeding large numbers of rabbits kept in pairs or small groups. Debby:

> Feeding colonies of community rabbits can present the volunteers and caregivers with challenges. Factors that will need to be considered include: how many rabbits there are, the environment and weather, availability of natural food sources, numbers of very young rabbits and lactating and pregnant mothers. The practical considerations of what the financial resources are, the numbers of volunteers and their commitment

to care also come into play. How the feeding and watering is managed is dependent on investigating all these variables.

In a temperate climate where dense food sources are plentiful and a large foraging area is present, most of the rabbits' basic food needs may be met naturally for a limited time. As the colony grows however, natural food resources become scarce even in the best of conditions. Where there are seasonal changes, finding nutritious food as harsh weather arrives leads to stress, disease and death of many unmanaged colonies of domestic rabbits. Most often these rabbits are in need of nutritional food and a clean water source.

As a beginning, large groups of rabbits can be fed bales of alfalfa hay or alfalfa blend hay and survive on this food. The hay must be protected from getting wet and moldy or being used as a nesting place by other animals. Two X bases made out of wood and 2" wire can be constructed with a hinged metal lid on top to keep the hay dry and a few inches off the ground. A quick container can be made out of a large sturdy plastic tub with a lid. Anchor the inside of the tub to the ground. Make a 4-5" hole in both ends about 2" off the ground, and keep the tub stuffed with fresh hay.

Most rescues and/or sanctuaries housing large numbers of rabbits will attempt to seek donors for as much of the food as possible. Easiest to obtain are usually donations of produce, although sometimes donors can be found for pellets and hay as well. The quality of some of these donations, especially of produce, may be marginal, so it should be carefully sorted. A reliance on donated foodstuffs also means that the rabbits will most likely be receiving a variety of food, such as multiple brands of pellets. For this reason it can be a good idea to mix foodstuffs after they are sorted. This way the rabbits are less likely to object to changes.

Rabbits, like people, may have different preferences on where they want to eat, so presenting the food in different areas and different ways (some in a pan, some directly on the ground, some in the open, others under cover) will allow the rabbits to choose.

At any colony, be sure to protect feed from rodents and raccoons, as fecal contamination from these species can have serious or even deadly consequences for rabbits. Keeping in well-sealed containers and only putting out enough food for the rabbits to eat that day will help keep from attracting too many other animals.

Costs

The costs of building a place to house colony rabbits and the maintenance costs (food, etc.) will vary depending on the geographical area and how many donors can be found. Most rescuers involved in large rabbit colony removal and relocation are able to find donors for at least some of the expenses, including some veterinary care, feed, and housing construction costs. But to give a general idea of expenses, here are examples of setup costs for 500 rabbits that were given in a Rabbitats general presentation, "Abandoned Rabbits: Review" updated December of 2018:

Spays and neuters: $37,500

Vaccinations: $1,500 to $5,000

Sanctuary housing: $31,500

Overhead and care: Approximately $4,500/month or $54,000/year

See the website of Rabbitats.org for more information.

Rescuers who responded to the survey Debby and I sent out all provided hay, greens and pellets to the rescued rabbits. The greens were the least costly; most of the rescues either grew or collected their own or found businesses willing to donate produce. Hay and pellets cost about the same to provide; hay was cheaper than pellets but more was given to the rabbits. Total feed costs ranged from under $500/month for smaller groups of rabbits up to $1,500/month for sanctuaries housing very large colonies.

Disease and other Medical Issues in Colonies

This is not a book on the medical care of rabbits, so only diseases or other medical conditions that may present problems in large groups of rabbits will be addressed. This includes facultative and obligate flystrike, mites, coccidiosis, Encephalitozoonosis, diseases that may affect the central nervous system (CNS), and rabbit hemorrhagic disease (RHD).

Flystrike (myiasis), facultative and obligate

Flystrike should be a primary concern to rescuers, as rabbits living outside are at high risk. Flystrike is usually painful to the rabbit and can be deadly. Flies are always a danger to colony rabbits or any other rabbits kept outdoors, and may also occasionally affect indoor rabbits. There are two groups of parasitic flies that are a danger to rabbits, facultative and obligate.

Facultative myiasis happens when a fly that does not have to lay its eggs on a particular host in order to complete its lifecycle does so because the opportunity arises. Flies that will sometimes lay their eggs on rabbits are sometimes called "blowflies" and include bluebottles, greenbottles, grey flesh flies, and – rarely – house flies. The female flies are particularly attracted by damp or soiled fur, urine, feces, rabbit scent glands, and wounds. Ammonia-rich compounds induce the female to lay her eggs – up to 250 at a time. In summer, larvae can hatch within two hours, although it may take up to twenty-four hours.

The hatched larvae (maggots) go through three stages: the first stages lasts about 24 hours, during which time the rabbit is not being fed upon; the second stage also lasts about 24 hours, and the larvae of this stage start feeding on both live and dead tissue; the third stage again lasts about 24 hours, the larvae again feeding on the rabbit's tissue. At the end of the third stage the maggots move away from the rabbit. The maggots are not always easy to see underneath the fur of the rabbit. Common places for this kind of flystrike to occur include around the perineal (anal-genital) area, on the rabbit's back just above the tail, and on the belly, although eggs may be laid anywhere on the rabbit.

Blowflies usually feed on dead tissue, but will also feed on living tissue. Rabbits with maggots suffer severe pain once the larvae begin feeding upon their live flesh, and the raw skin is open to bacterial infection. Rabbits may go into shock, especially if there are very large numbers of maggots present. Another danger is that larvae may enter a body opening. If this happens the body cavity may become involved or larvae may migrate through the central nervous system, in which case neurological symptoms may be seen.

All rescued rabbits should be thoroughly checked for maggots. Signs that a rabbit may have a maggot infestation include lethargy, grinding teeth, restlessness or reluctance to move, loss of fur, reddened and/or eroded skin, diarrhea, lack of appetite, weight loss, and fetid odor, although these signs will not be evident during the first 24-hour stage. If maggots are seen and a rabbit cannot receive immediate veterinary attention, the following steps may help:

1) Immerse the rabbit's hindquarters in lukewarm water or rinse affected area with running water; if the maggots are in stage 1 it is possible to remove most of them before they begin to eat the rabbit's tissue.
2) Pat infested areas with a warm, damp towel. This can cause maggots of any stage to leave.
3) Carefully blow warm air on the rabbit, using a hairdryer set on **low,** this will draw more maggots out. Be sure not to damage the rabbit's skin by excessive heat.
4) Hand pick any remaining maggots off using tweezers.
5) Clean the site and apply a cream such as topical silver sulfadiazine.

Antiparasitics that may be prescribed by a vet for flystrike include ivermectin, selamectin, moxidectin, and nitenpyram. Fluid therapy, antibiotics such as bicillin, enrofloxacin, or trimethoprim, pain medication (buprenorphine, meloxicam), syringe feeding, and fluid therapy may be necessary. In cases where there is extensive damage to tissues, especially where the larvae have penetrated into the dermis or subdermis, wound management is required. The wounds must first be cleaned and a hydrogel covered by a permeable dressing may be needed to prevent fluid loss and protect the damaged skin from bacterial infection. The area should be checked every 6-8 hours so any new larvae can be removed. Once larvae cease to be found a more permanent dressing can be applied.

A topical product to prevent facultative flystrike is available in the UK (Rearguard), but an equivalent product is not available in the US at the time of this writing. However, ivermectin, selamectin, and imidacloprid can be given prophylactically during fly season to control flystrike in smaller colonies of rabbits, or even larger ones where there are experienced volunteers capable of trapping the rabbits so the medications can be applied. Imidacloprid (Advantage) is effective for a longer period of time (about four weeks) than selamectin or ivermectin (about one week) and may also kill bot fly larvae. Biological control such as Spalding Lab's Fly Predators may also help control flies. Another way to discourage flies at a managed rabbit colony is to plant herbs such as mint, rosemary, oregano, basil, and lavender, which repel flies.

Obligate myiasis is caused by flies that must lay their eggs on a host in order to complete their life cycle. For rabbits in North American this is most often the rabbit bot fly, *Cuterebra cuniculi*, although other species of Cuterebra and the screw-worm fly (*Cochliomyia hominivorax*) can also attack rabbits. (The screw-worm fly was officially eradicated from the US in the 1982, but there was an outbreak in Florida in 2016).

Bot flies, sometimes called warble flies, are large black flies that may superficially resemble bumblebees because of their size. The females lay one to 1,000 eggs in groups of 5-15 near burrows, hutch openings, on bark, grass stems, other vegetation, or, occasionally, directly on a rabbit. After the eggs hatch the larvae enter the host through a body opening. (Larvae do not penetrate unbroken skin; they enter the body first and migrate from within the body to the place they form the "warble.") Larvae may stay in the region of the mouth, nose, and trachea for a few days, from where they move into the abdominal cavity and then to their final subcutaneous positions. There they each bury themselves in a "pocket," leaving a breathing pore to the outside. As the larva develops over the next 4-6 weeks the warble often appears as a raised lump or cyst on the rabbits jaw, neck, sides, or elsewhere on the body. Once the larva is fully developed it enlarges the pore and leaves the host.

The most obvious sign of bot fly infestation is the large cyst-like lump (warble) with a hole in the center. Secondary bacterial infections can develop in the larval holes. There may be only one bot fly larva on a rabbit or several larvae. Rabbits with more than nine bot fly larvae are at higher risk of dying. Rabbits with multiple bot fly larvae may lose their appetite, become weak, lame, and dehydrated. Larvae produce toxins, and in rabbits with many larvae present this may cause them to go into shock and die. Secondary infections may also occur in the larval pockets.

Although warbles are most often found in skin, larvae may rarely migrate to the eyes, mouth, nose, ears, and even to the brain, which last is fatal to the rabbit. Young rabbits are more likely to have warbles than older ones, although bot fly larvae may affect rabbits of any age.

A bot fly larva should only be removed by a veterinarian, as crushing or damaging a larva will cause a large release of toxins and the rabbit may have a severe allergic reaction (anaphylaxis) which may be fatal. If necessary, a larva can be left alone until it exits the rabbit on its own and the hole then treated as an open wound.

Researchers in one study found that up to 70% of cottontails in an area may be affected by bot fly larvae, and it is not unreasonable to suppose that an equivalent number of domestic rabbits might be affected in an outdoor colony of rabbits. In many managed colonies it is not feasible to check all individual rabbits as often as would be needed to prevent flystrike. At Best Friends, the decision was made to treat the Reno colony rabbits prophylactically with Revolution during fly season, a solution that was quite effective and which would help protect the rabbits from other flies and parasitic insects as well. Treating rabbits with imidacloprid (Advantage) may also be effective in preventing warbles. In the northern parts of the US, bot flies only mate and lay eggs once a year, often around June. Thus, in northern areas it is possible to prevent most cases of warbles by treating the rabbits once around June, but in southern areas bot flies may mate and lay eggs more than once and require more applications of an anti-parasitic.

Mites

Mites – especially ear mites and fur mites – also attack many dumped rabbits, but they are not usually as immediately life-threatening as blowflies can be. However, this does not mean mites cannot become a serious problem with time. In the 2018 fall/winter Rabbit Sanctuary Newsletter, the story of Babbit is featured. Babbit was discovered in the middle of a neighborhood street by a family of animal lovers on their way from a vacation. They stopped the car and jumped out to catch the rabbit, which was unusually easy because the rabbit's eyes were crusted shut due to mite infestation. His head, ears, tail, and paws were also encrusted, and there were areas of raw bleeding flesh on his back and shoulders. Babbit received medical treatment and now lives at the Rabbit Sanctuary where he has a "Home for Life."

If colony rabbits are treated prophylactically for flystrike, this will also help control mites. However, in general mites are not as seasonal a problem as flies. Should signs of mite infestation – excessive scratching, visible encrustation, fur loss, emaciation – appear in a colony rabbit it will be necessary to trap the rabbit in order to give medication. One medication that appears to be effective on mites and is generally safe for rabbits is a combination of moxidectin and imidacloprid (Advocate) which can be applied at the base of the neck and only need be applied every thirty days. For more information on mites and medical treatment for mites see Chapter Eleven.

Encephalitozoonosis (Encephalitozoon cuniculi, EC)

EC is a microsporidian parasite which has fungal-like properties and may be related to atypical fungi. In a UK study 52% of clinically healthy pet rabbits studied were found to have serological evidence of exposure to EC. However, only about 6% ever show signs because the immune systems of healthy rabbits keep the parasite under control. There are three strains of EC, one found mostly in dogs and humans, one in rodents, and one in rabbits. Interestingly, although no cases have been documented of the rabbit strain being transmitted to humans, the

dog/human strain can be passed to rabbits.

Signs of EC in rabbits vary, and can include: head tilt, rolling, star-gazing, cataracts, paralysis, weakness, incontinence, and behavioral changes. I found EC mentioned frequently in articles and on lists about large rescues of rabbits and colony rabbits. However, I was struck by the fact that many times EC was being *assumed* because of neurological signs – signs not only associated with EC but also with other medical conditions common in rescued and colony rabbits, e.g. raccoon roundworm, bot fly larvae that have migrated to brain tissue, trauma, and poisoning. I therefore thought it a helpful reminder to reprint an excerpt from a piece by William Kurmes, DVM, in my book *When Your Rabbit Needs Special Care*:

The symptoms of neurologic disease are often very similar despite many different underlying causes. This is because the symptoms are more related to the location affected, rather than the specific cause. Sometimes the specific symptoms can be used to determine the location of a localized lesion, while other, more generalized symptoms can be caused by many different or more diffuse diseases.

The following outline demonstrates some of the possible causes of neurologic disease in rabbits:

Infections:
- Bacterial – *Pasteurella multocida*, many other bacteria
- Viral – rabies, herpes
- Protozoal (single-celled parasites)– *Encephalitozoon cuniculi*, *Toxoplasma*
- Parasitic – *Baylisascaris*

Physical
- Trauma – brain, spinal
- Stroke (not well documented, but suspected in older rabbits)
- Heat stroke
- Spondylosis (arthritic degeneration of spinal joints)
- Neoplasia (cancer)

Toxic
- Metal poisoning (lead)
- Plant toxins (milkweed)
- Strychnine
- Drug toxicity

Metabolic
- Pregnancy toxemia

- Liver and/or kidney disease

Nutritional
- Vitamin deficiencies – vitamins A, E
- Mineral deficiencies – calcium, magnesium, potassium

Developmental
- Syringomyelia (progressive disease of spinal cord)
- Achondroplasia (abnormal development of cartilage)

In some cases, of course, neurological symptoms may indeed be caused by EC. There is still much disagreement over the best treatment for EC; many veterinarians still recommend the benzimidazoles (fenbendazole, albendazole). Others suggest ponazuril (Marquis) in conjunction with Panacur (fenbendazole). In one recent interesting article I found, fenbendazole was found to be effective in preventing EC in immunosuppressed rabbits, but not in treating the disease.

Coccidiosis

Coccidiosis, caused by protozoal parasites, is not common in companion rabbits, but may be encountered in colony rabbits. Multiple species of the genus *Eimeria* may cause intestinal coccidiosis in rabbits, and *Eimeria stiedeae* causes hepatic coccidiosis. Signs of the intestinal form include loss of appetite, weight loss, depression and diarrhea (may be watery or contain mucous or blood); signs of hepatic coccidiosis include jaundice, weight loss, a pot-bellied appearance, and diarrhea. Rabbits are infected by ingesting oocysts that are shed in the feces and can then contaminate food and the environment. Colony rabbits may be treated by putting medications (sulfaquinoxaline, sulfamethazine, sulfadimethoxine, sulfadimerazine) in food or water.

Raccoon roundworm (Baylisascaris procyonis)

This is an intestinal nematode common in raccoons. Oocytes are shed in raccoon feces; potentially anything that raccoon feces touches could be infective. Oocytes are extremely difficult to kill, remain in the environment for months, and can be tracked in on the soles of shoes, wood that raccoons have climbed on, plants they have walked through, or feed they have gotten into. Once a rabbit (or other mammal) is infected, migrating larvae may reach an eye or the brain. The disease is often fatal to rabbits. In some geographical areas (Northern California, the Pacific Northwest, parts of Missouri) a high proportion of raccoons carry the disease, and extra precautions should be taken. Some managed feral rabbit colonies are located where raccoons are common; all food and water at these colonies needs to be kept in containers the raccoons cannot open.

Rabbit Hemorrhagic Disease (RHD)

RHD is a relatively new rabbit disease but one all rescuers need to be concerned about because caliciviruses mutate easily and frequently. This has already happened with RHD; the original virus, RHD1, is being replaced in the UK by a second, more virulent form, RHDV2, which is now also found in North America. As Debby and I are writing this book the first confirmed outbreak of RHDV2 in the United States has been reported in Ohio (the disease had previously gotten a foothold in Canada).

Very young rabbits, which had some immunity to RHDV1, have no such immunity to RHDV2. RHDV2 also infects hares, which RHDV1 did not. The only positive appears to be that more rabbits survive RHDV2, at least at this time (the disease may be increasing in virulence).

One of the worries with RHDV2 is how easily it is spread. It can be spread by direct contact, insect vectors (blowflies, fleas, ticks, mosquitoes), and by fomites (objects such as dishes, shoes, bedding). It is also difficult to kill as it can survive freezing and also very high temperatures and persists in the environment. Feces of scavengers such as foxes and dogs can spread the disease, and perhaps most worrisome of all is that fly feces can carry the virus. Because flies are so ubiquitous and can range far from where they picked the virus up the flies could leave infective feces on plants in meadows, gardens, and commercial farms. Invasive species of ticks that are rapidly spreading across the US, such as the Asian long-horned tick (see page 249), are also a concern.

It takes three to nine days for the RHDV2 to develop after a rabbit is infected. Signs include lethargy, fever, convulsions, and bloody foam issuing from the nostrils and/or vagina. Rabbits that develop fever die within 12-36 hours. But more often, especially with colony rabbits that may not be under constant observation, rabbits that were seen healthy and eating shortly before are all found dead.

There is no treatment. Any rabbits that survive will need supportive care and will need to be kept separate the rest of their lives, as it is not yet known if such rabbits remain carriers. Vaccines that are effective against RHDV2 are available in Europe and Canada (Filavac, Eravac) but none legal in US at the time of this writing.

If an outbreak occurs at a rabbit colony, rescue, or shelter, lockdown is advised. No rabbits should come in or go out of the premises, workers should have separate clothing (especially shoes) for wearing on the premises and outside, and any objects leaving the premises should be sprayed with virucides. Three virucides (*virucides* limit the environmental spread of viruses, *viricides* are agents that destroy or deactivate a virus) that are said to be effective against RHDV2 are:

1) A 2% solution of sodium hydroxide (lye plus caustic soda).
2) Chloroform
3) Sodium hypochlorite (household bleach)

It is recommended that lockdown continue for a minimum of four months after the last death occurs.

Behavioral Issues

Behaviors that arise from colony living and/or being dumped and any trauma the rabbit suffered in early life may become an issue while a rabbit is living at a large rescue or managed colony. Sometimes a few rabbits may be so fearful they are unable to adapt to colony living; the best thing to do with these rabbits is to take them from the colony and either send them to an experienced fosterer or an adopter who can provide the supportive environment the rabbit will need.

Clicker Training for Fearful Rabbits

During the 2006 Reno rescue (see chapter 9), clicker training was found to be an effective tool in helping frightened rabbits. Rabbits from feral colonies frequently show fear of humans. Some of these fearful rabbits may be best dealt with by leaving them in a managed colony where the rabbits are allowed to live out their lives with minimal human contact. But others may end up at shelters or rescues where their fear of humans can be a roadblock to being adopted or even living a relatively stress-free life. Andrea Bratt and Jean Silva are experienced in using clicker training to help such fearful rabbits. Andrea tells of a specific feral rabbit she was able to help with this technique; that story is followed by a detailed explanation of clicker training for shy and feral rabbits by Andrea and Jean together.

Clicker Training a Feral Rabbit: Petunia's Story
by Andrea Bratt

I remember my first meeting with Petunia at the stray animal shelter where I volunteer. She was a tense black bundle of fur huddling at the back corner of her hutch. Every bit of her seemed to be saying "leave me alone, don't reach your hand in here, I really mean it!" But it was cage cleaning time and Petunia needed to go out to exercise. I moved my hand slowly into her cage, talking softly. She reared, growled and pounced. Score one for Petunia. After several patient attempts (and some nasty scratches) I was able to lift Petunia from her hutch. Her body felt tight with fear. She quivered as I carried her to an exercise pen. Getting her back in her cage was worse. Poor Petunia had no use for people and couldn't understand why we were bothering her.

This was discouraging. Would we ever find a loving home for Petunia? How could the other volunteers handle getting her out to exercise safely? We had six more rabbits that had recently come into the shelter with similar fear issues. Some of them would even scream and crash around in their cage when people walked by. These were adult domestic rabbits that seemingly had no previous contact with people. Some acted just as wild as any cottontail.

I had been learning about clicker training and had used this method to teach rabbits to jump hurdle courses and do tricks. At ClickerExpo we learned that clicker training could be used to train an animal to do anything it was capable of. This was inspiring knowledge. I wondered… could Petunia actually be trained to act like a tame rabbit?

I decided to give it a try. I took Petunia home to train her. She was set up in a comfortable hutch with hay and water always available. I began trying to hand feed her. I used long pieces of vegetable at first so she wouldn't have to come too close to my hands. As she came forward to eat, I used a clicker to make a single click. It didn't take Petunia very long to figure out that food always appeared within seconds after she heard that click. Then she figured out that every time she did certain things she would hear a click and get a treat. Amazing! She could actually make me click just by coming towards me.

I worked with her for about ten minutes at a time, four times a day. I measured out her pellets each morning into a cup on top of her cage. I chopped her carrot into pellet sized portions and used the pellets and chopped carrot for training. Whatever was left over became part of her dinner. By the end of the first day Petunia could earn a click and treat by touching my hand and even following it a few inches. Maybe my hands weren't very scary after all.

At the end of day two Petunia could make me click for getting pet on her head and letting me touch her ears and shoulders. She was still tense some of the time but seemed to like being in control of the game. If she got scared and hopped off, no problem, but no treat.

By the end of day three Petunia was earning clicks and treats by letting me pet her back, touch all four feet and doing gentle tail tugs. I could tell at this point that she was starting to enjoy her forehead pets. She would relax, lean into my hand and get that dreamy look in her eye. I started using forehead pets as a reward. If she let me touch her feet, I would click and rub her head. If I went too fast and scared her she let me know by thumping and retreating to the back of her cage. But she always came back to touch my hand with confidence as this had always produced a click and treat.

On day four I started putting my hand under her belly and then doing tiny lifts for clicks and treats. I started to say "up" before I lifted her slightly off the cage floor. I wanted Petunia to trust me so there would be no surprise about when she was going to be lifted. I used my mouth to make a clicking sound at this point because I needed both hands for lifting.

When she was comfortable being lifted, I put her in a four-foot square exercise pen. I put a stool in the pen for her to go under if she wanted and sat down in the pen with my clicker and treats. She hopped around exploring for awhile and when she started to approach me I clicked. She looked at me quizzically as if to say "the game works out here also?" We worked on as much touching and handling, as she was comfortable with and added clicks for jumping over my legs, putting her paws on my body and getting on top of the stool. Every time I clicked her for something new she would try the new behavior over again as if to test what was making me click. She jumped up on the stool several times. The more ways she learned to earn a click and treat; the more confident she acted.

Day five came and I was looking forward to training Petunia in the pen again. As I approached her cage with my training treats and clicker, Petunia began running back and forth and scratching on the cage door. She took a lap around her cage and happily leapt into her hayrack. She looked at me expectantly. It was the highest thing she could find to leap onto for a click! I was so amazed I almost forgot to click. Was this the same rabbit that huddled fearfully in the back of her cage not so long ago? What happened to the angry black rabbit that had no use for people? Now people were fun. They carried treats and gave massages. They played clicker games and politely said "up" before they lifted you.

On the sixth day I was petting Petunia in her cage. She began to tooth purr then sighed deeply and flopped onto her side for a good long massage. Although she still startled easily and could be quick to growl, she had definitely started behaving more like a tame rabbit. Petunia's success story laid the groundwork for rehabilitating many shy and feral rabbits that came to our shelter.

Taming Shy and Feral Rabbits with Clicker Training
by Andrea Bratt-Frick and Jean Silva of B.U.N.S.

The strategy in taming shy or feral rabbits is to associate all good things in life with you. All privileges, like time in the exercise pen, all toys, and all treats are accessed only through you. The rabbits' cage should contain only a litter box with hay, food bowl, water bowl, mat, and a chewing toy. Of course, this means that during the course of any 24-hour period, you should offer several sessions during which the rabbit does have access to an interesting – and rewarding, if challenging –

activity. Ideally, the steps outlined below would be undertaken in a one- or two-week period, the length of which should be most strongly influenced by the speed with which the rabbit is able to work and how much time you are able to devote to training.

We use a clicker to mark "tame rabbit" behaviors that we then reinforce with something the rabbit desires, usually a food treat. The click marks the behavior and lets the rabbit know that a reward will be forthcoming. Clicks should be delivered just before or at the moment of the desired behavior. If you consistently click after the desired behavior, you will reinforce the behavior that follows the actual behavior that you want. For example, if you want the rabbit to take food from your hand, you have to click on the approach or at the moment the lips touch the food, not when the rabbit is running away with the pellet. So it is better to click as the rabbit approaches you, which at least is a component of the desired behavior of approaching and accepting food.

Timing is important. The game should move quickly to keep the rabbit's interest and in the case of shy/feral rabbits to keep them too busy to think about whether they should be scared. Treats should be delivered within about five seconds after the click. You should try to deliver about 30 treats per minute. Treats should be bite-sized in order for the game to move along quickly. Even a long rabbit pellet may be a little large: break it in half if needed. Prior to the training session, sit down and prepare about 15 bite sized treats. If you are feeding a long vegetable, allow the rabbit to take a bite and then REMOVE the vegetable from the pen while the rabbit is chewing.

Cues

As a behavior becomes established, you can add a verbal cue. To add a cue, select one word to associate with one behavior. When the rabbit performs the behavior, say the word and click and treat. After you have done this for some time, begin to say the word before the behavior and click and treat when you get the behavior. Each cue can relate to only one behavior. One behavior can have more than one cue.

Confidence building and loading the click

1. The click, by itself, will not have meaning until the rabbit associates it with a reward. To do so, you need to associate (or load) the clicker with the reward. The reward we are using is food. When the rabbit takes a bite, click. This will associate the sound of the click with food. Click each time the rabbit takes a bite. The next items 2, 3, 4, and 5 are a discussion of the ways in which you can get the rabbit to eat from your hand. We get back to clicker training in item 6.

2. Hand feed any food the rabbit will eat. In most instances it will be long vegetables such as parsley, cilantro, parsley, kale, carrots, etc. A shy domestic rabbit may only recognize rabbit pellets as food. If one food does not work, try another. Try to feed up to 50% of the rabbit's diet by hand. Plan on several short sessions each day.

3. Hold the food pointing toward the floor with your wrist bent and the back of your hand at a level above the bunny's head. This position allows you to convert to a pet later. If the rabbit seems nervous about the hand position, use a long food and hold it so that it points toward the rabbit. Your hand and the food will form a >. You may need to point the food toward the rabbit.

4. If the rabbit will not eat from your hand you may find that sitting with your side to the bunny and your face averted will increase the rabbit's confidence. Sometimes feeding through the cage wire will be more acceptable to the rabbit, especially if the rabbit only recognizes pellets as food. If you are feeding through the wire, feed through the closed cage door. This positions the rabbit to eat from your hand at the open door later. Do not underestimate the power of a favorite food. If one food does not work, try another. If you are not sure that the rabbit knows an item is food, place a piece in the food bowl a couple of days in a row and once it has been eaten, try feeding it by hand.

5. As the rabbit eats more confidently from your hand, shorten the length of the food items by breaking off increasingly shorter lengths of the foods. A carrot can be chopped into about 200 pea-size pieces. If you are feeding through cage wire, offer some of the food items through the open door.

6. Call the rabbit's name and click as the rabbit moves toward the food item.

7. If the rabbit suffers a crisis of confidence, increase the length of your food items or close the cage door. Shorten the food items a little more rapidly this time. If you have closed the cage door, try one or two short sessions with the door closed and open it again. It will help to schedule your open door session for the first meal of the day, when the rabbit is most hungry.

8. Use bonuses. At the end of sessions give the rabbit several pieces of food, so that the end of training is not seen as a punishment. If you find that the rabbit is having a bad session, click and give several pieces of food for a desired behavior or a behavior close to a desired behavior. This use of a bonus keeps the rabbit from becoming discouraged. Give a bonus after a click when the rabbit makes big progress in performance or learns a new behavior, to impress on the rabbit that this is definitely a behavior worth remembering. Every few sessions, give a bonus just to keep the rabbit's interest.

Target training

1. When the rabbit is actively interested in your approach, begin target training. Hold your loosely-closed hand two to three inches away from the rabbit's head. Click and treat when he looks or moves toward it. Deliver the treat within five seconds of the click. Place your hand in different locations, to the left and right of the nose, above the nose, below the nose. Vary the pattern.

2. Work on this, gradually raising the standard, until the rabbit is touching your hand with its nose in order to earn the click and treat.

3. Add the cue "touch." At first, say the word when the rabbit is touching your hand; after a few sessions say the cue before the rabbit touches your hand, then click and treat.

Hand training

1. When the rabbit is confidently touching your hand for a treat, try nudging the rabbit with your hand as it touches you, turning the rabbit's touch into a gentle pet. Click as you do so and treat. The rabbit may retreat at the touch. Use the treat to return the rabbit to the desired training spot. (Click for behavior, feed for location).

2. Put some food in your hand and gently pet the rabbit as it is eating; click and treat. If it backs off, close your hand. Open your hand when the rabbit touches your hand again and continue trying to pet the rabbit.

3. Mix touching the rabbit with the rabbit touching a target and click and treat each time. Gradually increase the ratio of you touching the rabbit to the ratio of the rabbit touching you.

4. Try a variety of touches with the rabbit, followed by a click and treat. Touches to the rear, side, back, and shoulders may be more acceptable at first. When a certain touch becomes pleasurable to the rabbit, it can be used in lieu of food as a reward for a less pleasurable pat. In this case the click and treat would become a click and pat. Increase the length and pressure of the touch. Turn a touch into a longer and longer pat and click and treat. Turn a shoulder touch into a firm hold and click and treat. Add touches to the ears, belly, head, and feet followed by click and treat. Remember that each touch earns a click and treat.

5. If the rabbit becomes stressed, allow it to touch your hand for click and treat until it is confident, and then try touching it again.

6. If you progress too fast your rabbit may let you know by lunging, growling, attacking, or simply hopping away. Some rabbits won't accept treats when stressed. Don't reward aggressive behavior. Any aggressive behavior stops the game. Remove your hand and all those yummy treats and turn your back on the rabbit. Count to 10, take a deep breath, and try again. You may have to go back a few steps and regain your rabbit's trust. End training sessions on a successful note even if, to do so, you need to go back to an earlier behavior the rabbit learned.

Lifting

- When the rabbit seems very confident about being touched all over and allows you to hold it, say "lift," and lift it about one inch from the floor and click. Say "down" and as you are placing it on the floor, click. Follow with a bonus. Do not place the rabbit on the floor while it is struggling. If the rabbit struggles after you say "down" and begin lowering, stop. Wait until the rabbit is still, click, and resume lowering. Treat when the rabbit is on the ground.

- Add the occasional lift, click, and treat to each training session. Work on increasing the length of the lift and then the height.

- Start rotating your body during the lift so that the rabbit is outside the cage briefly before you click and treat and return it to the cage floor.

⌄ It may be helpful for some rabbits to work on lifting exercises on a small table. Be prepared to reassure your bunny, with treats and pats, the first time it is on the table. Do not let your rabbit jump off the table on its own.

Pen work

⌄ When the rabbit is comfortable being petted and lifted in the cage, you can begin training it in a pen. It generally takes about three days of training in a cage for the rabbit to be confident about being handled. Gently lift your rabbit and place it in a small, secure pen. A 4' by 4' dog exercise pen is ideal. Add a laundry basket with cut-out sides or cardboard box with doors for the rabbit to climb on or crawl under. Add a litter box if necessary.

⌄ Learned behaviors need to be re-learned in each new location. The learning curve in a new location will be faster than the original learning curve, but it is a learning curve nevertheless. Start with the earliest behaviors that the rabbit learned and move through all the behaviors as fast as you can until the rabbit is up to speed.

⌄ Practice hand targeting in the pen. The rabbit may ignore you until it gets used to the new area. Click and treat for the rabbit approaching you. Add the rabbit's name to the touch cue and move around the outside of the pen clicking and treating as the rabbit seeks you out and touches your hand.

⌄ Enter the pen and sit down. Click and treat for the rabbit making any physical contact with you. Don't try to touch the rabbit until it is confidently touching you.

⌄ Practice as many of the hand-training exercises above as the rabbit is comfortable with.

⌄ At this point you can start training silly tricks. Click and treat for the rabbit jumping on the box, standing up on its hind legs, jumping over your legs, putting its paws on you or anything adorable that your rabbit likes to do. Work on no more than one or two new tricks a session. After the rabbit is rewarded for doing a behavior a few times and seems to know that you will click when the behavior occurs, you can add a verbal cue as the rabbit does its trick. Gradually say the cue sooner until the cue occurs before the behavior. You can also use hand motions as cues to let the rabbit know what you want it to do.

 ⌄ Alternate between pen exercises 4 and 5. Some rabbits are going to be less interested in being petted in the pen, but may still want to play the clicker game and earn treats by doing tricks. Many rabbits seem more comfortable being petted when they are eating on top of the box. (Go figure).

 ⌄ Don't leave the rabbit alone in the pen for more than a few minutes. Keep the first few pen sessions to around 15 minutes. When you are done, gently lift the rabbit and return it to the cage and give it a big reward.

 ⌄ Increase the length of the pen training sessions as the rabbit becomes reliable about coming when called, accepting pats, being lifted, and doing silly tricks on cue. The size of the pen can also be increased at this time and more toys added.

 ⌄ If the tame behavior breaks down, which can happen if the rabbit is frightened by being grabbed, chased, etc., go backward in the training to where the rabbit is confident, and work forward again as quickly as possible. These "tune-up" sessions usually take a fraction of the time that the original taming sessions took.

Generalizing new behaviors

1. When the bunny is able to do most behaviors on cue, you can move the pen to a different location. Be prepared to relax your standards or start from the beginning when the environment changes. After training in a few different places, the rabbit will be able to transfer its new behaviors to other locations. You can help a rabbit to feel more comfortable in a new setting by training it on a blanket or mat, and moving the blanket or mat to each new location.

2. Switch trainers if possible so the rabbit will know that there are many people who can play the clicker game and can be trained to dispense treats. Start fading the clicker for the tricks the rabbit has learned well. Substitute a word such as "yes" or "good bunny" for some of the clicks. Continue to give the rabbit food rewards each time it does a trick. Gradually decrease the use of the clicker until you are not using it at all for established behaviors. Substitute pats and praise for some of the food rewards. Continue using the clicker to train new behaviors.

Mimicking behaviors

⌄   Rabbits learn by watching other rabbits. If you have a clicker-wise rabbit or a rabbit that is very comfortable with being handled, you can use it to engage a new rabbit. Simply allow the new rabbit to watch while the clicker-wise bunny is being trained. Often the new rabbit will volunteer to play "the clicker game." It can really speed up the first session.

⌄   As you train new behaviors, allow more experienced rabbits to demonstrate within the view of a new bunny. For example, cue and lift a bunny that is very confident with the lift in front of your new rabbit, just before you attempt a lift with the new rabbit. It can be very calming for the new rabbit.

Adopting Rabbits Out from a Colony

Many different factors will need to be taken into consideration when deciding whether or not to adopt rabbits out from a rescued colony. Debby Widolf:

> Every rescue is different and the rabbits within unique. Although some of the Reno rabbits were adopted out in pairs to homes as pets, their general temperament made the majority of the rabbits happier living in groups; small or large. After spaying and neutering, the frequency of the rabbits' fights was significantly decreased. Other large confiscations or feral/community rabbit rescues may vary in their collective temperaments. Factors that determine the personalities of rabbits living in a colony include: how long they have lived in a common group or alone after abandonment or neglect, their physical condition, age, and illnesses, predators in the area, presence of people, whether the rabbit was a former pet, and whether new rabbits were introduced by abandonment or inbreeding was dominant. These considerations will affect rabbits' behavior and are important as you plan the rabbits' futures and decide where the rabbits will be safe, get good care, and will be best suited to live.

Rabbits unable to adapt to colony living are probably best removed from the colony and fostered or adopted out. Nearly all the responders to our Domestic Rabbit Colony Rescue Survey reported that they adopted rabbits out and that only 10% or less of the rescued rabbits were considered unadoptable, although one respondent reported that between 31% and 60% of the rabbits in their rescue were considered unadoptable.Of course, finding enough homes for rabbits is never easy! Mary Marvin, of Rabbit Advocates in Portland, describes one way their organization reaches out to potential adopters:

> My husband organizes three adoption outreaches each month at local retail stores and invites all foster providers to attend with their choice of foster rabbits to present to the public. No adoptions are made out of the stores, but if potential adopters wish to adopt a particular rabbit, they may fill out an adoption application on the Rabbit Advocates web site. They are contacted by an adoption counselor and once their application is approved, the foster providers will receive a copy of the application and can make contact with the applicant to meet them and do a home check. It is up to the foster provider to choose the adopter.

Being Prepared for Natural Disaster and Emergencies

I learned the hard way about being prepared for emergencies when my community was evacuated due to a very fast-moving forest fire. Residents had fifteen minutes to get out when the final evacuation order came. I had taken my house animals to safety the day before, planning to come back the next day to figure out what to do about the two born-feral cats in my garage and my two tanks of tropical fish. I was not able to return to get them out, nor were many other people in the community able to get pets out, people who for one reason or another were not at home when the evacuation order was given.

Most cities and counties have plans for pets and farm animals during potential evacuations, but I found these are very limited in scope. There is usually a place a person may take pets and a place for farm animals, but these are unlikely to be places a person would want to leave rabbits. Furthermore, I discovered there are rarely any plans to help save animals that evacuees were forced to leave behind. In my situation, animal control picked up any free-roaming dogs they saw, but that was about it. I have been told by rescuers in hurricane areas that saving animals was low on the list of priorities for officials in many of those areas as well.

In my case I was not allowed back to my home for six days, even though the fire was past after the first day and the area relatively safe. During those six days – days I did not know for sure whether my house still stood or not – I frantically called department after department and official after official trying to get permission to return for an hour or so to take care of my feral cats and fish. I finally obtained permission from the sheriff's department to do so, provided animal control accompanied me. Animal control refused. They were willing to break into my house with my permission and try to care for the animals themselves, but would not allow me to go. I had explained to the various departments I had spoken to that both my born-feral cats and my fish required my specialist knowledge, but I suspect animal control either thought I was some stupid woman who thought they didn't know how to feed cats or that they were getting off on being "heroes" breaking into houses to get animals out. Whatever their reason, they refused to accompany me to my home despite my permission from the sheriff's department.

I later learned that many others in my community had been in the same position I had been, frantic over animals they had been forced to leave behind. They also were told animal control was willing to break into their home to get the animals out but apparently those with animals were not allowed to return even for the time needed to feed them or get them out, *although other people were being allowed to return to their homes under escort for other reasons, such as getting needed medication.* I was outraged by this and wrote over a dozen letters to various departments, politicians, and humane organizations afterwards, but I received not a single response.

Take my advice and be prepared. A fire, flood, tornado, hurricane, or other disaster can happen at almost any time, and saving animals is unlikely to be a priority of any officials. Saving the animals will most likely be up to you. The following suggestions apply for rescues, shelters, and individuals holding rabbits indoors.

1. Find somewhere you will be able to take the rabbits in an emergency ahead of time, selecting a place that is far enough away a disaster would be unlikely to affect them as well as you.

2.   Humane societies in some areas may be willing and able to help move animals in an emergency. Call and speak to a person in authority ahead of time; if they are likely to help have names and phone numbers in an easily accessible spot and make sure all volunteers know about it.

3.   Train volunteers for a potential emergency.

4.   Leave early. If you receive a pre-evacuation notice get your rabbits out immediately. Do not wait for the final evacuation notice.

5.   Have that stack of cardboard cat carriers Debby and I have mentioned previously, or Evacsaks (pillowcases will work in a pinch). In an emergency evacuation all rabbits will have to be moved, and you are unlikely to have that many hard-sided carriers.

6.   Take any needed medications for the rabbits with you. Plus always have supplies of bottled water and feed and any needed medications on hand. In some emergency situations the rabbits might not have to be moved but power and transportation may be lost and supplies difficult to get.

7.   Turn the settings on any refrigerators or freezers in buildings to a colder setting before evacuating (or if power is expected to be lost). Then if power is lost the contents will stay at a safe temperature a bit longer.

Early preparation for emergencies at a large colony

The brutal truth is that in a serious forest fire, flood, hurricane, earthquake, or other major natural disaster, rabbits living in large managed colonies will be not be able to be caught and transported. Therefore, the best way to protect these rabbits from disasters is to consider such disasters when the location for the colony is selected. Colonies located in or near forested areas should have an area surrounding the colony that has had trees, brush, and fire-carrying weeds removed. If an evacuation notice comes for the area, leave the rabbits extra water and food – those that survive will need it. In flood or hurricane areas include some structures that will provide a high place to which rabbits can retreat, be sure all structures are able to withstand strong winds, and have ditches and drainpipes to help divert flood waters.

CHAPTER 8: TRAP-NEUTER-RETURN/RELEASE FOR FERAL RABBIT COLONIES

Trap-neuter-return (TNR), the practice of trapping domestic animals that are living on their own, having them spayed/neutered and vaccinated, and then returning them to the area from which they came, began in the United Kingdom in the 1950's as an alternative to killing large numbers of feral cats. Early successes led to the idea being exported to Italy and other countries, and in the late 1960s TNR reached the United States. In the years since TRN began there have been many studies the results of which appear to support the claims that it is an effective and humane method of controlling the numbers of feral cats. However, not all people agree with using TNR to control populations of feral domestic animals.

Pros and Cons of TNR for Rabbits

As the numbers of dumped domestic rabbits continue to rise, it becomes increasingly difficult to find placements for those rabbits at rescues and shelters. There simply aren't enough shelters to take all the rabbits that have been abandoned; nor are there enough fosterers and people willing to adopt them. Supporting the rabbits in their colony is an option. Rabbits are social by nature and colony living is not unnatural to them. Staying in the colony after being spayed or neutered gives them the chance to live out their lives in as natural a manner as can be while the colony is prevented from getting larger. In study after study on cat TNR it has been found that having a TNR program results in lower numbers of cats entering local shelters and lower numbers of cats being euthanized in those shelters. In some studies it has been found that cat euthanization was reduced by as much as 80% after establishing a TNR program. Cats that have been altered are recognizable to animal control because veterinarians "tip" an ear (while the cat is under anesthesia) so volunteers and municipal employees will know if a free-living cat has been spayed or neutered. With rabbits, a tattoo in an ear serves the same purpose as a tipped ear in a cat.

Many of those who oppose TNR claim it is "inhumane" to let domestic animals live out their lives in the wild even if such a colony is supported with supplemental feeding and some veterinary care. They believe that letting cats or rabbits live on their own where they may suffer or die as a result of predation, accident, or disease is less humane than killing them through euthanization.

As a biologist, a family caregiver, caregiver of special-needs rabbits and as a person who has lived most of her life in the country, I disagree. Living in a home is no guarantee a person or companion animal will not suffer or be killed by illness, accident, or even predation (many rabbits have been killed by family dogs). Death and illness, however much people in this society may choose to avoid thinking of them, are part of life. I am also aware that euthanasia is not a guarantee of an easy, painless, stress-free death. The procedure may be done inexpertly by a vet with little experience, but even with a very experienced veterinarian, **any** animal, especially a young one, may react to the euthanasia procedure in unexpected ways and not simply "go to sleep."

To me, it is the life that counts. Rabbits, like humans, usually fight to live. Life as a feral rabbit may appear harsh to us, but look at the rabbits' behaviors. Do rabbits in feral colonies exhibit behaviors consistent with an enjoyment of life – running, binkying, flopping, eating with relish, cuddling with bonded mates? Yes, they do. Who, then, are we to say we know better than the rabbits themselves and insist they have miserable lives and need to be rounded up and euthanized?

Not all opponents to TNR feel that the animal's life is miserable and they would be better dead. Others feel that feral domestic animals are a nuisance and a threat to natural ecosystems. While it is true rabbits burrow and eat plants, altering the rabbits keeps the colony from growing and it would not be recommend for rescuers to attempt to manage a rabbit colony in an area with a delicate ecosystem. (In such a case the rabbit colony would be better moved.) Giving the colony rabbits supplemental food will most likely lead to the rabbits eating less of the natural and planted vegetation, and feeding the rabbits during the day can help keep raccoons and skunks from becoming a problem.

Some opponents of TNR for rabbits in particular believe it can never work because authorities will claim the rescuers are returning the rabbits to where they came from and therefore are "abandoning" the rabbits. While it is true some authorities may threaten rescuers with this if they do not want a colony in their municipality, in most places such claims are legally indefensible. I read multiple opinions on this point of law, and most agreed that caregivers cannot be charged with abandonment in most municipalities because the majority of animal abandonment laws specify the person must be the owner of the animal and must intend to relinquish ownership and intend to withhold necessary care.

Caregivers are not owners since the presence of the rabbit colony predates the caregivers' presence, the rabbits are not under the caregiver's control, and the caregivers do not have the rights of owners over the rabbits. Furthermore, the intent required under most abandonment laws is missing. Indeed, in most cases the caregiver is returning the rabbits to the place they came from, and is improving the rabbits' condition by providing some health care and food.(It is for this reason I prefer to use the term trap-neuter-*return* rather than *release*, although in cases where the rabbits are moved from their original location trap-neuter-release would be the proper terminology.) However, it may take some legal challenges before authorities stop threatening rescuers with claims the caregivers are "owners" and are "abandoning" the rabbits.

As large colonies of rabbits near and in cities and towns continue to increase, we as rabbit rescuers must find solutions. TNR can be a partial solution and help some colony rabbits in some areas where other options have not worked. Debby Widolf:

At this point in time, there are many colonies or herds of community abandoned rabbits living in unprotected environments, unspayed or un-neutered, totally on their own to find food, giving birth to young that must try to survive, thus continuing the cycle. The rabbit rescue community is faced with the distressing knowledge that room for these rabbits is not readily available in rescues or shelters. The community abandoned rabbit is often passed over for the needs of adoptable rabbits waiting for homes in shelters or rescues, and their situation is heartbreaking to those who want to help them.

A TNR does offer a step up for this group of abandoned rabbits. It is not a panacea that will make their existence a carefree one. But TNR will curb the colony population and give existing rabbits less competition for available space and food. A must in rabbit TNR is a dedicated effort to provide feed and water and minimal monitoring of the colony by organizations or individual volunteers. Signage can be placed throughout the area to warn that tampering with feeding equipment, harassing or harming the rabbits in any way is against the law.

Because rabbits are prey animals they are at risk living in minimally protected areas even though they are fed and monitored by volunteers. This type of living arrangement is NOT the same as the concept of colony living that provides protected areas: fencing, shelter from the weather, and closer monitoring and care from volunteers.

I believe these rabbits' lives are sacred and we are not to judge or set standards that are unrealistic given the expanse of the abandoned rabbit problem. Rabbits living in a TNR colony may not be as robust as a companion rabbit or have as long a life, but they will have more of an opportunity to live the life they know as rabbits. We can make a difference with this model; mistakes will be made, but we will learn how to do better in the future.

How to Set Up a Colony

Setting up a permanent TNR colony of rabbits is a bit different than rescuing and placing colony rabbits, although some of the steps are the same.

1. Site evaluation
2. Research
3. Define mission
4. Build coalition
5. Funding
6. Trapping, spay/neuter and holding
7. Maintenance/monitoring program

Site Evaluation

For the most part, the reader can refer to the section on site evaluation in Chapter 6 of this volume (getting permission to enter the property, estimating numbers of rabbits, etc.). However, there are a couple of additional considerations when evaluating a site for a permanent colony: Is the site feasible for a long-term colony of rabbits? Is there human population near enough that volunteers can easily reach the colony? Although in general it is better to leave feral rabbits where they were found for a TNR colony (the rescuers' legal position is better if the rabbits are being returned to the place they came from and the rabbits already know where food, water and shelter is), if the colony is located near a nature reserve of any kind, a TNR colony is probably not a good idea, and rescuers should think about relocating the colony. The distance from a population center must also be taken into account; TNR colonies require that a maintenance program with volunteers be set up, and if takes a long time to reach the colony fewer people will volunteer and stay with the program over time.

When evaluating the site the number of rabbits that appear to be recent dumps should be estimated. Sometimes recently dumped rabbits – especially the smaller, more popular breeds – can be separated out for adoption. This also helps reduce the population of the colony at the outset.

Research

Hopefully the person thinking of establishing a TNR colony for feral rabbits has read and taken to heart the advice in this book about seeking a volunteer whose only task is to research laws that affect animals in your area. There are many laws that may affect TNR plans in addition to those on ownership and animal abandonment that have been discussed earlier in this chapter. Laws regarding providing food for animals is one of these. Some municipalities have laws that ban feeding any animal outdoors (exceptions are usually made for birds and sometimes for squirrels). If this is the case it will be necessary to seek an exemption for the TNR rabbit colony. Some municipalities also require the registration of TNR colonies. This is normally for cats, but if the law doesn't specify cats it would be necessary to register a similar colony for rabbits. All these laws will need to be researched and hard copies printed out. If you don't already have that volunteer for researching such laws, now is the time to find one.

Laws are not the only thing that will need to be researched. The initial spays/neuters and health checks will be a large expense. Negotiate. Find a veterinary practice that is willing to do the operations for a lower cost. Ask other rabbit organizations in the area if they know of any vets that are willing to do low-cost spays and neuters.

Defining your mission

This is an important step, because you cannot build a coalition until you have clearly stated your mission. What is the purpose of setting up a TNR colony for the rabbits? Are you trying to reduce the population of feral rabbits, protect the environment, reduce shelter euthanasia for rabbits? Hopefully your mission will encompass all that and more. Write up your mission statement in a clear, concise manner, preferably in no more than one or two paragraphs.

Build a coalition

Trap-neuter-return programs cannot be instituted without cooperation from many different segments of society. You will need permission from the landowner and possibly from the municipality, animal control will need to know about it, the community in which the colony is located needs to understand and support what is being done, veterinarians need to be found who are willing to provide the medical help (hopefully for a reduced rate!), and you will need a place to house the rabbits during the spay/neuter phase of the program. You will need the help of several rabbit rescues and/or organizations (especially in the trapping and set-up stage), and you will need committed volunteers likely to stay on board with the project long-term.

The first step is to get the landowner and municipality to understand and approve what you are planning. Next, the community should be approached. This can be done through a combination of posters, offering a talk at a local adult education center, online avenues, mailings, and even by going door-to-door in those neighborhoods nearest the rabbit colony. Seek a volunteer whose only job will be to coordinate these educational efforts and continue them long-term. If you are able to get the support of the municipality and the community, you will next need to reach out to other rabbit rescues and organizations for help trapping and housing the rabbits during their spay/neuter operations and health checks.

A note of caution: what does *not* work well is for several different animal/rabbit organizations to all be doing their own thing with the same rabbit colony. This leads to confusion and arguments and ultimately does not benefit the rabbits. Frankly, it also makes the different organizations and rescuers look bad to municipal authorities and can negatively impact their willingness to cooperate with the rescuers. Setting up a TNR rabbit colony takes organization. One person or group needs to be in overall charge and have the final say, and all other efforts need to be coordinated so they go smoothly. Sometimes members of one organization don't like working under another, even temporarily, but *for the rabbits' sakes* egos need to be left out or the organization needs to stay out of the project if the members cannot tolerate not being in charge.

Funding

For the most part, funding is done using those methods presented in Chapter Six. However, TNR efforts can also be funded with grants through PetSmart Charities and similar programs. Some municipalities are willing to at least partially fund a TNR program. If a municipality is willing to fully or partially fund a TNR effort, **cooperate** (you need to appreciate how lucky you are) be sure meticulous records of all expenditures for the program are kept, and also make sure there are no frivolous or exorbitant charges. (Funding is far more likely to continue if a municipality sees the ones managing the program are financially responsible.) Smaller donations may result from appealing to the community where the rabbit colony is located.

Trapping, altering and holding

This step will be the most labor-intensive and will need a great deal of coordination to make things go well. Volunteers experienced at trapping rabbits are a must, as are organizations willing to lend the number of live traps that will be needed. Space must be found to hold the rabbits for the recommended days after surgery (five for spays and three for neuters) and sometimes prior to a spay/neuter event. If the colony is located near a municipality with a school of veterinary medicine, students at such a school are a potential source of volunteers and may even be able to get school credits for such volunteer work.

As the rabbits are trapped they should be triaged just as the rabbits are for a rescue where the rabbits are being moved to a new locations (see Chapter 7). After surgery the rabbits will need three (males) to five (females) days post-operative monitoring. The last day for male or female rabbits needs to be a day the rabbit does not receive pain medication. Rabbits are not safe to return to the location of their colony until they are eating, drinking and defecating without having received an analgesic. Additionally, the site of the surgical incision needs to be checked for infection and the rabbit's affect assessed – if the rabbit is not alert it may be a sign of something wrong,

Records are important. Each rabbit should be photographed and a record started for what veterinary treatment is received – the spay or neuter, pain medications and antiparasitics administered, etc. Keep a database with this information for each rabbit.

Colony maintenance program

This is one of the most critical points in having a successful TNR program, and can be the most difficult. When first setting up a program people are enthused and eager to help the bunnies. But after permissions are obtained and the rabbits have been altered and returned to their colony the initial excitement dies down, volunteers leave, and the grind of routine maintenance begins. This aspect takes committed volunteers, people who really care about the rabbits. It also takes good organization by the person in charge. A feeding, watering, and cleaning schedule needs to be set up. How much food, of what kind, and at what time? It is best for feeding in particular to be done mornings or during the day, because food remaining overnight will attract raccoons and other animals that may negatively impact the health of the colony. Containers will need to be cleaned at least once a week (weekends can be good as more volunteers may be available), and any spoiled food

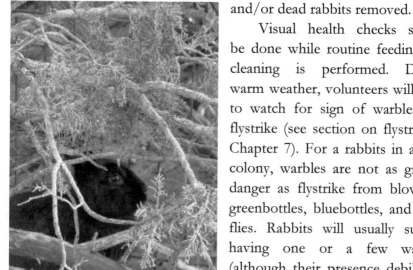

and/or dead rabbits removed.

Visual health checks should be done while routine feeding and cleaning is performed. During warm weather, volunteers will need to watch for sign of warbles and flystrike (see section on flystrike in Chapter 7). For a rabbits in a feral colony, warbles are not as great a danger as flystrike from blowflies: greenbottles, bluebottles, and flesh flies. Rabbits will usually survive having one or a few warbles (although their presence debilitates the rabbit), but the pain and shock of flystrike from the smaller flies can easily kill a rabbit. For this reason some kind of protection from flies should be provided. There are natural methods of fly control that can be purchased, such as Spalding Labs Fly Predators. Planting various herbs that repel flies (mint, oregano, lavender, basil) may be an option in some locations. For smaller colonies it may even be feasible to trap the rabbits during fly season and apply a dose of a medication such as Advantage (imidacloprid) or Revolution (selamectin). According to some sources, flea and tick medications (e.g. Advantage) may provide some protection from warbles, but many of these preparations are not safe for rabbits. Advantage is one product that is safe for rabbits, and the ingredient imidacloprid is said to provide at least some protection from warbles if the first dose is given early in fly season.

Another necessity is to watch for any new rabbits that are being dumped at the site. If dumping becomes a problem and threatens the success of the colony it may be necessary to use trail cameras or other security measures. Vandalism can also be a problem, and some people may try to hurt the rabbits themselves. Every volunteer should be trained to be on the watch for any human threats to the colony.

Given the variety of tasks involved in providing care for the colony rabbits, having a training program for volunteers is recommended. After the initial training, a new volunteer should work alongside an experienced volunteer at first. Allow adequate time for the new volunteer to become comfortable with the care routine before doing it alone. Although the routine of feeding, watering, cleaning, and health monitoring may sound complicated at first, it can often be completed in less than a half-hour unless the colony is an unusually large one. Additionally, training should be given on how to use live traps and how to watch for signs of new rabbit dumping and any tampering with the rabbits, their food, or water.

It is also helpful to provide some training on how to respond should a volunteer be questioned while providing care. In general, it is best not to give too much information and nothing should be signed unless an attorney has first reviewed the document. It is not necessary to even give one's name unless asked by a policeman or member of a sheriff's department. Remain polite, but give little information, as occasionally an official may attempt to trap a caretaker into saying they are the owner of or are responsible for the rabbits. It is often best to answer questions with questions. For example if a volunteer is asked what they are doing, a good response is to politely inquire if any law is being broken. If the response is yes, ask for the specific law. For more information on legal questions and situations that may arise, see Chapter Five.

A continuing community outreach program will also be necessary, for people will move in and out of the vicinity of the colony, and you will wish to keep people in the community open to the presence of the rabbits. Periodic programs offered through a local adult education program, brochures, mailings, and fundraising events are a few ways this can be done.

Nutrition for Colony Rabbits

When feeding colonies of domestic rabbits that live outdoors in a wild state it is first necessary to forget all one has learned about feeding companion rabbits, for the nutritional needs are quite different. To begin with, colonies of rabbits usually consist of rabbits of varying ages, breeds/mixes, and health. Since it is not possible to feed each community rabbit individually, the food provided to the colony needs to meet the minimal nutritional requirements of all these rabbits. Secondly, the rabbits in outdoor colonies expend a great deal more energy than companion rabbits. Dominance encounters, fleeing from predators, and surviving harsh weather all utilize a great deal of energy. If food is inadequate, rabbits become weak and more likely to die from disease and predators.

Generally, providing colony rabbits with adequate nutrition means providing high-protein high-energy foods, although this may vary a little by the location of the colony and what plants are growing in the environment of a particular community of rabbits. In most cases, a good alfalfa hay with lots of leaves (the more leaves the more protein, fat, and carbohydrates) is the best choice. If it is possible to provide pellets to a community of rabbits, alfalfa-based pellets will provide better nutrition. If the colony is located somewhere with lots of greenery for the rabbits to forage on, the alfalfa hay can be mixed with grass hay (again the more leaves the higher nutrition), but in arid areas where the native vegetation is sparse the hay provided should be primarily alfalfa. Keeping both hay and pellets protected (see section on feeding rabbits in Chapter 7) is extremely important since toxins from molded hay and pellets can be deadly to the rabbits. Because of the rapidity with which it can spoil outdoors, fresh produce is not recommended for community rabbits unless there are enough volunteers to check on it daily and remove any that is beginning to rot.

It is not recommended to feed rabbits late in the afternoon or early evening, because any remaining food will attract potential predators and animals that can spread disease, such as raccoons and skunks. Raccoons carry raccoon roundworm, which can be fatal to rabbits, and raccoons will also prey on the rabbits.

In addition to a high-energy staple such as alfalfa hay or pellets, it is essential to provide adequate clean water. Rabbits that depend upon hay and/or pellets as a primary source of food need more water than rabbits whose diets consist primarily of succulent green plants. Adequate water also helps keep the urinary tract healthy, especially when a rabbit is consuming a lot of high-calcium alfalfa hay and pellets. Large cat water dishes with a receptacle that holds a gallon or two work well. It is important to arrange with volunteers to clean water receptacles on a weekly basis to prevent the buildup of biofilm (the slimy coating that develops on the surface of water containers with time) to help prevent problems with toxins and disease.

TNR was initially used to keep an abandoned rabbit population at Long Beach City College, California from growing, although a permanent TNR colony was not possible because of college plans to build several parking lots which would have taken the rabbits' environment. Therefore the rabbits were eventually adopted out and not maintained in a colony on the campus. However, the following account of the Long Beach city College effort is a good example of how a TNR team can be set up:

Long Beach City College Rescue
by Donna Prindle

I must have been channeling my inner "Alice" when I took that leap down the rabbit hole and decided something had to be done for the hundreds of rabbits on the college campus I had made my second home for most of my life.

Long Beach City College (LBCC) had become known as a place to drop off unwanted rabbits....babies left over from Easter, older ones no longer loved, and the generations of rabbits yet to be born. I was surrounded by hundreds of these rabbits when I walked on the campus one evening, and as if on cue, they all sat up with every eye looking at me.

At LBCC, we seemed to always have rabbits on campus....not cottontails, but domestic rabbits...rabbits who should be in loving homes....safe and warm. It seems we had become known as a bunny sanctuary. By 2008, we realized that this population had grown out of control and our college was planning several construction projects which would endanger our rabbits. People would drive into a parking lot, open a car door and dump their unwanted bunny into the bushes. In California, not only is this inhumane but also against the law,

resulting in fines and possible jail time. Our bunnies were everywhere on campus…digging burrows under sidewalks, on our athletic fields, under portable trailers and basically anywhere they could find space.

The college realized that a Task Force would need to be formed to thoroughly and thoughtfully approach the issue. Our original task force was made up of members from the facilities department, grounds crew, environmental health and safety, public relations, and members of the faculty, staff, and long-time rabbit care volunteers. Here we all were….but now what?

Four years later and 500 hundred rabbits saved, our amazing team of community volunteers, rescue groups, and college faculty and staff popped our heads back up from that hole. Together we had accomplished the first known, successful effort to utilize TNR (trap/neuter/return) principles for a large rabbit colony. Here's how we did it!

Our first step was to contact Best Friends Animal Society to ask for help. They presented our college with the innovative TNR method to help control our rabbit population. Our first big challenge was to convince our college administration that this type of project would work. With the invaluable help and resources from Debby Widolf, Best Friends Rabbit Director, we were able to get the approval for this project with an additional promise of a $10,000 facilities rebate for help with some of the costs. The next big hurdle was figuring out just how to accomplish a TNR with such large numbers of rabbits. It could have easily become a Mad Tea Party!

The stars must have been in alignment because once again a solution quickly emerged. It seems a veterinary graduate from Western University, School of Veterinary Medicine had recently participated in a workshop at Best Friends. She was able to coordinate this idea of a rabbit project with her university. Soon we found ourselves in planning meetings with the veterinary staff of Western University, including experts from Best Friends, and local rabbit rescues. When asked at these meetings when we wanted to plan our first TNR, I always replied, "yesterday!" We were desperate to begin because of the rapidly growing number of rabbits on campus (females can give birth up to 12 rabbits at a time, every 28 days) and the impending construction plans.

Our first concern was where to house the rabbits once they were taken off the campus. Western University was planning on bringing their portable VACS unit (Veterinarian Ambulatory Laboratory vehicle) to perform spay and neuter surgeries on campus. We scheduled for them to come March 2010 for a two-day spay/neuter event hoping to be able to help as many rabbits as possible. Our college provided an abandoned workshop shop for us to set up our rabbit center. Best Friends delivered nearly 100 crates for us to use and it took some time to set up the crates, litter boxes, bowls, food and all the supplies needed. As the date in March approached, we then had to start rounding up rabbits. We would meet very early in the morning with our pens, carrots, greens and carriers and begin the process of catching every rabbit on campus. We ended up with 85 rabbits in our rabbit center after that first week, only to discover every day a new litter of babies was being born as we waited for the Western VACS to arrive. We had to set up a nursery to accommodate the 50 babies born that week, along with a hospital area for our bunnies that had medical issues such as abscesses, injured legs, infections, and other health issues. Fortunately our local rabbit rescues stepped up to help train us to recognize and treat our sick rabbits. More serious concerns were addressed by the veterinarians at Western University.

Western University showed up for our two-day event with four veterinarians and many veterinarian students to volunteer their time and skills. Debby Widolf from Best Friends also came to help. It was an amazing event. Despite working all day and obviously being very tired,

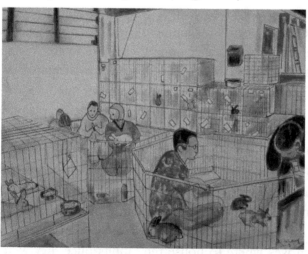

these skilled volunteers gave the last rabbits the same level of care as the first of the day. The rabbits continued to be cared for in our rabbit center after surgery to make sure they were recovering, eating normally and showing no signs of infection.

We also decided to use a small tattoo in one ear of each rabbit to indicate they had been spayed or neutered. Because our original plan was to return the rabbits and let them live out their lives on our campus, we needed a method to tell if a rabbit had already been through our rabbit center.

In May, Western returned once again for another two-day event. We were able to round up seventy-five rabbits this time. We knew that our project was working when we only had one litter of babies born instead of our fifty that week before they arrived. We returned several rabbits back to campus and continued to take small groups to Western University for their surgeries. Now that we had a better idea of the size of our

population, we realized that people were abandoning rabbits at an alarming rate. One morning we had eighteen babies abandoned in the middle of campus. It was depressing for us to realize that despite our efforts we might not be able to control the number of rabbits on our campus. We decided that we needed to start increasing our efforts to adopt our rabbits off campus. We started educating our community about the dangers of abandoning their rabbits and also about the possibility of receiving a fine and jail time for such actions. We were also able to convince our college to put up signs around the campus indicating this information. Our most experienced volunteer took over our adoption process which required people to fill our adoption paperwork, receive a thorough interview about what is required to care for a rabbit, and given bunny care handouts developed by Best Friends.

For the next four years, we continued to care for our rabbits in our center until they were all adopted. Some of the rabbits were bonded to another for companionship and all were eventually moved into larger pens. Every morning we would search the campus for any new rabbits that might have been abandoned overnight. Because out first event occurred near Easter, we received quite a bit of publicity. At first we were concerned that this media attention would increase the likelihood of people abandoning their rabbits. We decided to use every opportunity to educate the public to both the dangers of abandoning a rabbit and also the legal consequences of such actions. Whether that information was in our local paper, front page cover of the Wall Street Journal, local cable news, or Good Morning America programs, our message and mission were consistent. The publicity helped with adoptions and with increasing our number of volunteers. We had many people from the community come to help, along with groups of young students from local schools. Our own college students because very involved with our project as well. Many were able to receive volunteer service hours for their campus clubs and others came just to help out.

Many of our students would thank us for letting them be with the rabbits. Some students had never cared for an animal before, never held a rabbit. It was a very profound, memorable experience for them. Our rabbit center became a peaceful refuge for them away from the pressures of college life and a time to sit quietly holding a rabbit.

As our project wound down with the numbers of rabbits dropping on campus and in our center, we realized that our educational efforts were working. Fewer and fewer rabbits were being abandoned. Our entire campus was now on alert. If a rabbit was found, we were quickly called. Then a rescue in Colorado volunteered to take in some of our rabbits. We trusted them to find forever, loving homes for them. After several 16-hour road trips and the assistance of Best Friends, we were able to finally close the doors to our rabbit center. We no longer have any rabbits on campus, although we continue to have a single rabbit abandoned occasionally. We are still on call 24-seven to go rescue any rabbit dropped off. After making sure they are healthy, a trip to the vet for surgery is scheduled, and they are off to a rescue to find their forever home. We do this quietly hoping to not draw any attention and resurface any memories of the days when our campus was considered a rabbit sanctuary. It has now been a year since our last rabbit was abandoned on campus.

We are proud (and still a little amazed) that we were able to complete this rabbit project. From Debby Widolf and Victor Gutschalk of Best Friends, who were there from the beginning patiently teaching and sharing their knowledge, to Western University and their amazing veterinarians Dr. Diane McClure, and Dr. Frank Bossong and Dr. David Forster, who not only worked both of our S/N events, but continued to help our sick and injured rabbits. The amazing future veterinarians and students of Western University who helped during our events, Bunny Bunch rescue who shared their knowledge and provided supplies for our rabbits, our community volunteers who worked so many hours in the center, and our own college students who helped every day. Our project would not have been possible without their help.

We are proud the say we cared for every rabbit that came through our doors. We treated their wounds, infections, broken legs, and lovingly held some as they took their last breaths. We gave every rabbit at our college the love and comfort that they deserved and tried our best to give them a forever loving home...all 500 of them!

Now when I walk the campus, I recall many of the rescues that happened: The bushes near the English building where I found Jack, a black bunny with the biggest ears I have ever seen who ended up in Utah with the most wonderful family ever. And our newly constructed administration building where we found Reeses, who was so dirty you couldn't tell his coloring, missing one leg and the other injured. He ended up with the best bunny mom ever and became a therapy bunny comforting traumatized children and the elderly. And then of course my own Chipper...who is, of course, a white bunny who is maybe "the" white bunny from Alice's story. For you see, Chipper adopted me, as I was the only one he allowed to hold him.

Although we were successful in helping the hundreds of rabbits who had been abandoned on our campus, we realize that there are many, many other sites needing help. There are local parks and fields throughout our cities that have abandoned rabbits struggling to survive.

Hopefully our project will continue to give hope to others facing similar challenges.

CHAPTER 9: THE RENO RABBIT RESCUE OF 2006

Debby Widolf was the manager of the Bunny House at Best Friends Animal Society during the time of what has become known as the "Great Reno Rabbit Rescue of 2006." This has provided us with the opportunity to present the same rescue from the points of view of several different people who participated in it. We hope this will be instructive to readers.

My Reno Story
by Debby Widolf

We all have moments or events that spin our lives around, that mentally and physically turn what we thought we knew as reality upside down. Events that point our life in another direction or ignite a passion we had not known was within us. Mine arrived as a phone call at work on a cold winter morning. I had been hard at work as manager of the Best Friends Animal Society's Bunny House for only a little over a year; a change of career

spun from a love of rabbits. I knew I had a lot to learn about the world of animal abandonment and rescue, however the phone call from Reno threw me quickly into a situation that I could never have imagined.

In late December 2005 I received a call from a "friend of a friend" telling me that her friend had around 80 rabbits in her yard that she could not take care of due to an illness. I let her know that I would be willing to speak with the woman who had the rabbits and gave her some possible resources to share with her friend. All was quiet until mid-January when another call came in, only this time it was the "owner" of the rabbits. I will refer to her as "J" for my story.

I had a long and revealing conversation with J about her group of domestic rabbits. When I asked J about the number of rabbits she had I was taken aback, not sure if I had heard wrong during the heads-up call in December, for her reply was "around 800!" J explained that she had terminal cancer and wanted to find a place for the rabbits to go. Her family was unable to help with the rabbits and she was fearful that animal control would destroy them after her death. Her property would become a part of the expanding Reno airport when she passed on. J agreed to allow me as an employee of Best Friends Animal Society, to visit her home in Reno. My supervisors and administrators were alarmed by the plight of the rabbits and arranged for me and one of the Best Friends photographers to make the trip to Reno the following week.

After a short flight and drive we pulled up to a modular home in an ethnic, older neighborhood with encroaching new casinos up the street. J welcomed us to her tidy home, taking us through to the back door onto her deck which overlooked an approximate one-acre lot. There were two additional mobile homes and many sheds/outbuildings in various states of disrepair on the property. There was little vegetation that had not been eaten by the free roaming rabbits and a few trees. The yard was filled with hills of dirt, burrows and makeshift shanties. My jaw fell, and no words were said as I took my first look at over 1,000 rabbits! The rabbits were all ages, from the youngest venturing out of their nests for the first time to the older weathered and scared. The yard was a moving sea of darting, hopping, scrapping, chewing, digging rabbits. The general population seemed to be of medium size, five to six pounds and the dominant breed characteristics seemed to be blue-eyed

Dutch and English Spot with every variation imaginable. It was a confusing site to behold as the scene was one of dysfunction and a struggle for survival as well as great beauty and tenacity. I took a long, deep breath and knew that I would love each one and was committed to their journey.

J gave the photographer and me a tour through the backyard as she gave us a history of the rabbits. Her father had settled the property and did some farming and ranching. Although J was not in compliance with the current city regulations of how many animals were allowed per residence, the property had been grandfathered in to allow farm types of animals as long as she continued to live there. This clause worked in J's favor on the times she was cited for having too many animals (rabbits). Local children's groups visited the rabbits and according to J, wrote letters on her behalf when animal control threatened to have the rabbits removed. The domestic rabbits had been in residence at J's for around eighteen years. As is often the case, she started with a few rabbits and the population continued to grow. I asked if she had ever had any of the rabbits spayed or neutered. She replied that in earlier years she did but lost several of her females during the surgery and decided she would not attempt it again. She also had ongoing financial constraints which did not allow for any type of vet care.

J did say that when the population seemed to grow too large she would take some rabbits to a friend's farm and release them, and expressed some regret over having had to do this. She also told of rabbits being dumped over the fence at her home, and thought that people came to know that they could abandoned their rabbits at J's rather than taking them to the city shelter. I inquired about the various breeds she had. I learned that at one time she had a variety of breeds: Lops, NZW, Rex rabbits. I did not see any of these breeds with exception of some white rabbits. During the eighteen years the strongest survived. As stated earlier, a wide variety of Dutch, English Spot, solid black and agouti/ginger coloring emerged, all up-eared average size rabbits.

J had a person living in one of the mobile homes who did most of the rabbit care as J's health was declining. The rabbits were fed hay and seldom had pellets or greens except for the sparse native vegetation and bark from trees. Water was provided through a hose that filled long gutters. Hay and water had no protection from the elements. Vegetation, hay mixed with fur were gathered by the rabbits for nesting material, however, because of the over-crowded conditions some litters were born out in the open with no protection. The lot was filled with underground burrows dug by the rabbits, some so shallow that care had to be taken not to sink into them and injure rabbits below while walking the grounds. Besides digging into the ground, the rabbits lived under sheds, in old wooden lean-tos, in the bushes along the perimeter fence and beneath the mobile homes. On one occasion I saw rabbits that had dug underneath the mobile homes to the unfenced front yard and street. The backyard fencing was in disrepair with many exits to the outside and loose sharp wire that rabbits frequently became entangled in. J had rabbits living under her back deck and had several that had become comfortable enough to live on the deck itself. These were the luckier ones as they had a better diet. A few special ones, I saw five or six, lived in the house with J.

The herd of rabbits appeared to have established territories and an elusive invisible line to warn off their peers; lines in the sand that only the brave or foolish dared to cross. When boundaries were breached, fights ensued with regular frequency. I had never seen so many torn ears with missing pieces and short tails! At the initial assessment of the rabbits I estimated that around 10% needed immediate care or care in the next week by a veterinarian. I have no statistics to share in this account, so my estimate was based only on rabbits I observed in the initial visit. The most often seen physical concerns were large abscesses, fight wounds and eye problems. J said she observed that some rabbits survived the abscesses. Over time the abscess burst, dried up and the dead flesh fell away. How many rabbits had died from abscesses is unknown.

Because of the confinement, limit space and free roaming of the rabbits, the property provided a unique perspective of a "microcosm," if I can call it that, or an overcrowded, poverty-stricken ghetto type of neighborhood that was brimming with birth, life, death and an instinct to live that was tenacious, sometimes beautiful, and often tragic. The rabbits explored, the young ones "binkied", chased, and played. Territories were established, and re-established and dominant rabbits sought partners, females did their upmost to find or build a spot to give birth, obvious groups hung out together and strong bonds were evident. They were fiercely protective of their needs for survival, while also dependent on each other for the safety of living in a group, and for socialization and comfort. The marvelous photographer from Best Friends that went with me on the initial assessment had the general opinion that rabbits were not that interesting to photograph. I had to

chuckle when I observed him out in the rabbit yard very early in the morning snapping photos in every direction! I believe he was amazed at what fascinating subjects rabbits are to photograph in action. I regret I was unable to get permission to use photos from Best Friends for this book. His images are exquisite and speak volumes about rabbits as a species, as well as the plight of the Reno rabbits.

After obtaining an agreement of surrender of the rabbits from J, Best Friends Animal Society agreed to the monumental task of legal and financial responsibility, rescue, care and placement of J's 1,250 total rabbits on the property. I made two additional work trips to J's place. Vet techs and skilled rabbit personal were sent from Best Friends to set up a triage area in one of the vacant mobile homes on site. We provided vet care from local clinics and treated those with the most serious illnesses or injuries. A plan of action was set in place by Best Friends to establish: computer access, administration duties, project managers for the construction of pens to catch and contain the rabbits and the multiple other tasks needed to move the rabbits off the property. Rounding up the rabbits and separating them by sex was a stressful time for the herd of rabbits and hard physical work for the caregivers. A variety of means were used to move the rabbits into their designated pens: use of exercise pens to corral, bird safe nets in some cases, carriers and slowly walking/guiding them in to the spaces. Nests of kits in burrows were especially challenging when trying to determine which females were the mothers and to find the locations of the nests. The mothers with young and females that were obviously ready to give birth were kept in separate spaces. It was fortunate that there was ample time to get the rabbits sorted out and ready for transport to the ranch. Very few volunteers were onsite at J's, both because the conditions could be hazardous and because J needed privacy at her home. Rabbit transport began to the ranch site approximately one month after the initial assessment and continued until the process was complete. Efforts were made by Best Friends to remove all materials from construction and to clean up J's yard after all the rabbits were moved.

Best Friends rented a ranch house with land just outside of Reno which served as a temporary place to house the rabbits and to carry forth medical care and spaying/neutering. Approximately twenty-two 12x12 foot covered Priefert runs were put up with ground wire attached to the sides of the panels to keep rabbits from digging out and predators from entering. The ground wire was covered with the dirt and small stones. Shade cloth was put on the lower perimeter of the runs to act as a visual barrier against intruders. Other hand-constructed wood and wire runs were made, outbuildings and converted semi-truck containers were used for supplies to run the operation. Coyotes were plentiful in the area, so a perimeter 8-foot chain link fence was added to keep them out. The criteria for placing the rabbits in the new housing was to separate the males and females, which rabbits got along and to a lesser extent age or condition of the rabbits was also a factor. The rabbit groups generally co-existed well, with the occasional "bully" having to be pulled and tried with another group until a fit was found. The rabbit's diet was hay, pellets and greens.

The "ranch" also became the central port from which many Best Friends employees stayed while caring for the daily needs and comfort of the rabbits. Administration staff there worked at networking to find placements for the rabbits, managing paid staff and coordinating the out pouring of volunteers. Local volunteers as well as many from around the country came to the help the rabbits at the ranch site. Families with children, adults of all ages, employee's families, veterinarians, vet techs, vet students and vet assistants, volunteers from

other rescues, all came together to give their time, energy and goodwill in numerous ways. They were instrumental in making the rescue successful. The medical director of BFAS in Kanab was also medical director for the ranch site in Reno. One employee took on the job of cook, providing good meals and a lot of heart. We even had expert clicker trainers give a class on how to help the rabbits experience less stress. Many of the employees or volunteers were not experienced in rabbit care, but they were willing to learn and by the end of their time working at the ranch most all grew to love and respect their charges.

I made a fourth trip to Reno, my only one to the ranch site. My purpose for this visit was to do staff training on conducting home site visits for potential adopters. I was needed back at the sanctuary in Kanab to continue to manage the rabbit department at Best Friends Animal Society. I still served as a consultant on rabbit care for the Reno rabbits until the ranch closed after all the rabbits were placed. As a consultant I did not make administrative decisions regarding potential adoption sites or transfers to other rescues and adopters. However, I kept abreast of operations in Reno and had employees from the Rabbit Department rotate to Reno and later to a rescue in Washington State. Those employees reported to the BF supervisors directly managing those areas of the rescue at Reno.

The operation in Reno was concluded in approximately ten months. A total of 1250 rabbits were rescued from J's backyard. Prior to completing all the spays and neuters the rabbit population grew by several hundred rabbits already pregnant when taken to the ranch site. An estimated 1400 rabbits were placed in rescues and homes, adopted as groups, pairs or single rabbits. In 2009 three hundred plus rabbits were returned to Best Friends due to the financial constraints of the rescue that accepted them in 2006. This large group lived out the remaining years of their lives at Best Friends. The Reno rabbits were not mixed with the general population of rabbits at Best Friends Animal Society. They had a quiet location and lived in large covered runs or in yurts with indoor-outdoor access. The rabbits continued to live in groups, enjoying each other's company more so than the presence of people.

As each rabbit has their own personality, so it seemed that the Reno rescue "herd" had a collective personality as well. They were a unique group, a cloistered group, a group with a long history of interbreeding and a group relying on their instinctive nature and dependency on each other for survival. Over the eighteen years that the rabbits were on J's property the population was largely inbred, although new ones were occasionally added by people dumping their rabbits. Their contact with people was strictly limited. Little attempt was made to socialize them except for the few that lived in J's home and on her deck. Their world was primarily the interplay of relationships with each other with lessons passed down through the generations. They were vigilant about their territory and very leery of people. While there I found an injured baby that was close to dying. My choice to give him comfort was to put him into a litter of babies his size. This little guy snuggled down deeply into the center of the others and immediately seemed to feel safe. His need was to be with them and not me. Another day, I picked up a juvenile rabbit as we were gathering them into groups for transport. He screamed as I attempted to move him. I looked around me and there were about thirty rabbits standing up about fifteen feet away, clearly alarmed at his distress. I put him down to not cause

more fear. My lesson was to capture or move them with at least one other rabbit. The less handling the better for domestic rabbits that have had little human interaction. They need and want each other.

I was able to closely follow the personalities of the Reno rabbits when 300 of them returned to Best Friends Animal Society from previous sanctuary care. Despite having wonderful and respectful caregivers the group at large remained cautious and chose not to become friendly with the staff or visitors. There were exceptions of course. The rabbits with special needs or those that required long term medical care did become more tolerant of people. I would estimate that around 5% of the 300 rabbits were calm with direct human contact. From observations from the previous sanctuary, we were sure to bring in a favorite "well" rabbit friend from the group when one was confined for medical treatment. This practice seemed to calm and aid in recovery of the ill rabbit. Volunteers and special groups could help with the Reno rabbits care at Best Friends. They were instructed to speak quietly, to move slowly, and under no circumstances to pick up or expect to hold one of the rabbits. Children under age eighteen initially were not able to volunteer with this group when they arrived at Best Friends. We enforced this out of respect for the need to help the rabbits feel safe and to allow them to be who they were. The rabbit's needs for a private life had little to do with the staff and volunteers loving them and having favorites. Every rabbit had a name and was someone's little heart bunny. They were beautiful to observe, calming, entertaining and endearing.

The last of the Reno rabbits have passed away at Best Friends. They were dearly loved and never forgotten by staff and volunteers.

Housing the Reno Rabbits
by Michele Page

It amazes me still even though it was in 2006 how vivid my memory is in regards the Reno Rabbit rescue that took place while working at Best Friends Animal Society. Being employed at Best Friends for over 15 years, I've witnessed many rescues regarding a variety of animals.

However the Reno rabbits were quite a challenge to say the least! We received a little over 300 rabbits that were from Reno about three years after the rescue itself. The group that originally took the rabbits found themselves unable to stay afloat financially, and they could no longer care for the rabbits. Hence they were sent to Best Friends Animal Society, which could take over this costly endeavor.

I remember being involved in the construction of the facility. We had four yurt structures with open pathways from indoor to the outdoors that were enclosed by Priefert panels. They are 10x10 panels that can be put together for outside enclosures. You can interchange

them and make larger runs, which we had to do to house some of our outside rabbits. We had forty 10x10 foot, a 10x20, and a 10x40 runs on the outside besides the yurts. This was very challenging with snowy winter conditions and heat in the summer which would get to 100 degrees and sometimes more. We used straw bale houses on the outside runs for the rabbits to burrow into to keep warm since we would be in the minus-zero degrees some mornings. Shade cloth protected the outside runs from snow and rain. And metal roofs were put on the top of the Prieferts to protect them from the sun, rain and snow. We also had to lay hardware cloth down on the floor so the rabbits could not dig out and nothing (like predators) could dig in. This hardware cloth is metal and would be fastened with hog rings to be secure.

Many challenges were faced with having this many rabbits!

We had a medical yurt for the sickliest bunnies and medications would be given out as much as three times a day. This included everything from giving eye drops and shots to nebulizing, force feeding, and giving butt baths, just to mention a few. Feeding would take up to an hour and a half for the outside runs. Our routine included scrubbing water bowls, refilling them, bringing hay in for the rabbits to eat and feeding pellets.

We constructed hay houses in the corners with branches and hay so the rabbits could hide and get away and feel safe. In the larger runs that held 12 to 14 rabbits these were important as the rabbits would form small groups amongst themselves, establishing their own little territories. Rabbits are very territorial and will fight, sometimes resulting in serious injuries or even death, so placing rabbits together should be very well-supervised and can take some time.

In extreme heat we had fans set up throughout the hallways of the rabbit runs to ensure good circulation, and at times we would have to take hoses and water the ground to bring down the temperature. Also in the summer we would have bot flies which would attack the rabbits – another challenge.

We went through approximately ten to twelve bales of hay a day, four bags of Purina Rabbit Chow pellets and about six bags of wood pellets for the litter boxes. It was quite a huge undertaking. There are many challenges one faces on this size of a rescue. Even with the best of efforts, it can be draining financially. We had approximately eight caregivers work 8-hour days and we still found ourselves scrambling to get everything done by the end of the day.

We also made sure that each and every rabbit had his or her share of foraging toys in every run. This is so important for the health of their fast growing teeth. We used apple branches, hidey boxes, and wicker paper plate holders, to mention a few. The rabbits also received fresh greens every day, either Romaine lettuce or cilantro. We would go through approximately six cases of lettuce a day.

I was blessed to have had these rabbits in my life and so honored to have been a part of such a successful rescue. It has humbled me and really showed me what working as a team is all about. It was a huge group effort and couldn't have been done as well as it was without the cooperation of everyone involved.

The one thing I can't impress too much is, *do your homework*, all these guys need the best care you can give them.

When Bunnies Happen

by Renée Phelps

In the spring of 2006, something happened that would forever change my life as I knew it. It wasn't a birth, a death, a marriage, or any of the life events you would assume. What was it? Bunnies. Bunnies happened and they happened in a big way.

I was looking to adopt a bunny and found a local woman who did "rescue" (and I use this term very loosely) and decided to give her a call. She seemed like a very nice lady and we set up a time for me to go to her house and meet the bunnies to see if any of them were a good fit for our family. What I found when I got there wasn't what I expected. She did have many bunnies. The problem was they were all sitting in wire-bottomed cages, most had no food or water, and many were sick. The sick ones that were beyond help were put outside as prey for the wild animals. I was appalled by all of it, but had to at least question her on that point. She answered by shrugging her shoulders and telling me "that's nature." No, that is not nature. That is cruelty. Without a word, I turned on my heel, walked back to my car and left as fast as I could. The whole drive home, I considered all the possibilities of what could be done. When I arrived home, I called our local animal services, the Humane Society, the SPCA, a rescue organization in southern California, from whom I had previously adopted, and Best Friends Animal Society. And there it was…the moment that changed everything.

I spoke with a very kind gentleman from Best Friends and described the situation as calmly and accurately as I could, hoping they could somehow intervene and get these bunnies to a better place. When I finished, he asked me if this was located in Lemmon Valley, a small rural area just north of Reno.

When I answered yes, he just sighed and said "Oh boy." I didn't know at the time what was behind that "Oh boy." As our conversation progressed and confusion emerged, we realized we were talking about two very different bunny crises. As fate would have it, they were in the beginning stages of a very large rescue operation in Reno. A rescue of unfathomable proportions!

Because they had only shortly been on-scene, they were quite hesitant about taking volunteers. I don't think they even had their heads wrapped around the situation yet. It was truly an astonishing situation even for them, who to this point, had probably believed they'd seen everything. There were hundreds and hundreds of bunnies! It took some convincing, but he agreed to get me started as a volunteer.

The day I was to start volunteering, I arrived early and was very anxious and nervous. You see, to me these people were my idols, the people I respected immensely, the people I admired. I pulled into the driveway of the house where the bunnies were located, put my car in park and took a deep breath. I had no idea what I was in for, so I gave myself a quick pep talk.

When I stepped out of my car, I was stopped in my tracks. The smell. Oh, the smell. It wasn't hay, it wasn't even bunny poop or pee. It was sickness. It was despair. How could this be? Then I looked out in the back yard and found my answer. I've never seen anything so awful in my life. This wasn't going to be just a matter of collecting bunnies and finding them homes. It was a million times more than that and my head started to spin.

The Best Friends staff currently on site showed me around. Inside the trailer-made-makeshift-clinic it was an organized chaos. There were many bunnies in crates, stacked several high, suffering from various stages of illness and injury, an abundance of veterinary supplies, large amounts of blankets and towels, boxes full of dishes and water bottles, cleaning supplies, play pens full of babies with no mommies to care for them. Outside, simply put, there were bunnies. Everywhere. Two large lots full of bunnies. There's no real way to even describe it.  Bunnies of every color, size and shape, starving bunnies, injured bunnies, sick bunnies, social bunnies, feral bunnies, baby bunnies, adult bunnies, fighting bunnies, shy bunnies, terrified bunnies, incredibly brave bunnies, playful bunnies, bunnies resigned to a horrible fate and bunnies determined to not be. Strewn about the yards there was trash, pieces of sheet metal, camper shells, dead and fallen trees, pallets, a couple old sheds, barrels, stacks of straw and...more bunnies. It suddenly became quite clear why they didn't want volunteers yet. It was like a war zone.

Inside and outside. Hope and promise vs. heartache and helplessness. With my head still spinning, all I could manage to say was "What can I do?" Because they were still absorbing it themselves, the simple answer was "Can you feed these babies?" It seemed a fairly benign place to start. To their surprise, I showed up every day eager to help. I was taught how to do all the medical treatments, I helped capture bunnies, I ran errands, I took bunnies to the vet, I continued to feed the babies and I cleaned. I did everything I possibly could, but most of all I learned.

 In order to provide more thorough medical care, to keep the bunnies separated, clean and safe, to have a safer, more acceptable environment for staff, future volunteers and potential adopters, it was clear all the bunnies would need to be moved to another location and a ranch house was located in Lemmon Valley. Large runs were built on the land to house the bunnies. A surgical room, a pre-op room and a medical treatment room were all added on to the house and the living room was made into an administrative area.

Meanwhile, at the original location, through weeks of inclement weather and hazardous conditions, all the bunnies were eventually caught, separated and moved. Truckload after truckload of crated bunnies were transported. Sometimes we even unloaded more bunnies off a truck than we loaded because pregnant mommies gave birth on the way there!

The hard work continued at the "Bunny Ranch", as we jokingly called it. As word got out, more volunteers started showing up and it soon became a family affair. My father, my father-in-law, and my amazing husband all came to volunteer also. Hundreds of bunnies were fed and watered and hundreds of pens and crates were cleaned daily, sick and injured bunnies were treated and healed, dozens of spays and neuters were done a day. I continued to show up every day as well and I was eventually hired on as a Best Friends employee. What an incredible honor!!

Gradually, adoptions started to happen. Families from all over the country, other rescue groups and even some of the volunteers wanted to include these special bunnies in their families. One bunny in particular really stood out for me. He was found severely injured at the original location and brought in for medical treatment. Nobody was sure that he would make it and he spent almost three months in medical. I couldn't help but be inspired by his strength and determination. I named him McGill and he was our first adoption. His adoption was followed by twenty more.

After six months of working for Best Friends, my time there came to its natural end. During that time I saw so many bunnies find their new homes. I saw babies I witnessed being born grow and thrive. I saw sick ones get well and injured ones heal. I saw bunnies once terrified learn to trust and love. The people I worked with, whether Best Friends employees or volunteers, were incredible. We were all from different parts of the country, different walks of life, different backgrounds and experiences. We came with different ideas, different values and different strengths and weaknesses. The intense need to save these bunnies and give them the life they deserved served as a fantastic unifier. Friendships and bonds were formed that I'm certain will last a lifetime. A short time later, using all I learned from this experience, I started my own bunny rescue.

Fast forward ten years and my husband and I are still rescuing bunnies, McGill is doing great, the other "rescue" has long since been shut down and The Great Bunny Rescue of 2006 remains one of the most amazing times of my life.

From the Reno Rabbits...
by Renée Phelps

There was a lady named J,
we knew she meant well.
It was not her intent
To put us through hell.

But, day by day Our
numbers grew. After all,
we are rabbits, We just
did what we do.

She knew it was too many,
But what could she do?
A thousand rabbits?
This couldn't be true!

So she got on the phone And
called you, Best Friends. The
mistake she had made She
knew you could mend.

Before we knew
Our visitors came.
You cared for us
And called us by name.

Too many of us
Did not make it. The
sick and the weak Just
couldn't take it.

But our new best friends
Worked very hard
To make us well'
And clean up our yard.

The next thing we knew We
were moving somewhere. It
was away from here
So we didn't care where.

You put us in trucks
And drove to a ranch. You
knew we could thrive
Once given the chance.

We were then separated,
The boys and the girls.
We'd brought enough babies
Into this world.

We all went in
For a small operation
And when we got sick
You gave us medication.

People came from
All over to see us,
Until we were well
You weren't going to leave us.

Once well and relaxed
We started to play,
We actually looked forward
To each new day.

Then the day came When one
found a new home Which one
of us was next?
We were anxious to know.

Before we knew it,
We had all found homes.
We'd never again
Be scared and alone.

Some of us went in the sun,
Others went in the rain,
Many rode in a car
While some flew on a plane.

With our troubles now
In the distant past, We
are finally living Safe
lives at last.

So, thank you Best Friends
For all that you did, We
won't see you again, So
farewell we bid.

My Experience with "The Great Rabbit Rescue of 2006"

by Lisa Carrara

Television news, social media, the internet, ad campaigns, etc., place great emphasis on dogs and cats but often overlook other species. Dogs and cats are indeed a treasured and invaluable part of the animal kingdom; however, they are certainly not the only intrinsic beings that deserve attention.

I suppose my great love of animals was inherited from my wonderful mother. As a child I was blessed to have the opportunity to care for many different species, all of them rescues in one form or another. We were the "crazy animal people" that rescued every stray dog and cat we came upon as well as animals such as raccoons, squirrels, coyotes, squirrels, birds, field mice and even deer. Growing up in the mountains of Lake Arrowhead, California, wildlife was abundant.

Our hearts went out to the sick, injured and displaced. If any of them needed emergency or ongoing medical care, we did everything possible to provide it. We wanted each species to flourish in its natural habitat if rehabilitation was possible. Domestic animals became part of our family or were placed in loving homes, while non-domesticated animals were released back into the wild or placed in a sanctuary. Occasionally an animal's health wasn't optimal for them to be returned to the wild, so we came up with another solution: I've always enjoyed designing and constructing different types of habitats, so for these animals I would use a portion of our home or property and do my best to build a suitable environment for them to live a safe and happy existence.

My grandparents had a small farm with a bull, cow and eventually a heifer that was thoughtfully named after me! They also had a rooster, chickens and, low and behold, rabbits. I always gravitated toward the rabbits and would spend hours relishing in their adorability and observing their behavior. I was allowed to take one or two of the rabbits home and raise them myself. Inevitably, I became very attached and began to develop a curiosity about these adorable little scampers. Their antics and behavior absolutely fascinated me.

Thirty-plus years later I moved to Las Vegas and quickly became aware of the abandoned rabbit epidemic in that city. It was heartbreaking, and I spent many physically and emotionally draining hours rescuing as many as possible from the numerous "dumpsites" in the city.

My mother and I wanted to purchase an investment home, and while passing through a potential neighborhood one night, I noticed a rabbit far off in the distance near a bush. And then another. When I got closer it was obvious they were domestic rabbits that had either escaped or been abandoned. We did end up purchasing the home and the thought of those poor bunnies giving birth to litter after litter while in danger of predation, disease, poisoning, overheating, improper nutrition and much more, never, ever, left my mind.

After months of feeding the rabbits I attempted to gain their trust by several methods, hoping I could eventually capture them, but my efforts were futile. Their trust in humans was nonexistent and I knew I needed a "plan B." Being familiar with rabbit behavior I had an idea that I felt might be successful. I enlisted my mom as my fellow rescuer and decided to try one last scheme I thought might possibly work.

I always keep several types of safe, innovative trapping devices at home and in my rescue truck. During previous rescues I had fabricated a type of safe, large trapping net made from heavy-duty rolls of fishing net. It was a durable yet soft material with ¼" openings. Panels were cut and zip-tied together and SCUBA diving weights were secured to the bottom of each panel so when the rabbit charged the net it was less likely to get out from underneath the net. The 25-foot length made it possible to approach the rabbits from a distance without frightening them while keeping them contained. I designed the large net for one or two-person use. If I was solo I would attach one end to something and then walk the other end around the rabbit. Obviously with two people this was much easier!

The rabbits were grazing on one of the owner's lawns as they usually did that time of day, and we decided it was time to try and capture one. We knew we would probably only have one shot. One of us was at each end of the netting and I communicated to my fellow rescuer and mom where and how she needed to move her end of the net. After about an hour of repositioning the net around the elusive little critter we finally had him surrounded and slowly closed in on him. I slowly draped a towel over him, (frightened rabbits often feel safer with their heads covered) and put him in the correct position to be picked up without injuring his spine. After placing him in the awaiting crate we knew we had one more job – catch his mate.

But since she had observed her rabbit friend's capture, she was frightened and far more difficult to approach. After about two hours trying to steer her to a more enclosed area she ran into a yard where I knew there were no escape paths. As she crouched in the corner of a patio we repeated the same procedure with the net. Success! My prayers were answered, and my heart felt light.

My animal family at home was already complete, and it would not have been fair to either the bunnies I had captured or the pets I already had to keep these bunnies. I don't hoard animals; I rescue them. I strive to maintain the mindset that a healthy rescuer is altruistic and places the animal's best interest first. That being said, now what?

Fortunately, I was very familiar with Best Friends Animal Society outside of Kanab, Utah, and I knew they would be the best resource to contact to help me find a safe, loving home for these two precious bunnies. Best Friends put me in contact with the Bunny House Manager, Debby Widolf. Debby gave me approval to bring them to Best Friends where they would be happy and well cared for. Her knowledge, passion and dedication to the rabbits was very reassuring to me. and I felt safe leaving Mama and Chocolate in her care. Debby and I kept in touch and she became a dear friend and mentor.

This brings me to the story of my experience with The Great Rabbit Rescue in 2006, near Reno, Nevada. It was one of the largest rabbit rescues that had ever taken place in the United States, and I was incredibly honored when Debby extended the opportunity for me to volunteer.

I'd done animal rescue and volunteer work for over 40 years, but when I became a part of this rescue my life was forever changed. It was a hoarding case in which a well-intentioned woman had kept numerous unaltered rabbits on her property. Of course they bred, and the situation became a tragic example of hoarding and of over-breeding.

Ultimately there were about 1,600 rabbits in her yard.

Of course I brought my faithful rescue partner – my mom - with me to Reno! We arrived eager to begin, but neither of us were prepared for what we were about to experience. Seeing the innocent rabbits living their lives in an atrocious, inhospitable and unacceptable environment was devastating. In addition to the woman's self-created situation with her unaltered rabbits, her property was also a favorite dumping ground for others with unwanted rabbits. I think that hoarding issues deserve a far more extensive amount of attention than they are given. Public awareness is necessary before change can be made.

The conditions from which these precious, innocent bunnies were saved were incomprehensible. The rabbits suffered severe pain and anguish from untreated medical conditions and the consequences of overcrowding. There were many countless, unnecessary deaths. Again, the owner may seemingly have had good intentions trying to keep the rabbits, but a true rescuer is selfless, not selfish. Compassionate and responsible pet owners place their animal's quality of life equivalent to their own.

However, the impact of this gruesome situation was slightly tempered by the progress that Best Friends' had already made. The legalities with the rabbits' owner were underway so the volunteers were able to proceed with initial trapping and triage, the construction of predator-proof enclosures, medical and surgical units, and the separation of male and female rabbits. Many of the terrified rabbits were in extremely poor health, suffered from malnutrition, and had  injuries so severe that there were abscesses down to the bone and ears and genitals that were torn off. These ill and injured rabbits were prioritized for treatment and volunteers began the vast number of spays and neuters that were needed. Teams of veterinarians and veterinary technicians from around the country had gathered to take on this daunting task. Unfortunately, many rabbits were already pregnant when the rescue began, which resulted in hundreds more rabbits being born, bringing the total population to approximately 1,600 rabbits.

One of the many horrific things I experienced occurred while I was attempting to stabilize a very young bunny who was in critical condition. I sat with him for hours and at regular intervals I tried to raise his body temperature with thermoregulatory devices. In between periods of warming him, I held him in the palm of my hand, gently stroking him, talking to him and praying for his recovery. After several hours of this regimen, he suddenly screamed just before he took his last agonal breath and died in my hands. (A rabbit scream sounds eerily like a human child's scream but is more high-pitched. It is very disconcerting, and you can't ever mistake it. This occurs when rabbits are extremely frightened or in brutally intense pain.)

Another frightening incident occurred in the operating room during a routine spay. Rabbits under general anesthesia are high-risk. There is a very narrow margin between the dosage needed to induce and maintain anesthesia and the dosage that can produce toxic effects related to stress and cardiac or respiratory reactions. Exotic specialists or rabbit savvy veterinarians are essential. During the procedure the bunny suddenly went into cardiac arrest and quickly lost any heart rhythm. The amazing professionals performing and assisting in the surgery acted quickly. One of the best, most experienced veterinary technicians immediately started CPR. About a minute later the baby girl's heart began beating and she resumed normal respiration.

Another component of the rescue was several isolation trailers with rabbits of varying illnesses and injuries. One of them contained baby playpens with numerous bunnies that seemed to get very little attention. When I inquired about the reason behind this I was told that there was simply not enough staff to care for them. This hit me in a way that I really can't describe, and every fiber of my being told me they needed extra compassion. In between my regular duties of cleaning, feeding, etc., I chose to spend most of my time caring for them and ensuring they and their bedding were clean, and that they had fresh water, proper nutrition and loving human contact. I would stay long after most of the volunteers were gone, making my usual work period about fourteen hours per day. Debby would come in and say, "You have to go get some rest, we can resume tomorrow".

For a reason I'm not sure of, I was always drawn to a playpen which held seventeen babies that were approximately two weeks old. I would cry when I stood over them, knowing that they were suffering. I have never found the words to depict how devastating this was to me. I had horrible nightmares for many years after completing my part in this rescue.

Yet everyone tried to make the best of this ghastly situation, and there were occasional fun and exciting times. At one point a bunny had gone missing from his enclosure. Knowing that they feed at dusk and dawn, I set traps to try and catch him. I was eager to check the trap numerous times per day, and each time I did, from a distance I would notice a little critter moving about inside. I'd feel so thrilled to have finally trapped the little guy! I'd hurry over to the trap but it turned out every time this happened it was a darn squirrel in the trap gobbling up the hay! This little pesky squirrel had found his new banqueting location and became a regular in the trap. He was cute, but not who I was hoping would be there.

We finally located the bunny about two days later under a tractor trailer that stood about sixteen inches off the ground. We used a broom and sticks to gently steer him out and scoop him up, but it was impossible to catch him because of the many openings under the trailer. Debby, mom and I formed a covert plan. We blocked off all the openings we could find except one. Mom guarded the only exit that couldn't be blocked, and Debby kneeled behind a box next to the probable exit the bunny would try to use. The A-Team was in place! In full stealth mode, (wink, wink), I lay on my stomach and forced myself under the extremely confined space of the trailer. Inching through the mud I got close enough to the little guy to use a stick and steer him toward Debby. As soon as he was hoodwinked by our plan, Debby swiftly closed the box and we gained the peace of mind in saving one more.

As our time volunteering came to an end, as physically and emotionally exhausted as we were, my mom and I felt very despondent about leaving this amazing journey. We left the ranch late that night and checked into a hotel so we'd be ready to head back to Las Vegas the

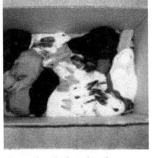

next morning. We got about fifteen minutes down the road the next day when we simultaneously looked at one another, and without speaking a word, we knew what we both wanted and needed to do. We quickly made a U-turn and headed back to the ranch in hopes that Best Friends would allow us to foster the seventeen babies in the playpen that had latched onto my heart. I was bound and determined they would get their chance to survive. so I signed a foster agreement, packed up the babies and we all headed home!

I immediately began to make plans to provide a safe, healthy and fun new existence for the bunnies. I built a predator proof pen on the grass in my yard where they could run, dig and play. As they grew a little bigger, so did their enclosure. I eventually fenced in the entire grass portion of my yard and built wooden ramps, obstacle courses and provided many other toys for them to experience.

At a young age bunnies get along well in a group, but as they develop they begin to form bonds, either in pairs or groups and will fight for territory. Not a problem! When they entered this stage, I determined who was bonded with whom, and it became clear that four separate runs were needed. I wanted to provide them with a life they

deserved but had never had so the construction began! I divided the yard into four enormous sections. Between each section I dug eight-inch trenches, pounded stakes into the ground, mixed and poured over 2,000 pounds of concrete to secure the stakes, and securely fastened configurable pet gates which separated each run. Since bunnies love to dig, I tunneled warrens at one end of the yard and buried eight-inch PVC pipe inside the burrows. Of course, they created their own warrens in the surrounding dirt for extra excitement!

Closest to the house was the covered patio where pet carriers with soft bedding were placed for them to hide, lounge and play in. Their hay bins, pellet dishes and water were secured here to ensure cleanliness and avoid contamination. They also had large litter boxes filled with hay. Rabbits are easily trainable to use litter boxes and often they instinctively use them with no training at all. All litter boxes, food dishes, water dishes and hay bins were thoroughly cleaned and replenished each day.

As you probably know, summers get very hot in Las Vegas and extreme heat can kill rabbits. So, a few modifications had to be made when summer arrived. I built 4' x 4' wooden cubicles with a lid, an entrance and exit, and a large cutout in the back where individual air conditioners were placed. Thermometers were placed in each box, ensuring the temperature averaged about 65 degrees. Crazy? Yes, but it was all worth it. These little guys were living the dream and they deserved it!

The second section contained several feet of brick that was kept continuously wet for cooling purposes. The bunnies loved stretching out those long bellies and lounging on the cool bricks. The third section consisted of a lengthy portion of grass. Because bunnies love to eat and dig in the grass, fresh sod was laid about every other month.

Every run contained safe, interactive toys and treats such as edible willow balls, sisal rope, apple sticks, hand woven timothy hay toys, wooden baby blocks, lattice jingle bell toys and freshly picked pine cones from local Mt. Charleston.

It probably goes without saying that at this point the bunnies already had names. Dot, Stacey, Milo and Peds owned the first run, Champagne and Freckles the second; Ming, Mei, Shi Shi and Fuzzy, (a.k.a. Fuzz Bomb) the third; and Jackson and Carmen the fourth. (The last five of the original seventeen bunnies had happily already found their forever homes!)

A rabbit's diet must be closely maintained, and the correct proportion of hay and pellets must be supplied to ensure a healthy digestive tract. They can have occasional treats but given too often, these can often cause blood glucose elevations, obesity and other serious health issues. But as every parent wants to spoil their child we figured out a way to do just that. On occasion, mom prepared a meal fit for a Los Angeles supermodel! Each group got a pie tin containing banana, apple slices, (without the seeds as they contain amygdalin, a substance that releases cyanide when it comes into contact with digestive enzymes), strawberries, carrot sticks, kale, cilantro and spinach. When the plating was complete, mom would walk outside and say, "Come get your yum-yums!", and every bunny raced for the patio at full speed! It became a very comical, sweet ritual. Happily, they lacked nothing. They were my pride and joy.

Fostering the rabbits was an emotional rollercoaster ride. All seemed to be going well when suddenly the bunnies developed signs of illness. They were infected with coccidia, tiny, single-cell organisms common to the intestinal tract of mammals. When these protozoa multiply they cause a disease called coccidiosis. Animals under stress or who were born sickly are at high risk, facing severe diarrhea, dehydration and even death. But with the personal and professional support of Debby Widolf, our local veterinary community, and a close friend and rabbit savvy veterinarian, Dr. Laura George, I was able to provide the care required. After three months of several treatments per day, the rabbits seemed to recover.

Soon after, the rabbits began to show symptoms of another disease and were diagnosed with pasteurellosis. *Pasteurella multocida* is the most common pathogen in domestic rabbits. Affected rabbits may develop pneumonia, rhinitis, conjunctivitis, genital tract infections, septicemia and abscesses. Again, several treatments per day for another three months were required. By  treating the rabbits with oral antibiotics and a nebulizer that administered medicated liquid mist to their lungs, these precious little bunnies survived yet again.

When the rabbits were just under a year old it was time to begin the sorrowful process of finding forever homes for these special bunnies. Yet another portion of the rollercoaster ride began as I tried to become emotionally adjusted to the reality that they would be leaving. Then one bunny, ironically named Dot, developed a spot in his eye. An ophthalmologist determined that he tested positive for *Encephalitozoon cuniculi*, (*E. cuniculi*). The spot was literally a hole being eaten through his eye, inside out. *E. cuniculi* is a parasite in which there is little known about. It's thought to be transferred, mother to offspring prior to birth, and possibly by the urine of infected rabbits. The organism travels through the body with white blood cells, the very cells that normally fight disease, and can infect a rabbit's brain, kidneys, spinal cord, heart, liver or lungs. As with Dot, it has also been known to damage the eyes.

I was told some of our other Reno survivors were also suffering symptoms from this disease and that this was the age when the indicators begin to appear. Just a week after this devastating news, another bunny showed symptoms, including head tilt, which is among the most serious problems with this infection. Symptoms can be swift and devastating, or slowly develop over time. Effects can range from a slight head tilt, rapid side to side movement of the eyes or a lack of balance which produces horrific body rolls.

I will never be able to thank my mom enough for the essential role she had in the rabbits' treatment. Sadly, she now has dementia and doesn't remember any of our journey, but I will never forget her dedication to the rabbits. During each bout of illness, I would gently restrain while mom administered oral medication that was compounded with grape flavor. After the oral medication they received medicated drops and then she gently placed them in their crates and made them comfortable while I prepared the next step of  treatment, placing a nebulizer at the opening of their crate. Never a better team. Mom is amazing!

Ultimately, we were able to provide the treatment and support that brought these bunnies back to health. At a little over two years old, our little family of bunnies went back to Best Friends where they would either be adopted or live permanently.

They are still missed every day. Sometimes I revisit the many pictures and videos that captured all the love, gratitude and loyalty they

showed us. Looking back on the memories warms my heart, and the gratification of having earned their trust and had them become attached to us is indescribable. I smile when I reminisce about their funny, interactive shenanigans, their occasional ornery behavior, the binkies they performed and so forth. I remember how on occasion I would sit outside with them in the evenings and enjoy a glass of wine. Fuzz Bomb did everything in her power to enjoy a sip. Dot learned to play catch and would catch the jingle bell ball and toss it back either using his mouth or paws. Jackson couldn't stand my partiality to him and would run from my attempts to cuddle him. Stacey, Peds and Milo always kept secrets in their private clique. Freckles and Champagne shared an incredible bond where they enjoyed each other's company over anyone else's. Jackson and the love of his life, Carmen, always lying side-by-side while they groomed and cuddled. Ming, Mei and Shi Shi tolerating and finally accepting Fuzz Bomb, the odd man out. Touching memories such as Dot feeling so secure with me that he would jump into my arms from the examination table when the doctor would enter the room. There are so many memories and not enough paper to write them on. Each and every one will be treasured forever.

I am very blessed to have been a part of the "Great Rabbit Rescue of 2006" and to have helped make the world a better place for those bunnies. We need to be more responsible as a human race and not let incidents like the one that necessitated this rescue occur.

PART III
INDIVIDUAL RESCUE OF DUMPED RABBITS

CHAPTER 10: CAPTURING ABANDONED RABBITS

Those rescuers who have taken part in large rescues and colony rescues are a special group whose collective knowledge is going to be needed more frequently as the dumped rabbit crisis grows. But it is the individual rescuers, those who rescue one to several rabbits at a time, who are the foot soldiers of rabbit rescue. They are the ones who often continue to rescue those rabbits who come into their orbit year after year. They are also often the ones who nurse the rabbits back to health, frequently paying veterinary expenses out of their own pockets, and if they are unable to find a home for the rabbit, adopt the rabbit themselves. Their contributions to rabbit rescue may appear small if viewed incident by incident, but taken collectively the number of rabbits they rescue is immense.

Some of these individual rabbit rescuers are associated with a rabbit group or shelter, but many are not. Some don't even know a thing about rabbits, but just happened on a situation from which they could not in good conscience walk away. Melissa Shelton agreed to share her experience in order to show that even those who know nothing of rabbits can help, and she hopes that other inexperienced people who find themselves in a similar situation will feel less intimidated after reading her story:

I live in Colonie, NY – a small street, not overly busy like some areas in Albany, but it still gets quite a bit of traffic. About a month or so ago I noticed two stray domesticated adult bunnies hanging around my street. After a couple of weeks I saw only one adult, and later found out from a friend that the other one was caught and sent to a foster home. Then I saw a baby bunny hanging around my stairs; the bunny proceeded to hide under my porch. I saw the baby and one adult for a couple days, thought there were only the two...

I am NOT a bunny person, I'm a cat person. I know nothing about rabbits other than they're cute - I thought they only ate carrots! But I know that domesticated bunnies living on their own will not survive, and I couldn't stand knowing no one else would help these bunnies except for me.

That Friday I bought some Havahart traps from Lowes (for $30 I got a large and small trap, so I bought three sets). I set up the three small traps near the three openings around my porch. I followed a rabbit expert's advice and used bananas as bait with

 a few pieces of green leaf lettuce. I made note of when I saw the bunnies outside so I could try and time setting the traps so the bait would be at its freshest. That night I caught **seven baby bunnies**. Five were in one trap and two were in another. At this point it had been days since I had seen the adult, but I kept putting the larger traps out with bananas as bait, and a couple baby carrots (I did  learn that carrots should only be an occasional treat because

 they're high in sugar). That Sunday night I caught baby number eight, and finally on Tuesday morning I caught the adult bunny

It was a very stressful experience, mostly because I care very much for animals and wanted to make sure they were safe. As I said previously, I have no knowledge of bunnies and never even touched one. The guidance from an expert on how to lure the bunnies into the traps and knowing where the burrow was located gave me the confidence to believe that maybe I could help. The adult bunny and the eight baby bunnies were given to the Mohawk Hudson Humane Society where they will all be neutered/spayed before being available for adoption. I hope I don't see any more stray bunnies in the area, and hope that people will learn **all** pets are a lifetime commitment

Meg Brown is one of the most experienced individual rabbit rescuers I know, and has saved the lives of countless rabbits, not only through direct rescue but by caring for rabbits for others after the rabbits have had operations, or seeing the rabbits through home medical treatments the caregivers don't have the knowledge to deal with. But even Meg started with one rescue:

My Journey with Abandoned Bunnies
by Meg Brown

My journey with abandoned bunnies began when I received a call about a black and white rabbit running loose on a nearby mini-golf course. I already had two bunnies, the first one bought from a feed store before I became educated and serious about rescue and adoption; not supporting breeders. My second bunny was adopted from the House Rabbit Society. I wasn't looking to adopt a third rabbit, nor aware of the common and tragic occurrence of rabbits being "dumped." I later learned that this happens  often, especially in the summer and early fall, after the novelty of their "Easter bunny" newness wears off, though bunnies are set "free" every month of the year.

I caught Lucky, the mini-golf bunny, a young and sweet Dutch rabbit, in a large net on the day I received the call about him. It was June, 2000, two months after Easter. Despite skilled and immediate vet care, he succumbed to the toxins that filled his body from numerous bot fly larvae and open wounds.

As destiny would have it, there were to be many more bunnies in my life, two more from neglect situations, before I learned about another abandoned bunny. This time the bunny was left in an empty apartment. Days after the tenant moved out, the little black bunny was found with nothing but an open bag of food and empty water bowl. My Bear was less than a year old then. He was neutered and soon bonded with the love of his life, Hoppity, who I had rescued at three years old. Bear lived to be 14.5 years old (see Bear's picture on p. 316).

The following spring I received a call about two bunnies running loose in a neighborhood, one white and one brown, who had been hanging around together from September through April. A lovely couple had been feeding them inside their garage. They were easy to catch: we just closed the garage door and set a large mammal net on the floor with greens in it. When the first bunny hopped in, I picked it up quickly. The other bunny was easily cornered and blocked by large pieces of cardboard. Sadly, there was evidence that the white female bunny had recently had babies. We scoured the area for two days after the rescue, but could not find them. I named the white and brown rabbits Lilly and Rusty, and they were very deeply bonded for many years. Rusty pre-deceased Lilly, passing quietly at home. Lily lived to be twelve years old and had hind-leg paralysis during the last year of her life. But she never lost her appetite for salad and always enjoyed a good massage.

I met one of my closest friends, Pat, when she contacted me, knowing that I was a wildlife rehabilitator specializing in cottontail rabbits. By then, I was also known as the domestic bunny contact person. She asked me for helped catching a large white rabbit that was loose in her very rural neighborhood. Though I brought a net and a trap, amazingly we were able to corner "Annie" in a neighbor's barn. I got my hands on her and walked her back to Pat's house. She immediately became part of the family and was beloved for many years.

Shortly after Annie passed, sometime in 2005, I received a call about a very small bunny running the  streets of Saratoga Springs, NY, not far from my home. The neighbors had all been feeding him, mostly bread, I was told. I enlisted the help of a good friend, who had a business in which he humanely handled nuisance wildlife issues by exclusion or removal from the property. Within minutes, he called me to say that the little roadrunner was in his truck, safely netted! Pat was happy to adopt Benny, a sweet, affectionate Himmie (Himalayan), who lived for ten more years.

By 2005 I was rescuing many dumped bunnies; it had been quite a journey since my first, Lucky, in 2000. Many were with me only long enough to receive proper vet care and move on to a foster home or (better yet), a forever home, although some have stayed to become part of my family.

How to Capture Rabbits as an Individual Rescuer

Readers who are not experienced with rabbits may be wondering just how one does capture a loose rabbit. Anthony Cimino offers a few simple tips:

1. Don't chase then unless you are gently herding them INTO an area of your choosing. Wild rabbit mothers do this with their babies.

2. Set up "walls" out of natural fencing, bed sheets, x-pen panels, baby gates. You want to entice, herd to this area. Cities with close together homes separated by alleyways are best, keep basement windows in mind.

3. Food – it is easier to catch a bun when there is less natural food.

4. ONLY set a Havahart trap or other live trap if you are sure a neighbor is watching it constantly. A bunny can panic and even die from stress, hypothermia or hyperthermia if left too long in a trap. An unwatched trap can be stolen or the bunny nabbed or harmed.

5. Yes, you might see them binky (jump high into the air) as they are evading you. Please don't give up on catching

them.

For those new to capturing rabbits, here are a few additional tips:

˅ Pieces of banana, sprigs of fennel, parsley, or cilantro, and slices of apple are good bait. One experienced rescuer recommends Honey-Nut Cheerios.

˅ A frightened or panicked captured rabbit can often by

calmed by covering a trap or carrier with a sheet or blanket

• If using a live trap, transfer the rabbit and trap to a safe place as soon as possible, and then transfer the rabbit into a covered cage or carrier to reduce stress.

• Nets should only be used under the supervision of a person who is familiar with their use. The mesh should be fine enough the rabbits' limbs do not get caught in the holes, a bird net with a wide soft rim and a very long handle works best. Set the net on the ground with food in the center. (It may help to camouflage the rim with dried grass or leaves.) Once the rabbit is within the net, lift straight up, move quickly to the hoop and close the net, then either pull the bunny to your chest or lower the closed net to the ground as you press your upper body against the bunny until you get a proper hold and are able to transfer the rabbit safely to a carrier. You must act quickly to prevent the rabbit from kicking and injuring himself. Catching a bunny on the run with a net is more difficult; try to gauge where he will run and have the net in his path. Close the net and immobilize the bunny as described above.

• When you handle a rabbit always support the hindquarters and have a firm grip – rabbits are likely to take flying leaps and appear to have no sense of the danger of heights. One way to hold a rabbit is to tuck the head into the crook of your arm with that hand on top of the hindquarters while the other arm and hand support the rabbit from underneath. If you feel that a rabbit you are holding is getting away while you are standing, *drop to your knees* so the rabbit has less distance to fall.

See Chapter 5 for a list of useful things to have on hand for capturing rabbits. Even if you haven't been asked to help capture a rabbit yet, you probably will be! It seems to be inevitable for anyone who has a rabbit or works with rabbits. And you never know when that day will arrive!

Nancy Furstinger, author of *The Forgotten Rabbit* (and many other books featuring animals!) describes capturing one of her rabbits:

Hazel Cadbury

by Nancy Furstinger

I must have a bunny radar beaming out from my soul. My furry family and I had just moved into a new home. My two pooches and male bunny were snoozing on the deck when a local kid told me that there was a loose rabbit cavorting around my new neighborhood. It must be an Eastern cottontail, I rationalized.

I took the dogs on a walk to validate my theory. Damn good thing

I did. There on someone's lawn was a beautiful white bunny, her coat flecked with filth and bones jutting out. She (I instinctively felt that the rabbit was female) was super skittish, having been on the lam for months after being set loose from a hutch: a conspicuous white rabbit one block away from the lake where bald eagles were nesting...not to mention other predators, loose dogs, feral cats, cars, parasites, and cruel humans.

When I returned to the house where I spotted the bunny, I encountered one of the latter. The guy who owned the lawn refused to let me put a Havahart trap on his property, claiming that he got a kick out of watching the rabbit race around his property. "But sir," I protested, pointing out the myriad of dangers and emphasizing that soon winter would blanket his lawn, obliterating her only source of food. He remained a cold-hearted bastard.

Undaunted, I did what any rabbit crusader would do: I rang the doorbell of the house across the street. Thankfully this woman was much more sympathetic. Soon I nestled a trap baited with carrots and lettuce underneath a big bush. I proceeded to check the trap numerous times each day, replenishing the bait. And I waited...and waited...and waited for weeks. But the bun wasn't grabbing.

Now I had captured dozens of rabbits before, in my volunteer gigs with The House Rabbit Society and my local SPCA. I had paired up with a pal and shepherded rabbits into ex-pens. I had dived under bushes and cornered rabbits in barns. And I had trapped rabbits in Havaharts after only a day or two. So why wasn't I having any success?

Then I had an aha-moment. I needed to create a bunny burrow that offered a safe spot for her to snooze. So I covered the trap with flakes of hay and a towel. I topped that off with a tarp and leaves and branches. And apparently my bait was not enticing enough, so I brought out the big buns, er, guns: bananas. Who could resist bananas?

Not this bunny. The next morning I was delighted to discover her inside the trap attempting a jailbreak!

At home, I picked off ticks, combed out fleas, and scissored out tar. I cried with relief as I watched the exhausted and ravenous bunny gobble food and sleep for days. Yes, she was a female, whom I named Hazel Cadbury for her green-flecked eyes and for the bunny of Easter candy fame.

After a vet check and spay, Hazel resided safe in my den; my lonely male bunny, Petey, romped throughout the great room. Won't it be fantastic if they would bond, I thought as I headed off to bed.

The next morning I discovered Petey and Hazel curled up together in front of the gas stove. Apparently he had opened the door to the den, introduced himself, and they proceeded to bond without a helping hand from me. They remained completely devoted to each other, spooning and kissing all day long, well into their elderbun years. And bananas always were their favorite treats!

Capturing a rabbit as an individual rescuer is often a solitary task, but occasionally others will join in and help. In the following story an entire neighborhood joined in to help capture a stray rabbit that had been running around a neighborhood:

Annabelle by

Meg Brown

Several years ago, North Country Wild Care (NCWC), a wildlife rehabilitation group, which I have been an active member of since 2002, received a call about a stray black and white bunny in the town of South Glens Falls, just north of me. I was the go-to person for help with questions regarding domestic rabbits. This was July. "Another Easter bunny dump," I thought to myself.

Lynn and Bill, members of NCWC, met me in the neighborhood. What was lovely to see is that men, women, and children came out of their homes and joined us, asking if we were here to "save the rabbit." It was apparently a tight-knit community of well-kept homes and close, friendly neighbors. The rabbit had been seen running through yards for several weeks, eating from gardens or lawns until she zoomed away, easily startled. The neighbors were relieved to see us walking with a net, exercise pens, and a carrier, hoping to bring this elusive, scared bunny to safety.

Before long, there was a group of ten of us. Someone ran back inside to get a sheet to hold between two people in order to form what would look to the rabbit like a wall. The bunny knew the neighborhood well. She had her favorite yards and escape routes. This was not going to be an easy capture. But the people who joined us said that the community was very worried about her. The people expressed concern that running the streets, being on her own, would lead to an eventual early death for this bunny. They were relieved to see someone try to save her and wanted to help. This is not always the case. I have run into several situations where I've gotten run off an area or not been given permission to set foot on a piece of property, even when the abandoned rabbit or rabbits were just feet away from me. It can be enormously frustrating, feeling so close but helpless to do anything.

The big English Spot rabbit who became dear to that small but caring community, got away from us that first night. She ducked under a garage, too narrow for me to slide under. We were done for the night. I returned the next night along with Bill and Joanne, members of the House Rabbit Society. The neighborhood posse had almost doubled. We were determined to save this bunny. Armed with exercise pens to form barriers, a large net, and our excited troop of dedicated bunny saviors, we quietly walked the neighborhood. "There she is!" She zoomed across street after street, in and out of alleyways. We split into three groups. I had my large bird/ mammal net. An older gentleman who had helped the night before said: "I once caught a feral cat with a net. May I?" Clearly he wanted to try. I said: "You're the net guy! Just hold it and let her run into it. Ok?" He beamed!

It took almost two hours of patiently watching and walking, slowly, closing in, then losing her. Everyone listened to my cautions not to run or chase her. Finally, as the big gal was running from one street to another, our "net guy" reached out, held the pole as she bolted across the street and into the net she went! "I got her! I got her!" We were jubilant, like old friends, cheering and hugging! We had accomplished a beautiful deed that bonded us all together, neighbors and strangers. We had saved a precious life.

At first I fostered that beautiful female English Spot bunny, who I named Annabelle, as a member of the upstate NY chapter of the House Rabbit Society. She seemed to settle into her bedroom with castles and enjoyed running down the hallway. But she was anxious about being touched, even for brief periods of  petting. I decided to adopt Annabelle and felt happy and relieved that she would live the rest of her life where she felt safe and as comfortable as possible. She and I had bonded as closely as she had likely ever been or would have with a human.

After two years, Annabelle let me pet her as long as I didn't make eye contact. She always came running over for her salad, grunting loudly. I loved being downstairs hearing her having fun bounding up and down the hallway, or going upstairs and seeing her relaxing under a hidey box or castle, all stretched out, no fear.

On July 15, 2018, when I went upstairs to feed Annabelle her breakfast, she was lying on her side, looking far away. I gently picked her up and held her. She was limp but still alive. I held her for two hours, feeling that she was in the process of leaving her body. There was no sense of urgency; Annabelle seemed restful and pain free. I felt a peaceful trusting energy from her. I told her that the other bunnies were here to guide her to the light. She rested gently on my lap. I felt grateful to have been able to "save" Annabelle and honored to be with her as she took her final breath.

Many individual rescues of dumped domestic rabbits take place in either suburban or rural areas, but they can also take place in cities. City rescues may require different tactics than those used in more rural areas, especially given they may run from property to property. Anthony Cimino tells of a rabbit rescue he once took on in a tough Albany neighborhood:

The Golden Net by Anthony Cimino

A number of summers ago, I was asked to check out a loose bunny situation in a rather rough part of Albany, NY. Without any care, I was in people's backyards and seeing members of a bunny family here and there. Neighbors began asking what I was doing with a net trespassing in
backyards. "I'm going to catch these loose bunnies and give them good homes," I explained.

At first, I don't think they understood what I was doing and they certainly weren't ready for the volunteers that took over the block. Before I knew it, the same people who had been watching us from their porches were now assisting. Neighbors began holding x-pen panels and bed sheets, herding bunnies toward the obstacles we had set up, and watching Havahart traps during the times I couldn't be there. I'd get home after bringing one of the babies to my house and a call would come in that "another baby is in the Havahart." There were many natural hiding spots; this section of Albany has garages with small spaces a bunny can squeeze through. Volunteers and I would be able to get a broom in that area and "push" the bun into a net that was waiting at the opening of the alley.

After I'd capture three, I'd drive them to a waiting foster space in Syracuse. We were able to capture seven bunnies total. No others were noticed by neighbors. As time went on, I always wondered what happened to them after I took them to Syracuse. One I do know what

happened, as she came back to live with me as a foster bunny.

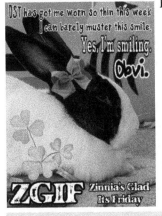

She may have been the baby that was binkying as she eluded our attempts to catch her that summer in Albany. She was adopted by Amanda Gilmore and named Zinnia-Gayl (in memory of Gaylord the bunny) and still lives a very happy life in her forever home. Once a week I still receive "Zinnia's Glad its Friday" messages. Her mom has taken well over 2,000 pictures of her.

One of the best rewards a rescuer (and one of the reasons we keep on doing it) can receive is to know a rescued rabbit has gone on to have a wonderful life. Amanda Gilmore's following description of Zinnia and her life gives insight into the behavior of a rescued rabbit and show clearly how Zinnia is treasured in her forever home:

Zinnia is a little over eight now (we estimated her age based on her approximate age at the time of her rescue. A few things about Zinnia that you don't need to include but thought I'd just let you know:

Zinnia has one blue eye and one dark brown eye (heterochromia).

· Zinnia's fav veggie is kale (with cilantro at a close second)

· Zinnia HATES being held or picked up (so we avoid it at all costs!)

· Zinnia is shy and doesn't like strangers (she doesn't even like to hear them talking in the house and will hide!)

·Zinnia loves having her mommy massage her morning and night. She's very picky about people she trusts so she basically only lets her Mommy touch her. Sometimes her daddy can touch her too but only usually a few pets on the head.

·She is the cleanest litter trained rabbit I've ever had – will only use one litter box and only one corner of this box and she almost never leaves a poop around in her room.

·She lives in a 200 square feet room(10 x 20) – it happens to be the only room in the house with a carpet. She will not go off the carpet as she hates slippery floors.

·Zinnia's middle name is Gayl (pronounced Gale) after her predecessor bunny brother Gaylord

·She loves the ramp her Dad made for her so she can safely get onto her bench and then jump to her table to look out the window.

·She binkies in the morning after her massage and when she gets food

·Her pellets are in a treat toy where she has to lift the little green lids off the round reservoirs to get to them. She probably wonders why I keep covering her food up with these little tops. Haha

·Because she is more of a cautious rabbit, I have only once caught her in the "bunny flop" pose on her side. Her relaxed pose of choice is the loafed back feet side kick pose.

-She can hear the TV when her Dad watches "This Old House" shows her common interest by making new interesting renovations to her room via digging in the corners and chewing on the moldings. Cardboard and gating now protect these areas from further Zinnia renovation attempts. Lol!

Not all rescued rabbits need to be captured; they may come to a person in unusual ways. As Debby once stated to me: "What we do to educate people and what we say on behalf of rabbits can have unforeseen results." That happened to me with my most bizarre rescue. I had offered to conduct short classes on rabbits and rabbit handling at the local humane society, and said I would also be willing to talk to people interested in adopting any rabbits. The humane society employees met my offer with blank disinterested stares, but they did take my phone number. Months went by without a single call, so I figured they had dropped my number into the nearest trash receptacle.

Then late one night I was woken by the insistent ringing of the telephone. A sobbing, mostly incoherent woman answered my groggy hello, telling me the humane society had given her my number and pleading for my help in saving her rabbit. I finally got the woman calmed down enough to understand what was going on. Apparently her brother had bought a rabbit with plans to kill and eat the rabbit later, but in the meantime had allowed her to care for the rabbit. As the months passed, of course she became attached to the rabbit. Then the woman's brother announced he was ready to kill and eat the bunny – on her birthday (I later spoke to the man; he claims that was not intentional as he had forgotten his day off that week was his sister's birthday). She wanted me to steal the rabbit. She further informed me that she was having a very difficult time as she was developmentally disabled.

I was in a spot. I could not go steal the rabbit; the humane society had given the woman my number and in a manner of speaking I was working for them. (Although obviously the humane society never really had anything to do with the rabbit; the worker must have remembered me and figured they could palm the hysterical woman off on me so they didn't have to deal with her.) I explained to the woman that technically the rabbit was her brother's property, and suggested she explain how attached to the rabbit she was and ask if he would give her the rabbit as a birthday gift or allow her or another person to buy him. Meanwhile I would endeavor to find someone else who could help her. She said she would try talking to her brother.

Apparently the conversation did not go well. The next I heard both the woman and her brother were in jail; they had gotten into a serious physical fight and threatened to kill each other. The case went before a judge, who ruled that neither of them could keep the rabbit; the rabbit must be sold. The woman begged me to be the one to buy him, and of course I agreed. I named the big Satin bunny Anthony and he was a beloved member of my family for many years. (He's the rabbit wearing an e-collar on the back of my special care book.)

The Unexpected

Sometimes when one gets involved in a rescue unexpected issues can arise that one does not know how to deal with. Reach out to someone who does. Davida Kobler, longtime House Rabbit Society Educator and Chapter Manager, tells of an unexpected situation she got into and the person who helped.

The Unexpected Rescue
by Davida Kobler

In mid July, 2017, I arrived home from work on a Friday to a call on my home machine from a gentleman who was clearly in distress about rabbits, but spoke very little English. Utica is a very multi-ethnic town, with an active refugee center. I called him back and gradually we were able to understand each other. He had gone out that morning to mow his lawn and found a box containing hay and eleven baby rabbits dumped in his backyard. No mama bun, just the babies. His daughters did not know anyone in the neighborhood who had rabbits. The babies been there perhaps overnight, and it was fortunate he discovered them when he did, because we had a torrential summer rain later that day.

Sometimes we fly by the seat of our pants in rescue work. I got his address, let the groceries defrost on the kitchen floor, and went to his home. He and his daughters were waiting outside with a shallow box which contained eleven baby domestic rabbits, furred, with eyes closed. One had rear leg paralysis. They had spent the day calling everywhere trying to get help and even went to the Humane Society and were turned away (although the Humane Society has my contact). This gentleman and his family were visibly upset, and were grateful for any response.

I knew that I did not have the skills to care for such young babies. So I called a phenomenal wildlife rehabber, Kim Jones-Skinner, whose area of expertise includes cottontails. This woman, despite having one arm in a sling from a torn rotator cuff, agreed to take in the domestics to give them some chance of survival. I got them to her house, she examined each one, and she set them up for hydration. We had no idea how this would go as she'd never done this with domestics. All I was certain of was that this was the only chance they could possibly have to survive.

This woman worked miracles. Of the eleven, the poor baby with the injured hind limbs passed first. Two others passed within the first week. But the others thrived, grew strong and started to "popcorn" around their enclosure and develop personalities. Kim's husband, Ron, tried to take photos, but nothing came out clearly because he could not stop laughing at the antics. The babies grew

up strong and healthy, and Kim actually adopted a pair, HazeBaze and Emmett (who like to disco-binky), one of our vets adopted a pair, and a good friend of Kim's adopted a pair. HRC helped us place the fourth pair in a good home.

Lives were saved because a dedicated, extraordinarily kind woman was willing to reach outside of her comfort zone. And because a kind man cared enough to not be deterred by people who were too busy to care or connect him with the right rescuers. The bunnies thank them both.

Other unexpected situations can arise in rescue than those to do with rabbits themselves. Meg Brown tells the story of a rescue that became a little too exciting:

Banjo

by Meg Brown

It was the summer of 2010. I had learned that twenty-two rabbits were "released" in a small country town, north of Saratoga Springs, NY. My friend and fellow bunny rescuer Anthony with me, I drove to the area. We located the crime scene, saw debilitated, old wooden hutches way back in the field, but no bunnies or people around, so we returned home.

I drove up the next day, alone. I saw four or five domestic rabbits, Lionhead and Dutch bunnies, grazing on a lawn near the country road. I also saw a group of men who could have stepped out of a scene from the movie, "Deliverance." I stopped my car, my heart beating hard. I asked them if the bunnies were theirs. They said they were but that they didn't want them. I said I'd take them with me. I had a net, pen, and carriers, and I was two feet from a couple of Dutch bunnies. The men said to go ahead. Then they grabbed shovels and rakes and ran after me. I was scared and jumped back in my car.

At that time, my license plate read BUNNIES. I was afraid that someone would show up at my door, a sloppy, scary man. But I called the police anyway. At first the police said to call the local animal control officer, who I learned only deals with dogs.

When I returned two days later, the hutch doors were closed and I saw no bunnies. I wondered if I had done a disservice to these poor bunnies after all. Would they have been better off not trapped in the prison of those tiny, filthy hutches? Did the men shoot them with the rifles lining the back windows of their pickups? Surely the bunnies would have died outside much sooner than later, but they might have had some nice fresh greens.

This scene haunted me for days. Then, twelve days later, I received a call about a Lionhead bunny caught in someone's yard, two miles from the place with the bunnies. Anthony and I drove up to retrieve the bunny, the one lone survivor of this horrible rabbit "dump."

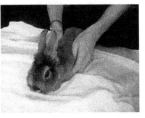

Driving back to my house with this sweet little guy, we passed a road sign, "Banjo." It seemed ironic, as I had likened the men to the rough, heartless-acting men in Deliverance. But I did love that once scene of dueling Banjos !"Banjo" it was! Banjo was adopted at an Upstate NY HRS adoption event by a wonderful woman named Laura, who totally adores him to this day. He is her little prince.

Obtaining Permission to Rescue a Rabbit

In some ways it is easier to rescue rabbits that have clearly been abandoned and are living on their own. Rabbits that belong to someone who is not providing adequate care can be more difficult to rescue. Such a person may flat-out refuse to allow anyone to take the rabbits or may agree to give a rabbit up only to change their mind a day later. It is not uncommon for people to change their minds multiple times. For that reason it is recommended that anyone involved in rescue to carry a blank rabbit surrender form (see Chapter 4 for an example) in their vehicle. Courtesy and persistence are a rescuer's most valuable tools in such situations. Plus a bit of good luck! Adrianne Lang tells the story of a difficult rescue where persistence won out:

Carwash Bunnies

by Adrienne Lang

I volunteer for Ohio House Rabbit Rescue, the only in-house rabbit rescue in the state of Ohio, located in Columbus. A few years back, in midsummer, we received a phone call from a Good Samaritan, informing us of a sighting of about 30 rabbits hanging around a car wash on a busy highway. It was determined they were coming from the house across the side street.

Two of our volunteers went to the home and spoke with the owner. She was not very welcoming and did not want to surrender her rabbits. A few days later, I went with two other volunteers on a Wednesday evening. We knocked on the front door, but no one answered. It was a corner home on a busy highway. Inside the tall

privacy fencing we could see the property had a couple of large dogs, a dog run and a rabbit hutch. Also, along the rear property line were a couple of sheds full of mis-cellaneous items stacked almost to the ceiling. Lots of great places for bunnies to hide among these structures within tall weeds and shrubbery. We decided to park at the car wash and observe for a while, hoping someone may soon return home. We walked along a few houses down the street in the neighborhood. We chatted with someone walking by, and they said almost everyone in the neighborhood has, or has had, a rabbit. They either caught one or got one from the lady who lived in the house. We saw several loose rabbits and tried to catch a few of them, but had no luck, as they quickly ran under the fence on to the property. We knew we would need to come back again, with more equipment and permission to access their property.

After about a half an hour, a man came out of the house and went to get in a nearby parked truck. I approached him and inquired, if I could buy one of his rabbits. He said he had an errand to do, but he

would be back in fifteen minutes. We waited. When he returned, he said that the rabbits were not for sale. They belonged to his wife who was at church. We asked when she would be home. He asked why we wanted a rabbit. I explained that we were with a rescue group and that we would like to get them medical care and find them good loving homes. He said that would be very nice, but he didn't know how he would explain it to his wife. He thought about it and finally said, just to go ahead and take them, and he would deal with telling her what he had done. The man invited us onto his property where we found four bunnies living in a ramshackle hutch with inches of filth on the floor, no clean water and no food. The man allowed us to take all four back to our rescue. I asked for his wife's phone number and told him I would call her.

We knew that we needed to go back and try to rescue the others, but we would need permission to access the property. I called the lady and explained to her what had become of the four bunnies and how they were now safe. She wasn't happy, but she was understanding. Her husband had explained to her that this was a good thing for the bunnies. She said that she knew she needed to do something, and had been thinking about it, but had not yet made a decision. She said that she was considering donating the bunnies to her church for a fundraiser. I explained how we would find very suitable homes after a veterinary check, and a spay or neuter. They would have a better future with us than a spontaneous adoption at church. She understood and agreed. She said that she and her grand-daughter started breeding the bunnies and wanted to continue, until "they had one of each kind." She

was disappointed that they didn't complete their goal. She wanted to achieve this for the granddaughter.

One of the four bunnies we brought back to the rescue that first night, was a handsome boy with bright blue eyes. He had a crooked- looking leg, many bite marks on his back, and appeared in pain. He was brought to the vet the next day, and it was found that he had four or five fractures in his front leg. He had no name at that time, and they named him Hutchkins at the veterinary hospital, based in part, on his intake description that he was found in the dirty hutch. He had surgery to pin his leg, by Dr. Susan Borders of Norton Road Veterinary Hospital, and he recovered nicely, wearing a little green jacket to keep his leg safe while he healed. Hutchkins was successfully rehabbed and found a fabulous home.

Another one of the four, a young brown bun, had a large wound on its neck. Maybe a dog bite? A Dutch mix, also among the four, was so recently pregnant that it was missed at her initial vet visit and she later had two babies while at our rescue. One dead at birth and the other died shortly thereafter. The fourth bunny was a beautiful white and black spotted mini lop, who was actually quite healthy. All the bunnies had ticks and ear mites.

On our second trip out there, we caught four rabbits. One was very pregnant upon her initial vet check. She had a tilted uterus. The vet spayed her and told us that she would have likely died a horribly painful death at childbirth had she not been spayed. She was carrying eleven babies!

While we never saw as many as thirty bunnies at one time, we did go back on many occasions, often catching two to four each time. Some volunteers from the local Humane Society also helped us. The property owners became very cooperative and would leave their fence open and bring their dogs inside to accommodate our hunts. On occasion, the lady would call me and tell me what bunnies she had recently seen and where to look for them. Between our rescue, and the Humane Society, we continued to rescue on the property until the week before Thanksgiving. I can't help think that many rabbits may have lost their lives by the car traffic on the busy highway corner. The last rabbit we caught was a beautiful girl, we named Zoey. I had the pleasure of fostering her. She surprised me just after Christmas, on Dec. 28, with a litter of five babies!

The rabbits had been established in this neighborhood long before we began rescuing there and are grateful to the Good Samaritan who brought them to our attention. We had an impact on ending this situation, and many rabbits were able to find safe forever homes.

Luck always helps in rescuing rabbits. Several times I have rescued rabbits from people who were planning to euthanize their bunnies; in each case I just happened to be at the right place at the right time to be able to give the rabbits another chance at life.

Meg Brown had a little luck rescuing a rabbit from an uncaring owner:

The "Lost" Bunny
by Meg Brown

I saw a "lost bunny" sign on a telephone pole near where I was working as a massage therapist at a spa. I called the number as soon as I finished working. A woman answered. "Oh, that damn bunny. She's nothing but trouble. She's back again; I guess she got hungry."

The "lost bunny" was being kept outside in a fenced-in area, with nothing for shelter but an overturned wooden box. The large Chinchilla girl repeatedly escaped from the enclosure by digging under the fence and then she'd come back to eat her pellets after a day or two. It was clear that the woman and her fifteen-year-old daughter did not care about the bunny. They had a large home for the two of them, and no other animals, but when I offered them a free exercise pen they scoffed at the idea of allowing the bunny even a sixteen square foot space inside their home.

As it turned out, their loss was my gain. As fall turned to winter, I couldn't bear seeing that poor bunny huddled under the tiny wooden box, seeking shelter from the rain and snow. The early December morning when I received a call that there was a grey bunny hopping around the adjacent street, I knew that it was her. I would capture this "lost bunny" one final time.

My friend Craig, who had swiftly caught Benny the previous summer, sprang into action once again. Within minutes, the gorgeous Chinchilla bunny, who I named Rosie, was safe and warm in my car.

That was almost fourteen years ago. Rosie and I became the best of friends and enjoyed twelve fun and happy years together. Eleven months ago Rosie stopped hopping due to severe arthritis and spondylosis. She remained bright and cheery and was a joy to care for as her body required more care. She bonded closely with her new kitty friend, Cowboy. Everyone loved her.

Rosie passed quietly in my arms in November of 2018, at home. There's an expression in rescue work; "We saved each other." It was never more true. "Rest in peace, RoRo. We got this."

Having compassion for people too.

Sometimes the most difficult aspect of rescue is the reaction – often anger – we may have to those people who have abused rabbits. Sometimes the abuse is intentional and our anger justified. But other times the abuse is not intentional, and although it is extremely difficult to remember this in our dealings with such a person, we need to make the effort. We should have compassionate for these people who, although they may in fact be harming rabbits, do so without *intent.* Anna Ehredt had to deal with this difficult aspect of rescue when she rescued Symphony:

Symphony's Story
by Anna Ehredt

We never planned on having four rabbits. Five months after my beloved Jujube passed away, I foster-failed with our Lionhead Buster; about a year later Jig swooped into our lives; and after another year passed Delilah came tumbling into our home, big beautiful dewlap and all. So there we were; bunny-mom, bunny-dad, Kitten the cat, and her three bunny siblings. Our tiny 650-square-foot home was full (literally) of love and binkies.

For about two years I've been consistently volunteering with a local no-kill animal shelter called Brother Wolf Animal Rescue (BWAR). I quickly became their Rabbit Mentor and carry out rabbit adoption follow-ups. I remember exactly where I was when I did my post-adoption follow-up call with Symphony's mom (we'll call her Beth for privacy's sake). Beth was an older woman in her 80s and from that very first phone call I could tell something was off – she repeated things over and over and seemed, well, spacey. At the end of a long, drawn-out, aimless conversation she said "oh, ya know, actually he's not eating much hay. What should I do?"

I gave her my usual spiel about troubleshooting hay issues. A few days later I checked in and she reported that there really hadn't been a change in his consumption of hay so I suggested I might come visit to be able to better assess the situation. She agreed, only to cancel on me multiple times. My gut knew something wasn't right and that I needed to get over there one way or another. So I got creative. I knew her bunny frosty had passed away right before she adopted Symphony. I knew it was still fresh for her and that she could use some consolation. I thought, what do old people like? Gifts! I B-lined it to the thrift store and bought her a rabbit figurine in honor of Frosty. "Beth, I have something I'd like to give you." I was heartily welcomed into her home the next day.

Walking into her kitchen, I was not-so-pleasantly greeted with the piercing caws of a pet bird. Below the bird on the linoleum was sweet Symphony. As I suspected, he had a case of sore hocks. His litter box was almost empty save a sprinkling of CareFresh but his hay was in a stainless steel bowl across the kitchen. He got daily greens but she oddly picked off the leaves of the cilantro claiming he didn't like the stems. I treated him with Revolution due to a case of fleas. Over the next couple of weeks we had conversation after conversation about proper rabbit care. I even went so far as creating visuals she could hang on the fridge like "Symphony's Daily Diet," because she would forget about 75% of what I told her. I had to be delicate in my guidance to ensure that she would allow me to keep coming back.

One day, after overhearing me ask what happened to the bird's feathers (or lack thereof), her sister confessed to me over a phone call that she was worried Beth had early signs of dementia and that she had had a compulsive disorder her whole life. Unprompted, Beth actually ended up confessing to me as well about plucking her bird's feathers. I calmly asked her why she felt compelled to do that (while simultaneously raging inside with anger over this clear abuse). "I don't know why, I just had to." This was the moment I knew, *really knew*, that

I had to get Symphony out of that home. I had to plan strategically and carefully; I had to stay on her good side. I felt like I was in some sort of Oceans' 11 movie, but the stakes were a sweet little innocent life in this movie, not money.

I never wish for GI problems to occur, but boy did Symphony plan it right! I had been trying to get over there for a visit, but Beth kept pushing it off – one time because she plucked her eyebrows too much and had embarrassing scabs she didn't want me to see. Finally, Beth called claiming Symphony was having diarrhea. True diarrhea is an emergency so even though I highly doubted it was true, I knew this was my "in," my chance, my golden ticket. She very hesitantly agreed to let him stay with me – "Just for one night! I'll miss him too much!" – to be able to monitor him and his "diarrhea" closely. As soon as I got him home, I noticed a large bald spot on his back. I called to ask her about it and she playfully laughed saying she must've brushed him there too much. I hung up the phone and immediately dialed BWAR. I didn't care if it was stealing or kidnapping or whatever it might be, I was under no circumstances bringing Symphony back to that home.

In the end, animal control got involved and the bird was confiscated. The officer told me I did not need to bring Symphony back. There were plenty of difficult phone calls with Beth as I guided her through her grief – at first she seemed confused, and then angry, and then apologetic. As much as I despised what had been done to symphony and her bird, I tried to hold on to my compassion for Beth. This story isn't long enough to describe her in detail, but Beth was old, alone, possibly experiencing early signs of dementia, and very obviously had a mental illness – a compulsive disorder. Through love, not anger, I was able to save symphony. Through love, not hatred, I was able to become friends with Beth and even help her understand why she was no longer fit to be responsible for animals. Because of love, Symphony became our fourth baby. And our house, although crazy and hectic and full, feels so much larger with him.

Feeding Rescued Rabbits

Most rescued rabbits will have been fending for themselves, eating whatever they could find. If it is summer in a temperate area the rabbit may have been foraging quite successfully, but in less hospitable climates and times of year abandoned rabbits may have struggled to find sufficient food to survive. Sometimes kind-hearted but uninformed people may have been supplementing an abandoned rabbit's food, but often such handouts are not rabbit-appropriate. One of my rabbits (see his picture on p. 279) was rescued from a perilous existence in the parking area of a tough bar district where he had been surviving on junk food tossed to him by bar patrons on their way to their vehicles. (How he avoided being run over is a mystery!) Even now, eight years later, he still goes crazy when he smells popcorn! So it should be no surprise that many rescued rabbits are suffering from malnourishment or digestive ills.

For those readers who are not very familiar with rabbits; rabbits' eating habits are very different from the dogs and cats we are used to in our homes. Unlike carnivores, which have evolved to eat larger, infrequent meals, rabbits are herbivores and need to eat lesser amounts more frequently. A rabbit's digestive system always needs to have food in it or digestive disorders may develop, some of which can eventually be fatal. Rabbits are *concentrate selectors*, which means they require high-nutrient foods to meet their energy needs. In wild rabbits this would be succulent green plants and occasional fruits, but in domestic rabbits this need is best met by a combination of fresh greens and commercial rabbit pellets. Rabbits also need to eat lower-nutrient high-fiber foods, such as hay. The important thing to remember is that they need **both** high-nutrient and high-fiber foods. Hay is not a high-nutrient food.

Digestive illnesses

Rescued rabbits, depending upon what they have been eating and what stress they have been under, may have digestive issues. One way to tell is whether the rabbit produces fairly good-sized fecal pellets that can easily be broken with finger pressure. If the rabbit is producing small hard fecal pellets or none at all, a vet or rabbit-savvy person should be consulted, as the rabbit may have gastrointestinal (GI) hypomotility (a slowdown of the gastro-intestinal tract) or a more serious digestive issue. A GI slowdown is often called "stasis," which is an inaccurate term because GI hypomotility is a *slowing* of the digestive tract, and does not normally involve "stasis," a cessation of movement, unless it progresses to the point that contents are severely impacted. Furthermore, there has been an unfortunate tendency for many different digestive ills to be lumped under the term "stasis," and this can lead to a digestive problem being treated in an inappropriate way. For example, if a case of acute bloat caused by an obstruction is treated as a GI slowdown by syringe-feeding and giving fluids and motility drugs, the rabbit may die.

There are many digestive problems that may occur in a rabbit, and more than one may be present at a time. A few of these digestive disorders are *intestinal dysbiosis* (imbalance in gut microflora), *gastrointestinal hypomotility* (slowdown of stomach/intestine emptying/movement), *gastric ulcers*, *acute bloat and blockage*, *cecal dysbiosis* (imbalance of microflora in cecum), and *cecal impaction* (impaction of cecum contents). See Appendix IV for a summary of the signs of selected digestive ailments in rabbits.

The stress of being rescued in and of itself may cause the digestive system of a rabbit to slow down (gastrointestinal hypomotility). In that case the rabbit may be fine once he or she has calmed down and feels comfortable enough to eat. In general, if a rescued rabbit is eating and drinking and producing some cecotrophs and fecal pellets, reducing the rabbit's stress and giving the rabbit proper food and adequate fluids will often keep the digestive system functioning properly. Tempt inappetant buns with a *few* fresh greens, herbs, and especially celery leaves (or chopped stalks), which contain a calming phytochemical. But if a rabbit ceases to produce any cecotrophs or fecal pellets at all or develops other serious sign of illness, it is a medical emergency and the rabbit should receive veterinary care as soon as possible.

The following entertaining story by Phyllis O'Beollain illustrates how a rabbit's eating habits can be affected by the stress of two moves within a short time:

Guillermo
by Phyllis O'Beollain

"He was just returned. The shelter is full, and I don't have room for any more rescues at my house right now. I was hoping you could give him a place to stay just until I can make other arrangements for him."

I drove home with the black and white lop eared rabbit and put him in an exercise pen in the kitchen.

Guillermo (way too long for a bunny name, I called him G) was a sweet, happy bunny who had been adopted from an area rabbit rescue's foster home less than six months earlier. He'd been returned because "it just didn't work out with the kids."

G wasn't eating; he was lethargic and depressed and apparently he had refused to eat all day. Going from his home of several months back to the shelter, then back to the rabbit rescue and then to my house all in the same day had been too stressful. Within minutes of his arrival at my house I had the bunny equivalent of a Las Vegas buffet set up in his pen to tempt him; all my gardening is bunny directed, so he had a wide variety of bunny herbs and vegetables to choose from. Nada. "I spit upon your greens" he seemed to say. I got out an assortment of fruits, and then began dragging out bunny treats. G wasn't having any of it; he sat in the corner with his head down.

A rabbit that does not eat for 24 hours is a veterinary emergency; their digestive system can shut down and they can die. After some tummy medicine, tummy rubs, prayer, and a few hours of lost sleep on my part, I was relieved to see him eating hay. He refused to eat anything else however; the rest of my bunny herd happily ate the untouched buffet leftovers. As it was well after midnight, I turned on the nightlight for him and G seemed to start to relax.

The next day, feeling better, G began growling and charging at me anytime I was in his exercise pen, or even when I put my hand in the pen to give him food or water. Rabbits can be territorial, and this was probably his way of saying he was tired of the company. Over the next few days, G became more comfortable, flopping down and rolling over on his back. I tickled his face with a carrot top; irritated, he nipped at it and discovered he liked carrot tops. He began to eat a few leaves of spinach, fresh basil, some food pellets and a tiny bit of apple in addition to his hay. He began to enjoy being brought out to the living room in his pen, where he could see the other bunnies. He continued to growl and charge at *us* however.

One day as I spoke to him, he looked right at me, picked up his water bowl with his teeth, and – still looking at me – turned it upside down, dumping water all over the carpet. When my daughter brought a rag to clean it up, he growled and charged at her. This, I thought, is just the sort of behavior that led Steve to make up that ridiculous story about not having room for another bunny. Puh-leese. I'd been to Steve's house a day before and there was not one single bunny currently living in his ventilation system.

Steve can be so selfish sometimes.

Guillermo continued to keep us on our toes (as we fled in terror from his growling and charging). Eventually, he was introduced to little Miko, a rabbit who had been severely neglected ("She would not have

lasted much longer" said the veterinarian). G was ever-attentive to Miko and groomed her meticulously each day. Guillermo, on the other hand, could grow dreadlocks for all Miko cared, but they were both very happy.

In fact, Guillermo was now perpetually happy...unless you touched his beloved Miko. Even a friendly skritch between her ears put Guillermo on alert: **WHAT ARE YOU DOING?!!** as he ran to protect her. Guillermo would look her over carefully for any signs of damage. Once he was satisfied that no permanent damage had been done by our petting, he would groom her and stand guard over her, ever watchful. Miko usually fell asleep during inspection.

Guillermo allowed Miko to eat first, before he even approached the food dish. Miko never objected to G's presence; never nudged him away from the food or water dishes, never commandeered the Cottontail Condo or dominated the litter box. Nonetheless, he allowed her first choice of food, water, the penthouse level of the condo, and waited patiently as she lounged in the litter pan. He was completely devoted to her and she to him, and I was very fortunate to have had Miko and Guillermo-the-growling bunny in my life.

Epilogue:

Guillermo passed away first; afterwards, even the veterinarian declared Miko was depressed. After twelve weeks with little improvement in Miko's behavior and appetite, she was introduced to Elliot, a bunny who had originally been destined to be someone's dinner and who was pronounced "practically feral" by the veterinarian. Nonetheless, Miko chose Elliot and while theirs was not the love affair Miko shared with Guillermo, the two were very happy together; both passed away at good old ages within a few months of each other. While I confess that I am still heartbroken, I am glad that Miko had the joy of these two wonderful bunnies in her life and that I had the privilege of knowing all three of them.

Elliot's legacy lives on in the company named for him: Elliot's Awesome Treats sells locally grown dried organic greens and twigs for bunnies.

Malnourished/starving Rabbits

A starving, malnourished rabbits is heart-breaking to see. If possible, take such a rabbit to a veterinarian immediately. If it is not possible to get the rabbit to a vet, offer the rabbit water and a sampling of greens, including herbs, and *small* pieces of fruit such as apple or banana. If the rabbit will not drink and you cannot administer subQ fluids, try giving the rabbit some liquid by eyedropper, being careful to drop the liquid into the side of the mouth to reduce the possibility of the rabbit aspirating any of the fluid. Something like Pedialite is best, since it contains electrolytes, but water with a little fruit juice will do in a pinch.

If the bunny refuses to eat any of the greens or fruit you offer, try offering a few rolled oats or even a cracker. An anorexic rabbit is at risk of fatal medical complications, and getting the rabbit to eat something is far more important than worrying about the rabbit eating a food with a little carbohydrate, sugar or salt. If the rabbit still refuses to eat, it may be necessary to syringe-feed, or, if you have no syringes, to put a little mashed food in the corner of the rabbit's mouth with your finger. Baby food fruits or vegetables with no additives (and no onion) will work, as will canned pumpkin. Syringe-feed small amounts every hour or so; do not syringe-feed a large amount at once. Meg Brown describes the care she gave Posie, a severely malnourished abandoned rabbit:

Once in a while, dumped bunnies get lucky, although that's not usually the case. Posie was left abandoned in a home, with no food or water. She was found emaciated and near death. Her

first photo is hard to look at. It was a long road to recovery for this little helicopter bunny. A bunny-loving vet at a local shelter then called me to ask if I would continue the bunny's care. Of course I agreed!

Because of her severe malnutrition, it was important to offer Posie food in small portions and slowly increase the amount over time. Posie gradually gained strength, weight and energy. Her spirit grew bright and playful over the next three to four months, and she was soon ready for adoption. It was love at first sight when potential bunny adopter Karen met her.

Today Posie is thriving in the loving care of Karen and Ed, who adore her and gave her a forever home where she will never be hungry and alone again.

CHAPTER 11: WHAT TO DO AFTER RESCUING A RABBIT

You've caught the rabbit(s) – now what? One of the first things you need to do is check for any medical problems – breaks, open wounds, sores, parasites such as fleas and mites, and lumps that could be a sign of bot fly larvae or an abscess. Obtain prompt veterinary care for any serious medical conditions. If you take the rabbit home, even temporarily, be sure you quarantine him or her, as you will not wish to expose other pets to parasites or disease (see section on medical problems later in this chapter). Once these steps are complete, it is time to find placement for the rabbit if you are unable to keep the bunny yourself.

Finding a Place for the Rescued Rabbit

If you are not affiliated with an organization that can help you find a place to take the rabbit, try calling local no-kill shelters, rabbit rescues, humane organizations, and the regional House Rabbit Society chapter. Even if they are unable to take the rabbit themselves, people from these organizations may be able to steer you to someone who can.

Fostering

Sometimes a person who rescues an abandoned rabbit ends up fostering the bunny through a rescue or other organization. Fosterers are not usually responsible for medical expenses, so this can be a means through which a person may keep a rabbit they otherwise might not be able to afford. However, the fosterer is responsible for providing food and other care, and of course must release their foster to a new home if a person is found to adopt the bunny. This last is not always easy. Author Laura CambyMcCaskill's story illustrates how the sadness over letting one foster-bunny go can be eased by taking on another:

Belk's Story
by Laura Camby McCaskill

When I first met Belk, I was standing in the shelter waiting to meet Agnes' new mom. Agnes was my foster bunny. She had been adopted the day before, and we were waiting to meet her new family. I cried when I handed Agnes over – for me, this is the worst part of the fostering process. I love to see them find their new fur-ever home, but it tears my heart out to watch them go.

Before I turned to leave, a lady at the counter directed my attention to a cage.

There he was – Belk, a five-pound white-and-brown bunny whose ears dropped to his sides like tired angel wings. He hid in his box when I spoke to him.

Belk's start in life had been a difficult one; he had been rescued from a hoarding situation. There were 50 bunnies crowded into one barn, and they were stressed. Because of this, the bunnies had begun to fight, and Belk was one of a few who had come in badly injured. His injuries were so bad he required surgery, and he also lost part of an ear. He was fostered by a few people before they sent him to a local pet store in hopes that he would get adopted. But being in the pet store, even though  he was behind glass, terrified him so bad that they had to bring him back to the shelter.

Belk needs a fosterer desperately, they told me.

I knew just by looking at him that he couldn't carry on this way for much longer. They told me he was showing the beginning signs of depression. He just looked at me as though he were saying, "Help me, please." I was still wiping away the tears I'd shed for Agnes when I told them I'd take Belk home with me.

It took about two weeks for him to adjust and relax in his new environment. My house, for the most part, is pretty quiet. Belk seemed to be happy in the new surroundings, which made me happy. Shortly after, I noticed he stopped eating his hay. He still ate his greens, pellets, and treats, but no hay. This worried me – first, hay is eighty percent of a rabbits diet and they should not go without it. Second, it is very important to watch your bunnies and learn their habits and their body language. The slightest change in these things, such as Belk avoiding hay, could be a big red flag. See, rabbits are prey animals, and therefore, they hide the fact that they are sick. They're masters at this. In the wild, animals that look sick or hurt are usually targeted first.

I alerted the shelter, and they sent me contact information for a woman named Anna, who would soon become my "bunny mentor" and friend. At first we thought that maybe Belk just didn't like the hay. So we tried different types. He snubbed them all. To be on the safe side, I made an appointment with a veterinarian where I live, in Asheville.

It took the vet thirty seconds to find the problem – Belk had an abscess under his chin. We couldn't see it because it just looked like fluff. Unfortunately, there are no veterinary offices in Asheville that can handle that sort of medical emergency. The closest one to us was in Knoxville, Tennessee, a two-hour drive from us.

On our first vet visit in Knoxville, they confirmed the abscess and prescribed antibiotics for the next two weeks. On our second visit, they did a CT scan, which revealed just how bad things were. Belk didn't have just one abscess – he had six. Hi entire right lower jaw was abscessed, and things were turning from bad to worse. Because of the abscess, he wasn't chewing on that side, which meant his teeth had grown out considerably.

A rabbit's teeth will grow its entire life, which is why they chew. Chewing on wood and hay grinds their teeth down, keeping their teeth from growing too much. Because of the abscess, Belk's teeth had grown so much on that side that there were shards of tooth stabbing into his tongue. It was painful for him to eat, which is what had made him stop eating the hay.

There was still worse news yet. Because of the abscess, his teeth had grown crooked, and there were shards growing in different directions. They were so long that they were penetrating his nasal cavity and would soon penetrate into the lower part of his eye.

After the CT scan, while he was still under sedation, they filed his teeth down. This doesn't hurt, I'm told. It's like them grinding their teeth down on wood. Because so many teeth were infected, the veterinarian decided against pulling them, as rabbits need their teeth both to eat and to grind their other teeth against. Instead, we were prescribed both an oral antibiotic and an injectable antibiotic. Belk took his medication willingly, which made things a lot easier. We gave him his oral medication twice daily and his injectable once a week.

It wasn't until I witnessed his first binky – the happiest expression a rabbit can make – that I knew Belk was feeling better. Once quiet and shy, this bun was now a force to be reckoned with. Yet he could give the best snuggles and bunny loves.

Belk continued his medications, and we traveled to Knoxville every six months to have his teeth shaved down until he passed away. Belk lived happily with me for two years until he succumbed to an unknown illness. Anna and I worked for over a week to get him better, from around-the-clock medication and IV fluids to temperature checks and other critical care. He was also seen by two different vets.

In the end, he decided to cross the bridge. He is one of many waiting for me there.

By taking care of rabbits until a forever home can be found, fosterers are able to give countless rabbits – especially those that need special care – the best possible chance for a good life. Many devoted rabbit rescuers will foster one rabbit after another (or even several at a time) for many years, steeling themselves to the pain of letting the rabbits go, pain they feel even when they know the rabbit is going to a forever home. But occasionally fosterers do adopt their charges, especially if they feel the rabbit is happy with them and unlikely to adapt to another home. Meg Brown's bunny Eva was such a case:

> Eva was found outside, recently born along with her six siblings. The Mom and babies were taken into foster care. The Dad was never found. However, the Mom delivered another litter before her first litter was fully weaned. All of the bunnies except for Eva found homes through the dedicated efforts of the volunteers of the Upstate NY chapter of the House Rabbit Society, The Rabbit Resource, but she sure didn't seem too sweet! Not at first...
>
> Eva charged, grunted, and scratched, bounding clear across the room when I entered. It was quite the greeting! But she quickly learned that I was the alpha bunny and I had the power to melt her with full-body petting, using lots of pressure.
>
> She had one adoption application, but she chased the lovely woman out the door during her meet and greet. Shortly afterward I told her I'd gotten the message: my rough and tough "smushy bunny" was in her forever home after all. Eva is very happy at Buster's Bunny Barn. While she still pulls the "charge and grunt" routine, she now stops short with a head push to the floor and melts, my big sweet white bunny.

Medical Problems Common in Dumped Rabbits

Dumped rabbits may have many medical issues, from injuries caused by predators or vehicles to illnesses to infestations of parasites. It will be necessary to examine closely and obtain prompt veterinary attention for conditions requiring. Mary Marvin, manager of Rabbit Advocates in Portland, Oregon, describes some of the medical problems encountered in just two months:

> In the last couple of months we rescued a two- week-old that needed formula feeding until she was big enough to wean and place in a foster home; and we took on the medical care of an injured young rabbit and his mom. The young one had a deep puncture wound and abscess of golf ball size that did not respond to heavy duty antibiotics and required surgery to remove. He did well with the surgery and is now placed in another foster home. Today's rescue (a four-week-old injured by a cat) did not survive. The list goes on.

For those who are new to rabbit rescue and may not have a rabbit-savvy vet to take a rescued rabbit to, please consult a rabbit-knowledgeable person or a rabbit organization for suggestions on what veterinarians are good with rabbits in your area. Although many more vets have good training in rabbit medicine now than in the past, rabbits are still considered exotics and not all vets are familiar with their needs. Two things in particular are red flags, and suggest a vet may not be skilled with rabbits:

1) Fasting before medical procedures. Rabbits should not be fasted before operations, as they are not at risk of regurgitating and need food in their digestive system at all times.

2) Prescribing oral penicillin. Although some penicillin may be safely given to rabbits by injection, penicillin antibiotics given orally (e.g. Clamavox, Amoxicillin) are often deadly to rabbits. Should a vet or an employee at a veterinary office suggest fasting or prescribe oral penicillin, please consider taking your rabbit to a different vet. His or her life may depend upon it.

Injuries

Many rabbits that are rescued have broken bones and other injuries, many caused by vehicles or predators. Sometimes these injuries

can be healed, at other times they require more drastic intervention, such as pins or amputation. One of the responders to our Domestic Rabbit Colony Survey told the story of a rabbit named Hutchkins who was discovered half-buried in waste in a filthy hutch with no food or hay in sight. The terrified rabbit had several fractures in a front leg that had to be pinned. The bunny recovered from the invasive surgery and a wonderful family was found for him (read his story by Adrienne Lang in the previous chapter).

Kim Dezelon describes another injury that can occur with young rabbits and which rescuers may encounter:

Kalle and her babies came from a hoarding house in Phoenix. The males were eating the babies as they were being born. We took in a litter that was two weeks old. Some of the babies' ears were eaten plus

Paisley had an abscess on her back. We ended up keeping Micah, Grayson, and Paisley. We still have Grayson and Paisley, both of whom (at nine years old) have lost the use of their hind legs.

Parasites

One of the most common medical issues in dumped or feral rabbits is parasites. Parasites are one of the reasons quarantining rescued rabbits from household pets is necessary. Every dumped rabbit should be thoroughly checked for mites, ticks, fleas, maggots, and lumps that might be caused by bot fly larvae.

Mites

There are several types of mites that may be found on rabbits. Ear mites (*Psoroptes cuniculi*) and the fur mite *Cheyletiella parasitovorax* (also called "walking dandruff") are two of the most common. Less common are the true fur mite, *Leporacarus gibbus*, and mites that cause mange (*Sarcoptes* and *Notoedres*). Although mites are not life-threatening, their presence should not be ignored, because unless steps are taken they will spread rapidly through a household, and once they have established themselves they are extremely difficult to eradicate from a home.

A rabbit with **ear mites** may shake his head frequently and kick or scratch at the affected ear. A crusted exudate will accumulate in the ears, and in bad cases, to the face, neck, and even down to the feet. Secondary bacterial infections can also occur. Very rarely, *Sarcoptes* may be found in a rabbit's ears.

Signs of infestation by fur mites include scratching, fur loss, dandruff, and sores/scabs, although a rabbit with only a light infestation may show no signs at all. Fur mites don't always show up in scrapings. If such a test is negative it doesn't always mean the mites are not present.

A rabbit with ear mites may shake his head frequently and kick or scratch at the affected ear. Crusted exudate will accumulate in the ears, and in bad cases, to the face, neck, and even down to the feet. Secondary bacterial infections can also occur.

Signs of infestation by **fur mites** include scratching, fur loss, dandruff, and sores and scabs, although a rabbit with only a light infestation may show no signs. The entire life cycle of *Cheyletiella* mites takes 35 days, but females can breed at three weeks. Female mites can also live up to 14 days off the rabbit. This – along with their activity – is what can make the mites so difficult to eradicate from the environment.

Meg Brown has had experience with *Cheyletiella* mites and knows how difficult they can be to deal with:

Dealing with Fur Mites
by Meg Brown

Stray rabbits are at risk of many dangers and health concerns besides the ones that might first come to mind, such as predation, flea or bot fly infestation, or starvation. They are also vulnerable to ear mite and fur mite infestation. Ear mites are generally easier to diagnose, and often present with obvious "dirt" in the ears. The ears themselves may be thick and crusty-looking, or even weighted down in more advanced cases. Fur mites can be far more difficult to diagnose and require extreme diligence to prevent them from spreading to other rabbits. A rabbit with fur mites may have obvious flakes of "dandruff" and possibly rough scaly patches on the skin. The fur may also fall out, leaving tufts or bald patches.

Revolution is my first choice medication for both ear and fur mites. When I capture stray bunnies, I quarantine them, do a full-body check, then often give them a dose of Revolution (a topical anti-parasitic).

Sometimes an older, immune-compromised rabbit can suddenly present with a fur mite infestation. This happened in 2010 with one of my well-loved and cared for house bunnies. I noticed that my Dutch bunny Lola had white dandruff-like flakes on her glossy black fur. Lola was nine years old and had been paraplegic for two years. She had a great appetite and was always bright and alert. Still, a vet visit confirmed that Lola had fur mites.

This was an especially big deal since I had ten other rabbits, two who lived in the same large kitchen as Lola, though they didn't have physical contact with her. I knew that *universal precautions* were of utmost importance, not only in their room, but both upstairs and downstairs, where the other bunnies lived. I hoped that I wasn't too late in being careful, as I handled Lola often to give her fluids, massage, and express her bladder.

I was a bit relieved when both of the bunnies sharing Lola's room tested negative for mites, but I wasn't taking chances and treated them also, as mites often do not show up in the tests. I moved the bunnies into another area while I took everything off the floor except the table. I cleaned the floor and replaced the rugs with cloth and vinyl incontinence pads, using a dozen of them at a time. I changed the other bunnies' litter boxes every day. I washed every corner of that room every day and washed my hands between handling bunnies. I also changed my clothes after handling Lola, 4-5 times a day

One dose of Revolution will generally kill the existing mites. But eggs will continue to hatch for several weeks, so the rabbits' environment must be cleaned daily. Litter boxes and any fabric must be changed daily. I changed out the pads that I used for flooring every single day. Because I know how persistent and contagious mites are, I continued with the diligent cleaning for six weeks. I was not going to risk the possibility that any female mites (which can survive up to three weeks off their host) might survive long enough to lay eggs and re-infest Lola or be unknowingly transported to any of my other bunnies. I also gave the bunnies a second topical dose of Revolution thirty days after the first, which is often recommended. I may not have needed to take my cleaning to that extreme, but it was worth it as no other bunnies contracted the parasite.

Six years later, in 2016, with my broken arm in a hard cast, my quadriplegic bunny, Frank, ten years old and immune-compromised, also presented with mites. He shared a bedroom with my sweet guy, Tupac, who liked to hop near him, though they didn't spend a lot of time together and weren't closely bonded. But they got close enough so that Tupac also got fur mites. Both bunnies were treated.

Keeping the parasites isolated to Frank and Tupac's room would have been a challenge under normal circumstances, but it became a much larger issue managing with one arm. I moved Frank into the kitchen and put Tupac in an exercise pen. He was used to having the entire room, so the confined space was quite an adjustment for him. I kept up the diligent cleaning for several weeks, using one arm. But it was again worth the time and effort as I was able to confine the mites and they did not spread to any other bunnies.

I'm sharing my two personal stories of dealing with mites in bunnies that had been house bunnies for several years. They are even more likely to be found in abandoned rabbits that have been outside. Rabbits with fur mites (*Cheyletiella parasitovorax*) may be without obvious signs of infestation initially, but it is important to check for signs of them on a regular basis, especially in stray or elderly rabbits. Bunnies with mites don't tend to scratch nearly as much as they do if they have fleas, if they scratch at all. Whenever I see dandruff, I get the rabbit tested for mites. It could be a little dry skin. But if not, I take quick and serious action to prevent an outbreak.

Fur mites can be a difficult and long-lasting problem, especially if the environment is not cleaned carefully every day. Food-grade diatomaceous earth is safe and helpful to sprinkle outside in the grass and in hard-to-reach corners and cracks of flooring and baseboard. Rabbits must be treated individually and quarantined from other rabbits whenever possible. A commitment must be made to clean everything that the rabbit comes into contact with, including litter boxes and flooring, every single day for up to six weeks due to the life cycle and ability of the female mite to live off the rabbit for many days.

Treating fur mites is easy; cleaning their environment takes time and consistency, but the mites can be contained. It's important to take action quickly, but don't panic. Mites are an inconvenient, time-intensive problem, but they are manageable. Before you know it the creepy "bugs" will be a memory and your home will be super clean!

Fleas

A rescued rabbit should be treated immediately if any fleas are found. If the rabbit has been living in the wild it is **remotely** possible that fleas could carry serious diseases if the rabbit is from a high-risk area, for example, south central US (tularemia) or southwestern US (plague). Some of the products used for flea control in dogs and cats, such as Sentinel or Frontline (fipronil), are not safe for rabbits, so consult a rabbit-savvy vet before using any medication. Although permethrin has been licensed for use in rabbits to treat fleas and other external parasites, rabbits can have negative reactions to it, including reddened skin, sores and fur loss where permethrin is applied topically, and neurological symptoms may appear in rabbits if permethrin is ingested or inhaled.

The original Advantage (imidacloprid) was generally safe for use on rabbits, but some people reported that Advantage II (imidacloprid and pyriproxyfen) was not tolerated as well and some vets would not use it on rabbits. Bayer's Defense Care for cats, which contained only imidacloprid as its active ingredient, was safe for use on rabbits. However, at the time of this writing it appears that the Defense Care line may be discontinued and Advantage II has been reformulated with moxidectrin instead of pyriproxyfen. The combination of imidacloprid and moxidectin (related to avermectin) has been found to be safe for rabbits. Selamectin, which is often used to kill mites on rabbits, will also kill fleas, but researchers have found that it takes a higher dose for fleas (15-20mg/kg). Another medication used to treat fleas on rabbits is nitenpyram (Capstar), which is given orally and kills all adult fleas very rapidly. Nitenpyram is related to imidacloprid, and although it is generally safe for use on rabbits, there have been rare cases where rabbits have had a negative reaction. (It should be remembered that this can happen with any medication since rabbits are individuals and may react differently to medications.) Flea collars should not be used on rabbits.

As with fur mites, the environment will need to be cleaned for several weeks if fleas are discovered on a rabbit being kept indoors. It has been found the number of adult fleas represents only about 5% of the total flea population. Eggs account for about 50%, larvae for around 35%, and pupae (cocoons) for ten percent. Fleas can live up to a year and are quite active, being able to jump as high as five inches and as far as twenty-two inches, depending upon the species. (Cat and dog fleas are most common on indoor rabbits, although rabbit fleas may be found on rabbits that have been rescued from or live outdoors.)Flea eggs hatch in the environment and larvae also live in the environment, such as carpet. Adults feed on the blood of the host and their dark-colored feces, called "flea dirt," may be the first obvious evidence a rabbit has fleas.

Because of their activity fleas are very difficult to eradicate from a home once they have become established. Using professional exterminators is risky because rabbits are highly sensitive to most commercial insecticides. Therefore, if fleas are found on an indoor rabbit it is essential to treat all household animals with a safe flea medication and immediately begin a thorough cleaning routine. All flooring and upholstered furniture should be vacuumed daily for two weeks, and bedding washed in hot soapy water once a week. To prevent fleas from escaping the vacuum bag, put a flea collar, borax or diatomaceous earth in the bag. Food-grade diatomaceous earth can also be sprinkled into crack and crevices of flooring and upholstery to help eradicate the fleas.

Ticks

Rabbits are quite good at removing ticks from parts of their body that they can reach with their teeth, but have difficulty removing them from their head and neck area. One of the dangers of ticks is that they can carry diseases, including some highly fatal diseases such as RHD. As new ticks such as the Asian long-horned tick (first discovered in New Jersey in 2017 and moving rapidly to other states) spread across the US ticks will become even more serious disease vectors. Any ticks found on

a rabbit should be removed immediately. The CDC recommends that ticks be removed with fine-tipped tweezers, grasping the tick as close as possible to the skin and pulling up steadily, without squeezing, twisting or jerking. Injuring the tick can cause it to regurgitate gut contents, increasing the risk of infection, and mouth parts may be left in the skin.

In all honesty, when I lived in a tick-infested area I tried a method of tick removal that supposedly does not work: I poured between 1/4-1/3 cup isopropyl alcohol over them. In every case, the tick released its hold and was washed off with the alcohol. Whether this was because I was consistently lucky or because of the species of tick in my area or because I am very diligent about watching for parasites and none of the ticks were deeply embedded, I don't know, although I suspect the last.

For rabbits being kept in outdoor colonies, most medications given prophylactically for fleas or flystrike are said to kill ticks as well.

Flies *(see Chapter 7 for more information on flystrike in rabbits)*

One of the greatest dangers to dumped/abandoned rabbits is attack by blowflies that lay their eggs on the rabbit. Greenbottle, bluebottle, flesh and, rarely, house flies, may lay eggs on a rabbit, especially if they are attracted by damp, soiled fur, the scent glands, or a wound. In just a matter of hours the rabbit can be covered with maggots. The maggots will eat both dead and living flesh, and may enter body orifices. This causes extreme pain to the rabbit, who will eventually go into shock from the pain and the toxins released by the maggots. Death can follow. In some cases a rabbit cannot be saved at this state of flystrike even if help is available. Meg Brown:

> I rescued a four-month-old abandoned English Spot rabbit with hind leg paralysis, who had been found on a lawn. I named him Scooter. A week after his rescue I was giving him a butt bath and gently using a blow dryer set on low to help dry his fur. Suddenly hundreds of maggots began pouring out of his anus and penis, stimulated by the heat. I got him to an emergency vet, but because the maggots had infiltrated Scooter's internal organs, the vet recommended euthanasia.

If you find a rabbit with fly maggots crawling on it, get the rabbit to a veterinarian as soon as possible. If you cannot get the rabbit to a vet immediately, follow the steps under "facultative flystrike" in Chapter 7.

Bot fly larvae are more common on rescued rabbits than the larvae of the other flies in many areas of the United States. The primary bot fly that attacks rabbits is a large, mostly black fly with some white underneath (*Cuterebra cuniculi*). A bot fly larva develops subcutaneously, causing a large cyst-like lump with a tiny hole in the center. Do not squeeze the lump and do not attempt to remove the larva – if it is squashed, broken, or injured it releases a flood of toxins that can cause a severe allergic reaction that may kill the rabbit. Leave extraction of larvae to a veterinarian or other skilled veterinary professional. If no such professional is available, leave the lump alone. In time the larva will leave, and unless the rabbit is covered with bot fly larvae, he or she will most likely survive. A bot fly is an obligate parasite, and as such does not normally kill its host (although having a great number of bot fly larvae on a rabbit may seriously debilitate the rabbit, resulting in death).

With both bot fly larvae and blowfly maggots, the more that are present on the rabbit the more the rabbit is affected by the pain and by toxins that both maggots and bot fly larvae release. Secondary bacterial infections can develop in bot fly larval holes and where maggots are eating tissue (and maggots are sometimes attracted to empty, infected warbles). Seriously affected rabbits may go into shock and die. Getting immediate veterinary care for the rabbit is essential.

Anthony Cimino begins the story of Dahlia, a rescued bunny with bot fly larvae:

> I was asked to go to a school in Saratoga, NY to look for a black bunny that children and teachers had noticed. With the assistance of a construction worker, we were able to coax this bun under a trailer. We then built a space with wood and x-pen portions on one end of the trailer and made tons of noise at the other end. This sweet doll bolted to the end with our ad-hoc space and we dove into it to block her from running back under. Children and teachers cheered, we knew this bun was going to get the best care.
>
> I drove her to Meg Brown's home and set up a space for the rabbit in her garage. I had to leave this bun there, but I knew she'd be cared for. When Meg arrived and looked over this doll, she was alarmed, this baby had Bot Flies. I'm sure Katrina Cutter can take the story from here:

Dahlia's Story
by Jeff and Katrina Cutter

The little black bunny came to us late on July 29th, a Thursday night. She had been abandoned in the Saratoga, NY area and had been outside for several weeks during the hot summer before finally being captured by Anthony. After an initial examination by Meg it was clear she needed immediate vet care. We got the call from Jude and agreed to do the transport to the vet. We were not really prepared to provide the unexpected overnight accommodations before the next morning vet visit and then the transport to her foster home. She was to be quarantined in our garage so as not to introduce the risk of spreading something to our current house rabbit, Cherry Vanilla. Meg came over with the bunny and some supplies to set up her temporary abode, a nice size ex-pen with a hiding box and litter pans. We watched her daintily nibble at some greens and explore around. You could see that she was quite swollen and sore from parasites but still showed off her affectionate personality right away. What a beautiful little girl she was with shiny black fur, large dark eyes, dainty feet and a generous dewlap. The little bunny needed a name. 'Dahlia Bea' came to mind, very feminine and delicate. And so Dahlia's journey with us began.

The next day at her early morning vet visit the diagnosis was confirmed as she had a festering infestation of cuterebra parasites. Four cuterebra were removed from her and she was released to us. This was unfortunately the first of many vet visits for her. She couldn't be transported to the planned foster home in this condition, so Dahlia

would stay with us for the time being. Over the next few days more cuterebra were discovered as we examined her and treated her wounds, and each time she was taken back to a vet for medical attention and removal. With much help and advice from everyone in the local house rabbit network, and thanks to Collette and Meg, we got a crash course on administering her bunny medications orally and giving sub-Q fluids. We followed the medicine regime several times a day for the next few days. Throughout her several times daily poking and prodding by us Dahlia was so easy to handle and willingly took her medications, never a grunt or nip from her. Thinking about her sweet temperament we began to realize that we would truly miss her when we took her to her foster home. We wondered what kind of family would adopt her and where? Would we ever hear about her full recovery from all this? We'd become quite attached to her, as if she was our own in a matter of days. What if *we* adopted her? But we weren't prepared to have two bunnies at the time. Finally after several days with continuing issues and serious concerns about a failed larva removal over Dahlia's eye, Davida of the HRS Chapter got an appointment at Cornell Animal Hospital and we took Dahlia on the long drive to have a more intensive exam done.

As we spent the day at Cornell while Dahlia was being cared for, more and more we knew we were head over heels for little Dahlia Bea. Cornell was great and took care of the failed removal and her other wounds. The prognosis seemed good but she needed daily wound care and medicine and would have to go back for a follow-up visit in a week. That evening before we got to Cathy's house, the fostering home, we knew that Dahlia Bea would be coming home with us. As we talked with Davida and Cathy, Dahlia Bea bounced around the couch and playfully arranged a small towel that was next to her several times. When she was done she settled down next to her new 'bunny dad,' Jeff, for some petting; she spread out on her belly, one dainty front foot extended and with a look of satisfaction on her face. She clearly was realizing what a special little princess she was and had chosen her family-to-be.

We didn't want to leave her but circumstances had us being away for a family vacation when she was to go back to the vet for her follow up visit. She was to stay with Cathy and Jeff for the two weeks and we would pick her up the Monday after we got back from vacation. What a perfect plan. We couldn't wait to get back home and do some bunny shopping the very next day. We hit the pet store and on-line shopping. Would Dahlia like this water bowl or this food bowl? She'll love the pink pet bed!  And don't forget the willow toys! Everything we/she needed was purchased or ordered up on-line and would be waiting for us when we got back from vacation.

Little did we know that that was the last time we would see our darling little girl. Her follow-up visit and surgery on Monday, August 9th went well but Dahlia passed away very unexpectedly late that night, unable to fully recover from going through the trauma yet again. Heartbreakingly, it's not known exactly why it happened but it did. It didn't seem fair that after all the effort, time and money put into giving her a second chance at life that she didn't get to enjoy it longer. We didn't get to give her the love that she deserved in her forever home. We'll never get to snuggle our sweet, beautiful little Dahlia again, but we can take comfort in knowing that the last couple weeks of her life were filled with people that truly cared for her and were intent on helping her heal and erase the horrors she had been exposed to by being dumped in the wild. One thing is for certain though, for the short time she was with us, Dahlia Bea may have been a tiny four pound bundle of fur but she left a giant hole in all our hearts and lives. We love and miss you, our little 'DB'!

Meg Brown has also had experience with rescued bunnies who have been attacked by bot flies, and her story shows some rabbits so attacked can be saved:

Betty Boop, later named Kayleigh Betty by her wonderful adoptive Mom, Stacy, was yet another discarded bunny. She was quite small, and had reportedly been seen running around the grounds of a retirement home for over a month. As often happens, someone found my number and I was ready to head off to capture the little black and white bunny.

But the second call I received was from two of the residents of the community saying that they had easily picked her up, and "Now what?" I asked them to meet me at my vet's office in Saratoga Springs. She was a tiny little bunny. The women named her Betty Boop. My vet determined that, other than being underweight and having a single bot fly larva in her, which she pulled out, Betty was basically healthy and would recover with some added weight and TLC.

I decided to foster her, not that I had much choice, as our foster homes were almost always full, especially in the summer with the post-Easter dumped bunnies. I was volunteering with the upstate NY chapter of the House Rabbit Society at the time, The Rabbit Resource.

A couple of days later, as I was grooming Betty Boop, very late at night, I noticed a hard scab-like area under her belly. It was moving. Oh no! My first live bot fly larva at 2 a.m! I called Caroline Charland, who encouraged me to get the hemostat and wiggle it out of there, of course without breaking it, as I could introduce toxins into the delicate bunny's system if the larva was damaged.

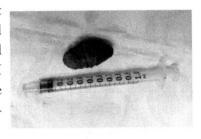

Remembering how bot flies had killed my first rescued stray, Lucky, I knew that I had to try. I was very nervous, but I did it. I pulled out the surprisingly fat, wiggly worm-like creature who had been feeding off the inside of my new friend's body. It left a gaping hole which I rinsed with chlorhexidine for a few days. But Betty Boop healed nicely and began to gain weight. She was adopted by a lovely woman who lives locally and who has become a

good friend, so I get to see how Kayleigh Betty has grown and hear funny stories about her. It's always heartwarming to know that our efforts continue to enrich the lives of both the bunnies and the adopters.

(Author's note: Meg Brown is an experienced rescuer with extensive experience nursing rabbits; unless a person has comparable skills to hers, bot fly larvae removal should wait until it can be done by a veterinarian.)

After reading about some of the parasites, injuries, diseases, and other problems that rescued rabbits may have, new rescuers may be feeling a bit discouraged. They shouldn't be. Kim Dezelon of Brambley Hedge Rabbit Rescue tells about a very special bunny, who survived despite multiple problems and went on to live a life as a treasured companion for many years:

Triscuit was adopted out at about six months old. In 2011, she was returned to Brambley Hedge Rabbit Rescue at five years old. She had been eating high-calorie high-fat pellets and had been kept in a cage, with the result she was fat with no muscle tone whatsoever. I remembered her as a baby and soon adopted her.

Triscuit was an English Spot/lop mix. She had lots of problems initially and we soon discovered she had megacolon, a condition affecting the digestive system that is more common in English Spots than other rabbits. I started treating her and after about a year got a normal protocol going so she wasn't always going into stasis (gastrointestinal slowdown). I also noticed she acted like she wasn't spayed even though she had been spayed. One of our rabbit-savvy vets suggested we do surgery to determine if the surgery was complete. It wasn't, as he found an ovary and part of her uterus. Later that year, she appeared to have bladder problems. After X-rays, our vet found a huge bladder stone and it was removed. My poor baby girl had been through so much!

Triscuit was finally was issue-free other than occasional megacolon problems. Rabbits with megacolon often have

recurring bouts, but I stayed on top of things. Triscuit was happy and active through most of her years. I lost her last July out of nowhere. Granted she was 10.5 years old, but she had been doing great. It took me by surprise as there were no signs.

Adopting Rescued Rabbits

Those who adopt rescued rabbits are just as much a part of rescue as those who physically capture abandoned rabbits. They are people willing to take a chance on rabbits that may have physical or behavioral problems stemming from abuse, neglect, or the time during which they were trying to survive on their own. At the same time, adopting such a rabbit can be extremely rewarding, for the adopter knows a rabbit with a neglected or abusive past is being given a chance for a happy life after being discarded by people unable to see the value of a rabbit.

Bonding

Many rescued rabbits are happier with a rabbit friend, and if you adopt one rescued rabbit you may wish to adopt another so the first rabbit is not lonely when you are not at home. However, rabbits are picky and will not accept just anyone as a friend. Unbonded rabbits that are left together may fight, sometimes viciously. Sometimes the process of bonding rabbits is easy, at other times difficult or nearly impossible. If you do not have experience bonding rabbits consult with a rabbit-knowledgeable person.

Anthony Cimino tells of a very difficult bonding challenge he overcame – after three years!

The Amazing Bond (Thank you Caramel!)
by Anthony Cimino

Two years before I knew there were so many humans working to protect bunnies, I adopted Patches from the Menands Mohawk Humane Society. Patches was given his own bedroom, but he was restless, he'd make circles with his front right paw. "He's bored, and we have plenty of room; let's get him a friend." We didn't know about "bunny dates," nor how hard bonding two rabbits can be. We innocently went back to the shelter with Patches, he hopped to Muffin's cage and they immediately began kissing. The second visit they were given a room to play in that included a huge fish tank with a snake. It was as if they knew it was their turn, they sat together and pushed their butts against the fish tank glass! "We will take her!" When I returned home from the vet after Muffin's spay we let her lie in the litter box. Patches looked at me, then at her, then at me again. "Yes, we brought her home so you can be with her all the time," I answered...he then jumped in with her and began grooming his recovering love, clearly wanting to make her feel better.

Fast forward to how I ended up getting involved with rescue: I was given Clavamox for Muffin when she started sneezing. This killed her. After shouting and crying, I realized nothing was going to bring her back to Patches and me, so it was time to fill the space that was left. After crying on the phone with Davida Kobler of the Upstate NY House Rabbit Society, I knew I had to help another bun. I adopted a red-eyed-white rabbit and named her SugarMuffin. She hated us! Patches and she would fight, battles that were so out of control I can only remember this: they developed a way to hurt each other by biting, then while holding the opponent with their teeth, they would flop and kick each other as hard and fast as they could. The only time they didn't do it was when they were in the car or a new place. I would say, "I know Patches can bond, because he bonded to Muffin. Maybe SugarMuffin just isn't the bonding type."

Then my mentor Meg Brown and I captured a bunny in the Stockade Section of Schenectady, NY that I named Caramel. Caramel gave my family what we all wanted so badly: through an act of aggression she broke SugarMuffin's resistance to Patches. I was cleaning Caramel's x-pen when she got out, and before I could catch her she was already in the bunny room where Patches and SugarMuffin lived in side-by-side x-pens separated by cardboard. As I entered the room, I saw Caramel go straight for SugarMuffin, and she cut her! I got Caramel back in her space, and then I had an inspiration. "Here goes nothing!" I thought, and I opened the x-pens of Patches and SugarMuffin. Just as he had with Muffin after her operation, Patches knew what to do with hurt buns! He began to groom the battered SugarMuffin and the bond I had waited for three years to happen occurred right there, on the spot. I removed the separate x-pens and two years of amazing bunny fun began.

Patches and SugarMuffin passed away twelve hours apart from an unknown illness we battled for two weeks. Caramel was bonded with a bunny named Moose and adopted!

Medical Issues

Although most minor medical issues in a rescued rabbits will have been dealt with by the time they are adopted out, some may have conditions or have had to go through procedures that will make them special needs rabbits for life, such as amputations. Meg Brown tells the story of her rabbit Caroline:

I received a call before Christmas 2017 that four Flemish Giant rabbits were running around outside. A neighbor was very concerned and wanted to try to catch them. Before I was able to help, the wonderful women at the spay/neuter clinic loaned him live traps and arranged to have the four bunnies split between two different shelters.

There was a male and female who went to the county shelter. Within days, the female gave birth to seven babies. To think that these babies would have been born outside breaks my heart. They are now almost three months old and being well cared for by the shelter staff.

The other two went to a different shelter; apparently they were a Mom and daughter. The smaller of the two, still a large growing Flemmie, had a compound fracture of her left metatarsal. I took her to my vet, Dr. Joy Lucas, for assessment. We don't know how long the bone was broken, but because it was an open wound, the entire foot was full of infection. Her leg needed to be amputated. This is not the news I expected. I also was not planning on adopting another bunny. But, we don't usually plan these things and I knew right away that she wasn't going anywhere! Dr. Lucas did an amazing job with the surgery. Caroline now bounds around half of a bedroom and  down the hallway on her three legs, as though she had four. I plan to bond her with her roommate, Tupac.

I've named my big silly girl Caroline after Caroline

Charland, my dear friend and first bunny mentor, and Caroline Mack, my young friend whose family adopted Midnight.

Behavioral problems

The behavioral problems of dumped rescued rabbits may stem from trauma during the time after they were dumped or from abuse and/or neglect they may have suffered with the owner who dumped them. Clicker training can be used for rabbits rescued by individuals as well as those with colony or large rescues. Andrea Bratt describes how clicker training helped a frightened and skittish bunny from a shelter learn to accept being touched, and even learn tricks.

The Story of Nicholas
by Andrea Bratt

I met Nicholas at the Bunnies Urgently Needing Shelter (BUNS) rabbit rescue where I volunteer. He came to our shelter with five other feral rabbits one summer. They were very scared and almost impossible to handle. Although Nicholas was a large white rabbit with pink eyes, he acted more like a wild rabbit. Just walking by their enclosures would sometimes cause them to scream and slam into the walls in a panic

trying to get away from humans. We put blankets over some of their hutches to give them a sense of security and tried hand-feeding them long pieces of vegetables such as carrot, parsley or kale through the wire of their hutches.

Over a few weeks some of them were eating vegetables from our hands and getting used to being handled by volunteers. We were able to very carefully, sometimes padded with towels, put them out in pens to exercise but it was difficult to catch them again to put them back in their hutches. Cleaning the hutches with a terrified rabbit inside was also proving to be a challenge.

One day Nicholas bit a volunteer and had to be quarantined for ten days. I offered to quarantine him at my house and give him a break from the shelter environment. I promised to be the only one to handle him and keep him away from everybody. During the ten days I had Nicholas, I began to clicker train him. I put his daily ration of pellets and a small bowl of chopped carrots on top of his cage. Three to four times a day I would have a 10-15 minute clicker training session with him.

The first thing I did was teach him to touch a target stick. The instant his nose touched the target, I would click and give him a rabbit pellet or a carrot chunk. He always had plenty of hay and water but my plan was to use as much of his daily food intake as I could manage for intensive training. Whatever food was left at the end of the day became his dinner. Gradually I began to slide my hand down the target stick so Nicholas had to touch my hand instead of the stick. I also trained him to touch my hand through the wire of his hutch so he could get used to approaching and touching hands without the opportunity to bite them. Animal trainers use this method for potentially aggressive animals and call this "protected contact".

The next step was getting him to touch my hand and hold there for a second or two before I clicked. After a few days he would park his nose under my hand for a several seconds and I was able to rub my hand up his face before I clicked and treated. Yeah, the first pet!

On day four, I began to take him out to an exercise pen. In the pen I clicker trained him to hop onto a box, jump through a hoop, spin right and left, and "Give me ten," (slap both front paws onto the palm of my hand). Training tricks is valuable because the more behaviors that a rabbit learns, the more options it has to respond. Training an incompatible behavior is one of the ways that animal trainers can modify aggression. Nicholas could not be biting my hand at the same time that he was parking his nose under my hand. He couldn't be scratching or boxing at the same time he was "Giving me ten". Now hands coming near him were cues to do certain behaviors for a treat, not a signal to bite or scratch in order to get rid of the scary hands.

I also began desensitizing Nicholas to being touched all over his body. I would rub my hand up his nose and touch his ear. If he stayed still and accepted the touch, I would click and treat. If he pulled away, there would be no click and treat and I would try again after 5-10 seconds. I was gradually able to handle his ears and paws and tail and pet him all over his body. The wonderful thing about it was he began to not just accept the petting but to enjoy it. At that point I could touch his back leg gently and reward him with a nose rub instead of a food reward.

At the end of the ten days, Nicholas was a much calmer, braver rabbit. He would still spook at sudden noises and movements but he wasn't panicking or trying to bite people anymore. I continued to train him and a few months later was invited by Animal Planet to bring a rabbit to a promotional event in Santa Monica, CA. I brought Nicholas and he was comfortable enough to perform his "Give me 10" trick live on the KTLA morning news! Everyone thought the trick was amazing but what truly amazed me was the whole journey of a remarkably resilient rabbit and the fact that Nicholas was able to perform his trick in front of horses, a roller skating parrot, several barking dogs, a pig and TV cameras.

Jean Silva offers some simple clicker training techniques that can be used by individual rescuers. (For more detailed instructions on clicker training, see the article by Jean Silva and Andrea Bratt in Chapter Seven.)

Socializing Rabbits with a Clicker
by Jean Silva

We use behavior to get the things we want or to avoid the things we don't want. Rabbits are just the same. If you are late with dinner, does your rabbit look back and forth from you to its pellet bowl? If so, your rabbit has learned a behavior that reminds you to serve dinner. A bunny may run or hide from a scary person. If so, that bunny has learned that flight or hiding can make a scary person go away.

All training, including clicker training, relies on this principle: Behaviors that result in desired outcomes increase. The opposite is also true. Behaviors that result in unwanted outcomes decrease or disappear.

Sometimes a rabbit will wrongly decide that a behavior causes an outcome.An excited rabbit that begins running in a circle just as dinner is served may conclude that dinner comes after he runs in a circle. Each time he gets dinner after he circles increases the odds that he will continue to circle before dinner.

We need a way to tell the rabbit which of their many behaviors will give them a great outcome: that is, a way to mark which behavior we want to see repeated. You can use a sound like a mechanical clicker, a tongue click, or a word. In the beginning the sound has no meaning for the rabbit. You need to pair the sound with an outcome that the rabbit wants.

When you are working with a feral or poorly socialized rabbit there are outcomes that they naturally want: food, safety, access to companions, and access to fun or safe spaces. There are outcomes they naturally don't want: scary people, predators and unknown animals.

Your first task is to pair the click with something you know they want, like food. Train just before a meal when they are hungry. Feed part of their meal using your clicker. If the rabbit will eat from your hand, use small items like pellets. If not, try long food like parsley or cilantro. Some rabbits prefer to have a fence or barrier between the two of you. You may need to lure the rabbit over to you by holding out the food before you click. Make the click sound as the rabbit eats. Gradually make the clicks before the rabbit takes a bite. Continue clicking and feeding until the rabbit looks for food when he hears a click.

Once the rabbit hears the click and thinks food, you can use the clicker to teach a rabbit behaviors. You may "capture" a common behavior like periscoping. You may shape a behavior like following a target or sitting on a mat.

Capturing refers to reinforcing a natural behavior like periscoping. When the bunny periscopes you click and treat. It is easiest to capture a behavior that the bunny does often, at a usual time, or in response to something you do.

Shaping refers to creating a new behavior by reinforcing a sequence of component behaviors.

I have shaped a head lowered for a pet using a clicker. I place my cupped hand on the ground about ½" from the rabbit's nose. When the rabbit lowers it head to sniff the hand I click, remove the hand, reach for a pellet and feed. I do 10 repetitions and end the session. I repeat the session several times until the rabbit consistently lowers it head close to the hand. Then, after the click, as I remove the hand I lightly touch the forehead and deliver the treat. Over the next few sessions, I turn the touch into a light pet and eventually into several pets. When the rabbit relaxes during the pets you can use the pets rather than the food to reinforce the behavior. If the rabbit backs away or shows other signs of discomfort, go back to the beginning and start again.

After the rabbit lowers its head for a pet you can teach it to hop onto your lap. Sit on the floor near the rabbit. Offer your hand and stroke the rabbit when it lowers its head. Gradually move your hand closer to your leg in small increments, petting after each head lowering. Eventually you will reach your leg. Place your hand on your leg near the floor. Gradually work your way up the leg, petting after each head lowering, until the rabbit places his front paws in your lap for a pet. When the rabbit is comfortable with that, move your hand until the rabbit jumps onto your lap for a pet.

Some rabbits will run away when you approach. They want you to leave. That's OK, because they are telling you that they want something you can deliver. As you enter their space pause and if they stand still, click and then leave or back up. Do this ten times, each time getting a little closer than before. Do this session multiple times over several days. Make your approach from as many directions as possible. If the rabbit moves away while you approach, stop and wait until the rabbit stops moving. Click and leave or back up. If the rabbit is consistently moving away as you approach, you are coming too close too fast. Back off. When the bunny stands still 90 percent of the time you approach, you can take a step closer. The rabbit will learn that you will leave if it stands still and it will gradually allow you to get close.

A group of feral rabbits can be taught to come to return to their overnight space. Choose a highly preferred food item and a feeding spot within their overnight space. Make the feeding time coincide with the time you would want them to return. Begin training while they are still in their overnight space. One of our volunteers says "Oh, my babies!," and rattles the pellet container while standing next to the chosen spot. When the first rabbits approach you give some pellets. The other rabbits will see them eating and come over. Give more pellets until their evening meal has been served. After multiple repetitions, the entire group will come on hearing your call and the pellets. Then you can give them access to a larger space during the day and get a reliable return at night. Our shelter has a group of twelve that is allowed to run in the large fenced yard during the day. At night, the door to their smaller play yard is opened and they are called to go home.

As rabbits learn with clicker training, they often become more engaged and confident. We think we are training the rabbits to do what we want. Meanwhile, they are training us to give them something they want. And, so they have gained greater control over their world. A world in which there is never punishment and rewards are plentiful and reliable.

Clicker training is also an enrichment activity. Clicker training is a lot like the child's game of hot and cold. When you play with the rabbit, the click says "hot" and silence says "cold." Rabbits enjoy the game. My rabbits will come to me in the morning and ask to train. Like any game, though, there are rules for clicker training. Experienced trainers learn to use the rules for elegant ways to get useful or fun behavior.

Adopting a small group for a yard or country property (micro-colonies)

A few adopters of rabbits take on the challenge of adopting a group of rabbits – anywhere from about twenty to a hundred – from a rescued colony of feral/dumped rabbits for outdoor living. This can be ideal for people in suburbs who have large yards or for those with rural properties. It can also be ideal for people who love rabbits but cannot have them in their houses because of allergies or other reasons. As the problem of dumped and feral rabbits increases, people willing to adopt small groups, also called micro-colonies, will be needed more than ever.

Quan Meyers, who started Rabbitats for Humanity, a non-profit center for unwanted rabbits that was located in Maine, was one of the first to promote having groups of rabbits in a backyard. Quan's rabbitats were predator-proof enclosures with small buildings or hutches where the rabbits could go to eat, sleep, and hide if they chose. The enclosed area had multiple houses/hutches, allowing rabbits a wide choice of places to hide, and recommended that in areas with snow hutches should be off the ground, with ramps for ease of access. She suggested solid perimeter fencing so that predators and rabbits cannot see each other even if they can smell each other.

The predators that could be a danger to a group of rabbits living outside will vary with geographical region. Choosing the correct fencing for your area will be the key to having a safe enclosure for a group of rabbits. I have lived in the country for over 35 years, and base the following recommendations for people living in areas with high predator populations on my own personal experience in fencing various predators out. I recommend extending hardware cloth 24 inches into the ground below the perimeter fencing to deter predators from digging in (and rabbits out), and also recommend the fencing be a minimum of 6' 8" high. Foxes, dogs and coyotes are capable of leaping up and pulling themselves over fences under this height. Fences with roller bars (sometimes called coyote rollers) on the top can also help keep dogs, coyotes, and foxes out. Electrified fencing is another option.

Raccoons can be a more difficult predator to defeat as they can climb almost anything. I have found that adding a floppy overhang works best. This is something like doing a cat fence in reverse (with the overhang outside the enclosure), only the overhang ends with 12 inches of inexpensive large-hole chicken wire that will sag if the raccoon attempts to grab it and climb over. There must be no holes in the base fencing if raccoons are common in an area; raccoons will stick their 'arms' through holes, grab prey by a leg or ear, pull the animal part they have hold of through the hole, and proceed to eat the animal alive. Another thing to watch if you have grey foxes, raccoons or felids in an area are trees: be sure no tree branches overhang your rabbit enclosure; grey foxes, raccoons and cats will enter an enclosure via overhanging branches.

Rabbits in the enclosure should have plenty of fresh water available at all times, plus hay, garden produce, and pellets provided in the hutches. Keep all feed and hay in predator-proof containers. Quan gave her rabbits a Ritz cracker a day. This was both a treat and a way for her to know if there was something wrong with the rabbit (one small cracker a day will not harm a healthy adult rabbit). As she gave each rabbit the treat she could check on the rabbit's condition, and if a rabbit did not come running for the treat when the cracker package was opened she knew she needed to check on that rabbit. Quan Meyers is retiring, and Sorelle Saidman's Rabbitats will take over educating people about keeping small groups of rabbits. See Sorelle's website: www.rabbitats.org.

Groups of rabbits do not have to be set up in rural areas. Lisa Carrara has had experience setting up a yard in Las Vegas for a small group of rabbits after what came to be called "The Accidental Rabbit Rescue." A woman who originally had one rabbit in her yard ended up with about twenty-five, at which time she contacted Best Friends Animal Society through the Community Animal Assistance Program. The staff of this program contacted Debby Widolf, who was then manager of Rabbits at Best Friends. The coordinator of the Community Animal Assistance Program in Las Vegas did not know how to trap rabbits, so Debby put her into contact with Lisa Carrara, a volunteer at the Great Bunny Rescue of 2006. The rabbits were all safely captured and altered.

Where this story is a bit different than most of this type is that the woman who had the rabbits on her property was willing for them to stay there if the yard could be set up to house them safely. Lisa designed and built a backyard habitat for the rabbits:

Housing for "The Accidental Rabbit Rescue"
by Lisa Carrara

 I didn't build traditional "housing" per se, if there is such a thing. The property in question was fairly big and the resources were limited, so I tried to provide shelter, safety, entertainment and diversity all in one using various materials. The majority of the rabbits stayed outdoors but the woman who owned the property did keep several in her house.

There was massive clutter in the yard; trash, debris, you name it, everywhere. The owner and I became pretty close as I spent a lot of time there, so eventually I was able to talk her into letting us sort, clean and dispose of everything she allowed us to. The hazardous material and trash needed to be discarded so it would be safer and cleaner for the rabbits and easier to construct more housing.

First, we worked on the patio closest to the house, using numerous sized x-pens and large used window screens that we secured together and covered with solar screen material. Inside each of the enclosures we put large tree stumps, logs and dog crates for hiding and playing places for the rabbits. Some of the large trees in the yard provided shade, but there was only one near the patio so I installed a mist system  to cover the entire patio to keep it as cool as possible. Las Vegas summers can be hot!

In one of the far corners of the yard there was an existing awning, which probably had been used to shelter horses, hay or something. The  rabbits had already dug some burrows underneath the existing pallets there, so we pulled all of them, cleaned the area, returned the pallets, and then put 1/2" plywood over them. On one side of the awning there was a chain-link fence; we lined up more plywood and large tree stumps/limbs to enclose it a little better.

At the center of the backyard was a shed. The rabbits had made a warren underneath it, and that's where the last bunny who needed altering was hiding. The shed was a disaster and the only way to reach the rabbit was to clean it out, lift it up and crawl under. It was still quite a challenge to find exactly  where the rabbit was, so I drilled several holes in the shed floor and used a flexible borescope with a camera to find him. He was the cutest, funniest, little bugger in the bunch and *not* happy about his extraction, lol.

The shed kept the rabbits as safe as possible and seemed comfortable for them, so I roughly duplicated the shed flooring in four other locations. Using 4' x 4'x 8' untreated pine posts, we placed four "beams" about two-and-a-half-feet apart and cut out sections in the beams for the rabbits to jump in and out of. Over the beams we attached a type of plywood/strand board that has radiant barrier sheathing on the top. There weren't any trees in this area of the yard, andthat's all I could think of to hopefully keep it a little cooler. Of course the nosey little critters quickly inspected each one and began burrowing underneath.

Once the housing was complete and the buns were released into the yard I knew it was only a matter of time until they started to establish territory. We were pretty nervous because we did not want any

serious fights to break out that might result in injury. The others laughed at me because I had this crazy idea to – hopefully – minimize any fighting. I'm not sure if it did any good in the long run, but it seemed to work at the time. I had this amazing dog, Dillon, who was one of the sweetest, most docile dogs I've ever seen. He loved any species of animal he had ever been around and was very submissive. He also hated any type of confrontation, to the point of getting on my lap and shivering...poor little (big) boy. My idea was to take Dillon with me in the yard when the bunnies were released, because I was certain he would never harm any of the rabbits but his presence might keep them leery enough that they would not fight much. If there was a scuffle I didn't see I knew Dillon would come running to mom and then I could stop the fighting, at least temporarily. Sure enough that's exactly what happened!

(*Note from authors: It is not ever recommended that a dog be left unsupervised with rabbits. Even without intending to a dog can seriously harm or kill a rabbit. Stay with the dog at all times he or she is with the rabbits, as Lisa stayed with Dillon.*)

CHAPTER 12: STAYING STRONG IN RESCUE

Animal rescue is not easy. Only those of us who have done it know what it is and how difficult – as well as incredibly rewarding – it can be. While I was writing this chapter my friend Meg Brown happened to read a post about people who run shelters. She read it to me, and I thought it so moving and well-written that I felt I had to get permission to include it in the book. The author, Carly Thorpe, has volunteered at shelters herself so she has first-hand knowledge. Although Carly wrote about those who run shelters and specifically about shelters for farm animals, most of what she recounts also applies to those who have rabbit shelters, and much pertains to individual rescuers as well:

Sanctuary Life

by Carly Thorpe

I've met so many animal lovers, advocates and activists recently who say it's their dream to open their own farm animal sanctuary. And I totally get it, it's mine too. But I don't think they all understand that sanctuary life is hard. It's not glamorous, romantic, or even enjoyable, sometimes. Of course it's worthwhile, but it's also incredibly difficult. And I say this as someone who hasn't even lived it full time, but as someone who only helps regularly and has seen some of the behind-the-scenes things that most people aren't aware of.

Sanctuary life is day after day of grueling physical work in sun, rain, snow, or ice. Sanctuary life is more than a full time job, with no pay, sick days, benefits, bonuses or pension. Sanctuary life is heartbreaking, recognizing the animals you can't save and losing loved ones who have been. Sanctuary life is finding unexpected injuries and deciding whether they warrant an expensive call to the vet. Sanctuary life is administering care to the animals they might not enjoy (first aid, medication, grooming) that you can't explain to them but is in their best interest. Sanctuary life is sacrificing every day luxuries most people take for granted, like sleeping in or going to a birthday party. Sanctuary life is wanting a break, and even if you have someone you trust to take care of the animals, you feel too anxious to leave them. Sanctuary life is struggling to make ends meet, giving up things you yourself might need or want in order to afford the next order of hay. Sanctuary life is seeing the worst things humans are capable of doing to animals and having to keep going even if your heart is breaking. Sanctuary life is trying to educate the public about animal exploitation without losing support of those who don't want to listen. Sanctuary life is coming to the aid of other sanctuaries, even when your own to-do list is miles long. Sanctuary life is trying to find a balance between your family, your job, your friends, and the never-ending work you do for the animals. And so much more...

It's not all pig cuddles, cow kisses, and chicken hugs. In fact, that's a very tiny piece of a huge puzzle that sanctuary owners are continuously fighting to keep together. That's why I revere them so much – they are heroes. Please be mindful when talking about sanctuary, and please support our local sanctuaries in any way that you can.

The Toll Rescue Takes and How to Cope

As is obvious from the above piece, caregivers tend to put the needs of those in their care before their own needs. (Perhaps it is telling that I have placed this chapter at the end of the book!) This phenomenon has been well-studied, both for human family caregivers and animal caregivers. But this selfless giving takes a toll.

I know only too well the toll caregiving can take. For the last 25 years my life has centered on caregiving, both for human family members (mother, brother, and father) and special-needs companion animals. I have repeatedly watched those I love decline, suffer and die, assisting them throughout. The toll it has taken has been profound, not only on my health, which dramatically deteriorated over those years, but on other aspects of my life. Friendships have dropped by the wayside, either because I did not have time to nurture them or because the other party did not like being around a person so involved in decline and death; pastimes important to me (e.g. gardening) have suffered because I did not have enough time to devote to them, and vacation breaks have been almost nonexistent because I had no one to take my place and do the caregiving should I be absent.

Rescuers have additional difficulties too, because we must so often deal with the horrible results of human cruelty and neglect on companion animals, and afterwards must dredge up the strength to go on and keep rescuing and keep dealing with the horrors time after time. Not only that, rescuers must often be courteous and friendly to the persons they are trying to rescue the rabbits from in order to have a chance of getting the rabbits away from a bad situation; a necessity which can be extremely stressful.

Once the rabbits have been rescued the caregiving begins, for many rescued rabbits require medical treatment, some long-term. It is difficult not to become emotionally attached to the rabbits one caregives, and this adds another dimension of stress if many of them die before they can be placed into new homes and have a chance at a good life. It can be very difficult to forget some of the things a person sees and deals with as a rescuer and caregiver. I feel it worth repeating the following paragraph from Lisa Carrara's Reno story:

> For a reason I'm not sure of, I was always drawn to a playpen which held seventeen babies that were approximately two weeks old. I would cry when I stood over them, knowing that they were suffering. I have never found the words to depict how devastating this was to me. I had horrible nightmares for many years after completing my part in this rescue.

Debby Widolf also found that some difficult Reno memories could not be forgotten:

> Several months after leaving Reno I was at a dance workshop and needed fresh air and went outside during a break. I glanced at the sidewalk and there lay a Wrigley's chewing gum wrapper. In an instant the wrapper flashed in my mind as one of the many dead rabbit babies I picked up from the ground in the Reno backyard. I understood then what flashbacks are. There is always, however, collateral beauty. Remember it.

Healing can be found. Debby finds healing in remembering the beauty, Lisa finds healing in her memories of the rabbits she helped; I am finding healing in writing this book, and I always find peace in my rabbits and the other animals with whom I share my life. I've also found making friends in the rescue and caregiving communities helps, because they understand. People who have not rescued and have not caregiven cannot understand however hard they may try.

Debby Widolf offers her suggestions for dealing with the aftermath of a difficult rescue:

Staying grounded, continuing on in rescue. I will speak only to my own emotional struggles during the Reno rescue, its aftermath and healing, as it is a very personal journey we must all travel in our own way. I know that all of you involved in animal rescue will have similar stories to tell. Reno had hundreds of stories. Rescue work will be one of the hardest journeys you could undertake and the one you will be most grateful for experiencing. I certainly found it life changing. The early weeks in Reno were physically challenging for me and that was compounded by the emotional stress. Despite years of rabbit rescue on a small scale, I was not prepared for a rescue of this size and operation. There were times when I felt powerless, unheard, and doubted my own knowledge and ability to make the wisest decisions. Other days, things moved too fast for me, decisions were made by others that I disagreed with or did not understand.

During an early two weeks stay in Reno, the daily morning task for my co-worker and I was to comb the property and pick up the rabbits that had died the night before. Most of the dead were newborns that were birthed out in the open yard. My highest death count one morning was 45 little ones and a few adults. We did what was in front of us; what was needed and required, but the stress caused some meltdowns. Best Friends wisely rotated employees in Reno, which was helpful in those early raw months. One thing that helped a co-worker and me was to go late night shopping after our long day ended. Trader Joe's never looked so good! I immersed myself in the color of fresh produce and blooming orchids. Life was continuing, and the rabbits were being helped to a better existence.

In summary, I will say that healing for the rescue worker may not come easily and will require work, as it did for me. You may have to reach, search to find your peace. Over the ten years post-Reno I used art to heal and restore. I felt the need to honor the rabbits lost and wanted them to be remembered. If you visit Angel's Rest Pet Cemetery at Best Friends Animal Society, you will see a headstone for the Reno rabbits and a large mosaic that I made of a brave boy named "Lego" as a memorial. When the tenth anniversary of the Reno rescue was close, I again used art to help me celebrate their lives. I folded 1250 origami rabbits, one for each rabbit removed from J's backyard. I hung them from paper umbrellas and felt their spirits as I stood underneath. I believe the rabbits send their gratitude to the many that gave unselfishly to their care. I know this is true; the love they left in my life opened the way for me to love more. Godspeed everyone.

Two highly qualified individuals experienced in the field of rescue have generously donated pieces for this chapter: Davida Kobler, who has a BSN in Nursing and a MSW in Social Work and has been a rabbit rescuer and an Educator, Fosterer, and Chapter Manager in the House Rabbit Society for over twenty-five years; and Dr. Linda R. Harper, clinical psychologist, author, speaker, and founder of Blessed Bonds, a foster-based program that keeps people and pets together. I think their contributions make the perfect end to the book.

Compassion Fatigue

by Davida Kobler, BA, BSN, MSW

Compassion Fatigue was initially described by Figley and Roop, as a consequence experienced by caregivers, as natural, expected, preventable and understandable. Whereas Post Traumatic Stress Disorder is primary and is defined as the individual's first-hand experience of trauma, Compassion Fatigue is secondary and generated from being recurrently exposed to the trauma of others. Most crucial is the concept of trauma stewardship, described by Laura vanDernoot Lipsky in Trauma Stewardship as referring "to the entire conversation about how we come to do the work, how we are affected by it, and how we make sense of and learn from our experiences."

We each come to animal rescue work for our own reasons. Perhaps we wish to educate that animals love unconditionally, they provide a myriad of health benefits, that it is morally reprehensible to exploit, or injure, or neglect those who depend upon us. Our level of involvement varies depending on time and physical and financial constraints, our networks and our access to support. No matter what the driving force, nor the ability to participate, we all desire to make some difference. What we may not expect is that in accepting this labor of love, we face challenges which may derail us unless we understand the process and have avenues with which to validate our efforts.

Many volunteers start out with the best of intentions, participate for a short interval, and fizzle because of the difficulties inherent in the work. For some, the anticipated joy of the work is dashed by the ugly reality of the cruelty, ignorance, lack of empathy, and often mind-boggling conditions we see. Being a rescuer for any significant amount of time involves not just ideals and dedication but being able to face heartbreaking scenarios without coming apart emotionally, understanding that in many cases, neglect/cruelty or hoarding is allowed to exist and continue because either protection laws are poorly defined, inadequate, or those charged to enforce are sometimes not trained properly and usually not backed up by any legal consequences when the perpetrators face a judge. I have dealt with superb Humane Investigators as well as one who told me that the humane laws in New York State did not cover rabbits, because "rabbits are not mammals" (his words). One huge cruelty case in which we assisted, in 2004, involving five humane investigators, volunteers from multiple organizations, confiscation of the remaining live and injured rabbits, evidence taken of the large number of bones and carcasses on the property, resulted in an anticipated 90+ counts of misdemeanor animal cruelty towards the perpetrator. Even after depositions were given, the case was dropped because the DA thought it insignificant to prosecute.

Such outcomes allow horrible abandonment, cruelty and hoarding situations to thrive, often frustrate rescuers beyond words. We grieve for the animals suffering; we lose sleep, neglect ourselves, feel (justifiable) anger at the people who create the suffering. How do we cope and not destroy ourselves?

We can start by being mindful – of our own emotions, of our purpose, of the indisputable reality that whatever we try to do we ARE making some difference. Large victories are rarely ours to claim, but the small victories (the "starfish stories") have a cumulative effect. We need to be realistic about the time and effort we can commit, understand that flexibility is often key, and reach out for support from those who share our experience and can validate us. We value the volunteers with whom we share our commitment, at every level of participation, and we must network with other rescues, to assist in larger scale confiscations. If we can individually recognize what we are experiencing and feeling as real, valid, and understandable, we can manage our own Compassion Fatigue.

Personally, I use that starfish analogy. It helps me to think back to how many rabbits we made a difference for in the last month, or year, or whatever time frame. I reach out to friends, co-rescuers, for support, and to support them. I am thankful for our local volunteers who make this lifesaving possible; without them there would be no fostering, no rescuing on site, no educating. And I have my heroes, those who never cease to amaze me, even in the face of adversity – the rescuers whom I admire for their ceaseless selflessness and drive, the vets who help us perform miracles. But what pushes Compassion Fatigue away when rescue work becomes overwhelming, more than anything else, is to hold and look into the eyes of the rescued bunnies who own me.

Facing the Inevitable Challenge of Grief Overload
by Linda R. Harper, Ph.D.

Saying goodbye to our beloved bunny friends is an inevitable part of the journey of the compassionate heart. Since you will connect with many rabbits, some directly under your care, in your home, and others that evoke your love and concern from a distance, you are likely to experience the grief of loss multiple times in your life. Cumulative grief is defined as a lasting sadness from multiple and frequent loss. In other words, Grief Overload! What can you do to begin to heal, find peace, and continue to do the lifesaving work that you love?

1. Honor your feelings. It is normal for animal lovers to report feeling deep pain when they lose an animal companion. Rescuers feel heartbroken when they are not able to save a rabbit in need. Feeling deeply sad, distressed, and empty are normal responses of a compassionate heart. Accept the feelings one day at a time. The love that you and your rabbit friends have shared has grown inside of you and will continue to give you the strength you need to get through these challenging times.

2. Listen to what you need to heal. It will be different for each of us. For example, some people want to take a day off work while others may prefer to work extra days. Some people may put more pictures up while others may prefer no reminders. On some days you may want to talk about your sadness, and other times you may want to just be alone. Listen to what your heart needs without judgment.

3. Observe your thoughts without believing them. It is normal to experience guilt and regret from thinking about the

past and wishing the loss did not occur. There can be an over-focus on the details and what you think went wrong. Dwelling on the past, along with thoughts anticipating your inability to face the future, can get in the way of the healing process. You can choose to let go of the thoughts that block your peace of mind. Here are some examples of how you can replace peace-blocking thoughts with peace-restoring thoughts:

Peace-Blocking Thoughts vs.	Peace-Restoring Thoughts
It takes a long time to feel joy again.	I can also feel joy NOW –along with sadness.
A terrible thing happened to ME!	I am facing a challenging aspect of loving animals
I must keep telling the detailed story.	I can choose how I tell this story.
I need others to understand to heal.	Self-compassion is always available and heals.
I must address all my thoughts that come.	I will honor my feelings, & question my thoughts.
I am helpless to the replay of sad images.	I can choose the images I want to focus on.
I must fully let go of this rabbit forever.	I can choose to connect in a new way.
If I am not sad enough, I didn't love enough	I can celebrate a life with joy!
I need to "get over this."	All experiences are part of the Journey.

4.   Stay connected to the work you love: take time to enjoy your own furry family and the bunnies you are helping. Be open to the support your like-minded friends and co-workers offer. Embrace all the new experiences ahead: Yes, there are challenges but also take in the adventure, the love, and that deep feeling of fulfillment. There is always joy in our journey with the animals. Every time we allow ourselves to find it, we are paying tribute to their lives.

Finally, remember that you honor those who have passed on by continuing to work together to change the conditions for rabbits and giving them a chance for a better life. Compassion toward yourself, others, and the world, are all part of the same love that will continue to grow and move us closer to our shared vision of a kinder world for all living beings.

APPENDIX I: RESOURCES

Websites

These two websites are recommended for information specifically on rescuing rabbits:

1) dontdumprabbits.org Articles on rabbit care, rabbit rescue and other related topics.

2) rabbitats.org The website of Rabbitats Rescue Society has information on housing abandoned rabbits as well as rescue stories and other information pertinent to rescuing rabbits, especially large colonies.

The following websites are highly recommended for information on rescue in general, fundraising, legal issues related to animals and rescue, and trap-neuter-return:

1) Best Friends Animal Society www.bestfriends.org/

2) Humane Society of the United States www.humanesociety.org/

3) American Society for the Prevention of Cruelty to Animals www.aspca.org (look under ASPCA pro sections)

4) Alley Cat Allies www.alleycat.org

Rabbit Tracking Map

There is a great tool for rescuers, a "Rabbit Tracking Map" on the site www.abandonedrabbits.com that flags abandoned rabbits, feral colonies, and RHD virus deaths. At the time of this writing it only covers parts of western Canada, but it will be expanded to cover the US and abroad. People are able to report sightings through a form on the website. Eventually Sorelle Saidman, who put up the map, plans to have it set up to track rabbit colony size increase and decrease, and for people to be able to list a single stray rabbit, its location, and if rescued.

Workshop

Best Friends Animal Society conducts an excellent workshop, "How to start and run an animal sanctuary," three times a year. Information presented at the workshop is varied and is useful to those who already have a rescue as well as those desiring to start a rescue. People who do not have a rescue but volunteer at one or who rescue animals on their own will also benefit from the workshop.

https://bestfriends.org/events/workshops/how-start-and-run-animal-sanctuary

APPENDIX II: Low-Cost Spay and Neuter Clinics
by Judy Books

I have created a state-by-state list of contacts for those looking to find lower cost surgery options for their rabbits. This list is just a start. It is based on research over the past year or two, on contacts I have made with other rescue organizations, shelters, and the website wabbitwiki.com. Due to the immense scope of this project, I cannot assure everyone that the information is completely current or up-to-date. But at least what is provided is a start. Please also note that what is provided is a listing only. I cannot testify to the credibility or professional experience of any vet or clinic shown here.

When considering the option of using a listed resource, remember that cost should never be the only consideration in selecting professional medical care for rabbits. Experience is equally, if not more, important. I hope the following listing, as preliminary as it is, will serve to benefit many people who have rabbits still in need of this surgery, and that it will be shared widely.

For those readers who are relatively new to rabbits: Spaying or neutering a rabbit offers numerous benefits for both a caregiver and his or her companion. Many people end up neglecting, abandoning, or simply surrendering their companions to shelters and rescue groups because they have not had their rabbits spayed or neutered.

Rabbits that have not had this surgery tend to develop unwelcome behavior patterns as they mature, such as acting territorial, nipping, spraying, circling and mounting their caregiver's legs, or becoming otherwise aggressive. Without this surgery, female rabbits have a high likelihood of developing uterine or other reproductive cancer. In addition, both male and female rabbits are more difficult to litter box train if they are not spayed or neutered.

Yet many people may choose to delay or even skip this procedure due to what can be the prohibitively high costs for the surgery. There are also those who never learn of the benefits or who believe the surgery is unsafe. These same individuals have never heard of low cost spay and neuter clinics that work with rabbits, and they don't know that the surgery is safe when done by vets that are experienced in the care of exotic animals, like rabbits; a vet that normally only cares for dogs and cats is not considered experienced enough to do the surgery safely.

Alabama
No known clinics at this time.

Alaska
Anchorage Animal Hospital, Anchorage, AK
907-563-2305

Alaska SPCA Spay/Neuter Clinic, Anchorage, AK
907-562-2999
(may only be neutering rabbits at this time, please check with staff to confirm)

Friends of Pets Anchorage, AK
907-562-2535

Homer Animal Friends, Homer, AK
907-235-SPAY

SOS (Save Our Steward) Pets
Steward, AK 907-224-7495

Gastineau Humane Society
Juneau, AK 907-789-0260

Ballaine Veterinary Clinic
898 Ballaine Rd., Fairbanks, AK
907-479-3641

Mt. McKinley Animal Hospital
425 Harold Bentley Ave., Fairbanks, AK
907-452-6104
(may not be the least expensive in the area, but the clinic apparently has a phenomenal small animal specialist and multiple vets that care for rabbits – also, their prices are considered still to be less than the lower 48 states)

Arizona
North Phoenix Spay & Neuter Clinic ,1610 E. Bell Rd., Suite 108, Phoenix, AZ
602-787-4240 Spay $79 – Neuter $69

Arizona Spay & Neuter Clinic, 6835 E. Thomas Rd. Scottsdale, AZ
480-947-4270, Spay $70 – Neuter $58

Arkansas
No known clinics at this time.

California, Northern:

Alameda County
For Paws Spay and Neuter Clinic, 40501 B Fremont Blvd, Fremont, CA
510-573-4660 By appointment: Monday & Wednesday 9am – 6pm
$125-150 female, $100-120 male
Females: Must be 4 months, Males: Must have visible testicles

Contra Costa County
House Rabbit Society – Rabbit Spay/Neuter Clinic, 148 Broadway,
Richmond, CA 94804. 510-970-7575
2018: SURGERY SPACE CHANGE, NOT CURRENTLY BOOKING
APPOINTMENTS

Santa Clara County
Humane Society Silicon Valley, 901 Ames Ave., Milpitas, CA 95035
(408) 262-2133 x108, $160 female/male, Available to anyone
By appointment: Monday-Saturday. Drop-off 6:30-7:30am, pick-up 4-6pm.
1. Call or come in to the medical center to schedule your appointment.
2. A non-refundable deposit is required to hold your appointment date.
3. Rabbits must be in carriers.
4. Please let us know if your pet has any medical conditions or is currently
taking any medication.
5. Rabbits must be at least 3.5 lbs and six months of age

San Mateo County
Peninsula Humane Society, 12 Airport Drive, San Mateo, CA
650-340-7022, $100 female, $70 male, Available to anyone
By appointment: Monday-Friday 7am-6pm

Marin County
Marin Humane Society, 171 Bel Marin Keys Blvd, Novato, CA
415-506-6268,$75 female/male (includes microchip)
By appointment: Mondays, Available to anyone

Sonoma County
Montecito Veterinary Center, 4900 Sonoma Hwy, Santa Rosa, CA 95409
707-539-2322, $113 male, $178 female + new patients must also pay for initial
vet visit, to ensure rabbit is healthy & ready for surgery: $61
Available to anyone

Napa County
Humane Society of Napa County, 3265 California Blvd, Napa
707-252-7442, $75 male/female (microchip with registration available for $11)
By appointment: Monday, Tuesday, Thursday, Friday, 8:30-4:30
Available to anyone

Sacramento County
Sacramento SPCA, 6201 Florin Perkins Road, Sacramento, CA
916-383-7387, By appointment: Monday – Friday 7:15am-5:30pm
$130 female/male, Available to anyone

Placer County
Placer SPCA. Voucher program – surgeries at participating Placer County
veterinarians, $30-35 female, $20 male, Placer County residents only

San Francisco
No known clinics at this time.

Santa Cruz County
Santa Cruz County Animal Shelter: PlannedPetHood, 2200 7th Ave., Santa
Cruz, CA, 580 Airport Blvd, Watsonville, CA, $75 female/male +$10
microchip required). First-come, first-served – sign up in person at either
Santa Cruz County Animal Shelter location. Santa Cruz County residents only

Friends of Santa Cruz County Animals: Vouchers
Free voucher for low-income Santa Cruz County Residents (see income
thresholds).

California, Southern:

San Diego House Rabbit Society offers a list of low-cost spay and neuter
clinics on their website. They also offer a rebate program for those who have
this surgery. For more information, please visit their website link:
http://www.sandiegorabbits.org/vete...

BunnyBunch
http://www.bunnybunch.org/spayneuter2.html

Many clinics also listed near the bottom of this website page link:
http://wabbitwiki.com/wiki/California

Colorado
htt p://color adoanimalwelfare.or g/.../wher e-can-i-find-low-co.../

Humane Society of Boulder Valley, 2323 55th Street Boulder, CO
303-442-4030
http://www.boulderhumane.org/pet-he.../spay-neuter-information

Downtown Animal Care Center, 1041 Galapago St., Denver, CO
303-595-3561. Special pricing also available for rescue groups who are
501(c)3's and hold a PACFA license.

Spay Today, Neuter Now! 1864 S. Wadsworth Blvd #2, Lakewood, CO
303-984-SPAYhttp://www.spay2day.org/services.html

Connecticut
House Rabbit Connection
Email: info@hopline.org for more information and to apply

This clinic does not offer "low-cost" surgeries, however, their fee is
considered quite reasonable in comparison to others:
Quinebaug Valley Vet Hospital, Danielson, CT. 860-774-7650 qwh.com

Delaware
No known clinics at this time.

Florida:

Broward
Humane Society of Broward County SPOT Program
http://www.humanebroward.com/http://www.broward.org/ANIMAL/PRO
GR...

Ft. Pierce
Tri-County Animal Hospital, Fort Pierce, FL 34950, 772-461-1311
Tri-County Animal Hospital is a bit north but when the other clinics are full it
may be worth the drive if you need to get your bunny fixed quickly.

Tampa
Animal Coalition of Tampa
http://animalcoalitionoftampa.org/

Several clinics are also listed near the bottom of this website's page:
http://wabbitwiki.com/wiki/Florida

Miami area:
http://www.projectpetsnip.com/

Georgia
Windward Animal Hospital. Stewart Colby, DVM. (770) 569-7298
11895 Jones Bridge Road, Alpharetta, GA 30005

Hawaii
The Animal CARE Foundation of Hawai'i
6650 Hawaii Kai Drive, Suite 105, Honolulu, HI, 808-396-3333

Idaho
Idaho Humane Society, 4775 Dorman St., Boise, ID, 208-342-3508

Illinois
Check the following website for clinics that work with rabbits:
http://www.spayillinois.org/find-a-clin.../s pay-neuter-clinic/

Fox Valley Animal Welfare League. Surgeon: Susan A. Brown, DVM
11 John Street, North Aurora, IL 60542, 630-800-2254. Please see website for
surgery schedules and more information on pricing and procedures:
www.fvawl.org

Hartz Second Chance. Dr. Megan Baebler, 119 United Drive, Collinsville, IL
62234, 618-975-4434

Vanderburgh Humane Society, Inc. 400 Millner Industrial Dr., Evansville, IN
812-426-2563.
htt p://www.vhs lifes aver .or g/r es our ces /news   detail.html...
Available to anyone who can drive to their clinic Surgeries are $75, for either
males or females. No other fees apply.

Animal Care League, 1011 Garfield St., Oak Park, IL 708-848-8155

Wonder Lake Veterinary Clinic, 4405 E. Wonder Lake Rd, Wonder Lake, IL
815-653-3586

Indiana
Vanderburgh Humane Society, Inc., 400 Millner Industrial Dr., Evansville, IN
Available to anyone who can drive to their clinic Surgeries are $75, for either
males or females. No other fees apply. Clinic information is listed here:
htt p://www.vhs lifes aver .or g/r es our ces /news   detail.html... 812-426-
2563

S.P.O.T. Spay & Neuter, 612 S. Main St., Cloverdale, IN
765-795-4336

Iowa
Iowa Humane Alliance Regional Spay/Neuter Clinic
6540 6th St SW, Cedar Rapids, IA, 319-363-1225

Kansas
No known clinics at this time.

Kentucky
Vanderburgh Humane Society, Inc., 400 Millner Industrial Dr., Evansville, IN
812-426-2563.
Available to anyone who can drive to their clinic. Surgeries are $75, for either
males or females. No other fees apply. Clinic information is listed here:
http://www.vhs lifes aver .or g/r es our ces /news   detail.html...

Lexington Humane Society, 1600 Old Frankfort Pike, Lexington, KY
859-233-0044

Louisiana
Azalea Lakes Veterinary Clinic, 15225 Jefferson Hwy., Baton Rouge, LA
225-755-3838. Customers can get a $20 coupon in addition to the discounted
rate from Magic Happens Rabbit Rescue

Jefferson SPCAFix-A-Rabbit Program
Offers low cost spay & neuter for rabbit caregivers in Jefferson Parish only.
www.jeffersonspca.org/low-cost-rabbit-spayneuter.

Maine
The Animal Refuge League of Greater Portland,
449 Stroudwater St., Westbrook, ME
207-854-9771 ext. 400

Maryland
Please see this link for some low cost opportunities in the state...
http://rabbitsinthehouse.org/?page ...

Massachusetts
House Rabbit Connection
Email: info@hopline.org for more information and to apply.

MSPCA – Angell (Boston, MA) sometimes offers low-cost clinics, please see
the following website link for contact information and to get more
information: https://www.mspca.org/contact-us/

Country Cat Clinics, 1 Fruit Street, Westboro, MA (508) 322-1788
They spay/neuter cats, rabbits, dogs and other critters. They rent space at a local clinic. Get specific directions when booking an appointment.

Pet Partners Veterinarian, Dr. Debra Gehrke, DVM
139 Shaw St., Fall River, MA 02724, 508/672-4813
General Information: info@petpartnersne.org

Dakin Pioneer Valley Humane Society, Leverett, MA

Animal Rescue League of Fall River – Sylvan Animal Clinic
474 Durfee St., Fall River, MA 508-679-6122

Michigan
http://www.allaboutanimalsrescue.org/spay-michigan/

Cedar Animal Hospital (offers surgery at a reasonable cost), Dr. Nauta. Cedar Springs, MI

Cedar Creek Veterinary Clinic, 2295 N. Williamston Rd ,Williamston, MI 517-655-4906

Minnesota
Mobile Clinics (only eligible for low-income individuals)
Kindest Cut Services the Minneapolis/St. Paul, Minn. area. 763-489-7729

Minnesota SNAP
612-720-8236

Mississippi
No known clinics at this time.

Missouri
No known clinics at this time.

Montana
No known clinics at this time.

Nebraska
No known clinics at this time.

Nevada
Bonanza Cat Hospital. Dr. Lemmon (retired vet does surgery on Tuesdays)
6620 Sky Pointe Dr., Las Vegas, NV, Phone: 702 438-7000
Cost is $50 per spay/neuter

New Hampshire
Animal Rescue Veterinary Services.
194 Rockingham Road, Londonderry, NH 03053, (603) 425-3928.
Dr. Kim Trahan
http://www.arvsonline.org/spay-neuter/This is a spay and neuter only clinic
and they do spay/neuter rabbits.

Fremont Animal Hospital, 125 South Rd, Fremont, NH 03044 (603) 895-0618
Controlling Overpopulation Pet Services,
15-05 Warwick Rd., Winchester, NH 603-239-3133

New Jersey
Please see the following website for a listing of participating vets that
participate in NJ House Rabbit Society's lower cost Spay/Neuter Program:
http://www.njhrs.com/spayneuter.htm.
Those wishing to participate should visit this website first to understand how
to purchase and use a certificate.

All Pets Low Cost Spay Neuter Mobile Clinic. Dr. Lori Duggan, VMD
Check https://m.facebook.com/AllPetsLowCostclinics/?fref=pb&hc_loc
for locations, dates, and registration information.

New Mexico
Santa Fe Animal Shelter & Humane Society offers low-cost spay/neuter clinic
for rabbits by appointment only. $75 spay /$50 neuter, rabbits must be at least
6 months old.
http://sfhumanesociety.org/animal-h.../s payneuter vaccinations /

New York
The Center for Avian and Exotic Medicine,
562 Columbus Ave., New York, NY, 212-501-9281

The Humane Society in NYC
http://www.humanesocietyny.org/about/services.php - make sure you ask for
Dr. Malka – he is the only rabbit-savvy vet here presently

North Carolina
http://www.spayneutercarolinas.com/

Low cost spay and neuter vouchers can be purchased through the SPCA of
Wake County. Here is the website with more details on this program:
htt p://s pcawc.convio.net/.../Spay% 2.../Spay Neuter mainpage.html

Once purchased, these vouchers can be used at the following two hospitals:

1. Animal Kingdom Veterinary Hospital, 329-G N. Harrison Avenue, Cary, NC 27513, 919-460-9111
2. Dixie Trail Animal Hospital, 3044 Medlin Drive, Raleigh, NC 27607. 919-781-5977

SNIP Regional Spay/Neuter, 131 Crosslake Park Drive, Building 200, Suite 206, Mooresville, NC, 704-799-7647

Spay and Neuter Clinic of the Carolinas, 8045 Providence Rd, Suite 450, Charlotte, NC, 704-542-9997

North Dakota
No known clinics at this time.

Ohio
Please also see the bottom of this website page for a list of participating clinics: http://wabbitwiki.com/wiki/Ohio

Oklahoma
No known clinics at this time.

Oregon
Rabbit Advocates will provide up to $100/$150 reimbursement upon request for neuters/spays for the general public. Rabbit Advocates strongly suggests taking your bunny to a rabbit-savvy veterinarian for any medical issue, including spays and neuters.
Please see the Rabbit Advocates website for more information:
http://www.rabbitadvocates.org/
Rabbit Advocates, PO Box 14235, Portland, Oregon. 503-617-1625

Pennsylvania
Please see the bottom of this website page for a listing of participating clinics:
http://wabbitwiki.com/wiki/Pennsylvania

Animal Friends, 562 Camp Horne Road, Pittsburgh, PA, 412-847-7000
http://www.thinkingoutsidethecage.org/site/c.elKWIeOUIhJ6H/b.9244089/k.9C4E/Pricing_Guide.htm

Rhode Island
Providence Animal Rescue League, 34 Elbow St. Providence, RI
401-421-1399

South Carolina
Birds and Exotics Animal Care, 814 Johnnie Dodds Blvd, Mount Pleasant, SC
843-216-8387

Spartanburg Humane Society, 150 Dexter Rd, Spartanburg, SC, 864-583-4805
(has plans to begin offering this service soon, please contact them to see when
or if this service is offered)

South Dakota
No known clinics at this time.

Tennessee
No known clinics at this time.

Texas
Please see the bottom of this website page for a listing of participating clinics:
http://wabbitwiki.com/wiki/Texas

Kingsland Blvd. Animal Clinic. Dr. Richard Croft, 20701 Kingsland Blvd.
Suite 105, Katy, TX 77450, 281-578-1506.
Please note: This clinic does not offer "low-cost" services, however, their charge
for this surgery may be considered quite reasonable. The cost of a neuter is
$95, and the cost of a spay is $222).

Utah
Spay and Neuter of Salt Lake City, 160 East 4800 South, Salt Lake City, UT
801-262-6414

Vermont
No known clinics at this time.

Virginia
Blue Ridge Veterinary Associates. Drs. Valerie Campbell & W. Behm
120 East Cornwell St., Purcellville, VA, 540-338-
7387http://www.blueridgevets.com/
Note: BRVA provides low-cost spays/neuters only via 'Spay Today' vouchers.
You can go to www.nhes.org or call (304) 728-8330 for details about how to
purchase them. Please see the bottom of this website page for a listing of
participating clinics: http://wabbitwiki.com/wiki/Virginia

Washington
Please go to the bottom of this website page for a listing of participating
clinics: http://wabbitwiki.com/wiki/Washington

West Virginia
Briggs Animal Adoption Center Spay Today program:
http://www.baacs.org/sections/view/179 (based in VA, but can benefit residents of W. Virginia as well)

Spay Today's low cost program is available with participating vets, including Blue Ridge Veterinary Associates, 120 East Cornwell Lane, Purcellville, VA 540-338-7387 http://www.blueridgevets.com/

Wisconsin
No known clinics at this time.

Wyoming
No known clinics at this time.

APPENDIX III: ANTIPARASITIC AGENTS

AVERMECTINS

Selamectin, ivermectin, and doramectin fall into this class. Moxidectin (a milbemycin) is a close relative. Ivermetin is reported to give good control of the *Psoroptes* mite, but is not as effective as selamectin for *Cheyletiella* mites. The combination of moxidectin and imidacloprid is effective on both mites. Both ivermectin and selamectin can be given prophylactically to rabbits to control flystrike by blowflies and bot flies, but imidacloprid has been found to be more effective. Selamectin will kill fleas, but a researcher found a higher dose is needed (15-20mg/kg). Selamectin was found to be less effective against sarcoptic mange in the ears of Angora rabbits than was doramectin following moxidectin. The avermectins are also reported to kill ticks.

BENZIMIDAZOLES

The benzimidazoles, especially fenbendazole and albendazole are sometimes prescribed for EC. A combination of fenbendazole and ponazuril (see triazines below) is preferred by some veterinarians.

NEONICOTINOIDS

Imidacloprid and nitenpyram fall into this class. Nitenpyram is sometimes prescribed for flea control, as is an imidacloprid/moxidectin combination. Both treatments are generally safe for rabbits, although some vets have reported occasional sensitivity to nitenpyram in rabbits. The imidacloprid/moxidectin combination is also reported to be effective against flies (blowflies and bot flies), mites, and ticks.

SULPHONAMIDES

Frequently used coccidiostats. Sulfaquinoxaline is reported to be the only one effective against hepatic coccidiosis, and the most effective against intestinal coccidiosis as well. It may be added to rabbits' water at 1-3mg per liter water. Sulfamethazine, sulfamethoxine, and sulfadimerazine are also prescribed for intestinal coccidiosis, but effectiveness is variable and coccidia are sometimes resistant. All may be added to rabbits' water. Trimethoprim/sulfamethoxazole, given orally, may be prescribed to control coccidia in individual rabbits.

TRIAZINE DERIVATIVES

Toltrazuril and ponazuril (Marquis) fall into this category. Toltrazuril is a highly effective coccidiostat, especially when used with ivermectin, but at the time of this writing is not available in the US. Ponazuril may be prescribed for use in combating EC, sometimes in conjunction with fenbendazole.

APPENDIX IV: SIGNS OF SELECTED DIGESTIVE DISORDERS

	Acute bloat, total blockage*	Severe GI hypomotility	Non-obstructive GI hypomotility**
Pain	Sudden onset of signs of acute pain	Rabbit may have been exhibiting signs of pain, now pain is acute	Gradual onset of pain as condition advances
Abdominal distension	Abdomen swells rapidly, becomes tight and balloon-like (or doughy if rupture has occurred).	Abdomen may have been larger than normal; now becomes tight and distended.	Gradual distension of abdomen. May be few to no stomach sounds.
Fecal pellets	All fecal production suddenly ceases.	Fecal pellets decrease in # and size; then suddenly cease.	Fecal pellets gradually decrease in number and size.
Food consumption	Rabbit suddenly stops eating; will not even accept favorite treats.	Rabbit may not have had much appetite; then stops eating at all.	Rabbit will at first continue to eat, often preferring fresh greens and hay.
Water consumption	Rabbit suddenly stops drinking	Rabbit may not have been drinking much, now stops.	Rabbit drinks normally at first; then intake decreases or increases.
Body temperature	Usually low; 99° or less.	Usually low; 99° or less.	May be normal or below normal.
General demeanor (affect)	Extremely depressed; may sit hunched/ grinding teeth.	Extremely depressed; may sit hunched and unmoving, grinding teeth.	May be alert or depressed, active or inactive.
Other clinical signs	Rapid heart/ respiration rates, shock	Shock	No specific

Note: Signs may overlap and vary in specific cases. This chart is provided only to give readers an idea of possible symptom (sign) differences among the listed digestive disorders.

*Acute bloat and blockage is a serious medical emergency

Intestinal dysbiosis	Cecal Dysbiosis***	Cecal Impaction
Varies from no signs of pain to signs of severe pain	Usually none unless cause other than diet.	Gradual onset of pain as condition worsens
May be some abdominal distension from gas	Usually none unless cause other than diet.	As the condition develops a hard mass can be felt in abdomen. This can cause rabbit to look "lopsided" viewed from back.
Watery or mucoid diarrhea is often (but not always) present.	Cecotrophs may be unusually large, soft, and malformed	Reduced or none produced as condition advances. May void mucus.
Often ceases to eat normally.	Appetite usually normal unless cause is other than diet	May eat tiny amounts or pick food up and drop it without eating.
Variable	Water consumption usually normal unless cause is other than diet	May be reduced.
May fall below normal.	Usually normal unless cause is other than diet	May fall below normal.
Lethargic	Usually normal unless cause is other than diet	Lethargic; may sit in hunched position.
Shock	No specific	No specific

**Non-obstructive GI hypomotility is the GI disorder usually referred to as "stasis," although the term is an inaccurate one that is commonly used to encompass many of the listed digestive disorders, each of which requires a different medical treatment.

***Most cecal dysbiosis is caused by alterations in diet or routine, but there are several more serious possible causes, Soft, mushy cecotrophs are not "diarrhea" – true diarrhea is a medical emergency in a rabbit and requires prompt veterinary attention.

APPENDIX V: AN EIGHTEENTH-CENTURY LAGOMORPH ADVOCATE

Rescuing and keeping lagomorphs as companions in the home is not a new practice, although sometimes we may like to feel we are amongst the pioneers. Rabbits and/or hares were kept as valued indoor pets in Renaissance Italy and in other countries over the last centuries by various persons who recognized and appreciated the delightful qualities of rabbits and their kin. One of these was William Cowper (1731-1800): poet, hymn-writer, and keen observer of the natural world. I first wrote the story below for inclusion in a book I did with Kathy Smith, but I felt it appropriate to include in this volume for a bit of fun and to show that reasons for giving up a pet lagomorph have not changed over the last 300 years – Cowper's first hare companion came to him because children tired of their pet. The following account, although containing fictionalized details and conversation to make it into a readable story, is based on Cowper's own words.

Three Hares and a Gentleman Poet

by Lucile Moore

William Cowper's quill pen scratched erratically across the page. "With few associates, and not..." The quill stopped. "And not...and not...and not what?" Cowper muttered, and irritably shot the pen back into the inkstand. It was no use. The melancholy which had set in after his brother's death two years ago had still not lifted. The words would not flow. It was useless to even try to write. He put his face in his hands and gave in to his dejection, becoming lost in a swirling world of dark thoughts.

"Beg pardon, your honour," a voice roused Cowper.

"Yes, what is it Coleman?" Cowper asked his servant with a touch of irascibility, raising his head.

"It's your neighbor, your honour, come with something for you. He is waiting in the parlour."

"Tell him I will be there directly," Cowper sighed resignedly. He rose from his chair, pulled the wide cuffs of his morning coat straight, and set his shoulders determinedly as he left the room.

"Good morning John," Cowper said as he entered the parlour where his neighbor, John Newton, sat waiting with a hemp sack near his feet. The sack moved slightly.

"Good morning William," his neighbor returned the greeting, rising. "I am sorry to disturb you this early, but I have a boon to ask of you. You know my daughters were given a young hare to play with?"

Cowper nodded. He had seen the girls with the hare since midsummer. At first the tiny animal had held the girls' childish interest with its novelty. But as the weeks passed and the hare had grown they had lost interest as children will, and once but a week or so ago in September he had seen them teasing the poor creature with a stick.

"They pay it little mind any longer, and although it is but a hare, it is one of God's creatures and it has pained me to see it grow thin and ill with their teasing and neglect," John continued. "I thought you might take the poor thing and give it a home in your garden. My girls have had their amusement and are happy to relinquish him to you." He handed the sack to Cowper.

Cowper took the sturdy cloth sack and carefully peeked inside, not wishing to frighten the animal further. A thin young hare cowered at the bottom. Cowper had always had a soft spot for the wild creatures of God's marvelous creation, and the sight of the poor hare in such a state touched his heart. Certainly there was room here in Orchard Side for one small hare.

"Indeed, John. I shall be pleased to take on his care. I am rather in need of something to engage my attention at this time," he acknowledged frankly.

"God will reward you for the care of the least of His creatures," his neighbor commented piously as he straightened his hat and picked up his walking stick. "I had best return home now; I have sermons to write. Good day to you, my friend, and may God bless you."

After his neighbor left, Cowper gently carried the sack containing the hare to his large back garden, where he set it down and arranged the sack's folds so the hare could venture out when he wished. Cowper sat on his heels a few paces away, watching. In a few minutes a wiggling nose poked out, followed by two bright eyes and large pink-white ears. He looked at Cowper warily and then, apparently deciding this new being was no threat, hopped free of the sack. Cowper remained still, and the hare approached him slowly, neck outstretched, ears forward, nose wiggling. He sniffed cautiously at Cowper, then visibly relaxed and hopped slowly off to sample some of the garden's goods.

Cowper watched his new pet, feeling a connection to the young hare. His interest was engaged and he began to make plans. He would study the hare's needs, be sure they were provided for, tame it, and return it to health. Perhaps this creature was just what he needed to draw himself out of his black melancholy.

When word spread in the town that Cowper had taken in a hare and was keeping him in his garden, others came to offer young hares they had found. Cowper could not take them all, but undertook the care of two more in addition Tiney, the one he had gotten from his neighbor. The two new hares he named Puss and Bess. The poet spent hours studying the habits of the three hares so he could give them

proper care. He sought to provide them a diet that would give sufficient nutrients, beginning with wheaten bread in milk and adding oats, thistles, lettuces, twigs of hawthorn, carrots, and apple peels to their meals over time. Occasionally Cowper would leave the door to the garden open so the hares could come into the house, where he was greatly diverted by their cautious explorations. He rapidly accustomed the hares to his presence by moving slowly and quietly and talking to them in a low, gentle voice. Puss and Bess were more accepting of him than Tiney, who apparently could not forget his early teasing and totally trust a human. But Cowper loved Tiney as well as the other two, despite the occasional nips and stubborn wildness.

"Well, my friends," he commented one day early in mid-autumn as the three hares poked about his parlour, "it is time you have your own quarters here. I fear the cold of winter is just around the corner. I shall build you your own chambers so you may come inside and escape the winter cold."

A talented carpenter, Cowper enjoyed designing and constructing a wooden home with three separate chambers and a common hallway. He lined the chambers with straw for the hares' bedding and moved their new home into the parlour.

"What do you think, my friends? Are your quarters satisfactory?" he asked as the three hares thoroughly sniffed their new home and marked it as their own by rubbing their chins on all the corners. "I shall need to keep you confined in them during the day while I am busy, but you like to doze through midday in any event. I promise you that you shall have every evening to share the parlour with me and days to frolic in garden when the weather is fine."

The hare Cowper had named Puss hopped over to where Cowper sat on a chair watching them. He eyed Cowper consideringly for a moment, and then, to the poet's surprise and delight, jumped into his lap.

"Puss, Puss, you are a bold one," Cowper said, overcome by this obvious expression of gratitude on the part of the hare. Slowly, he dared to raise his hand and stroke Puss's head and back. Puss graciously allowed this intimacy for several minutes before jumping down and rejoining his companions.

The next evening, during their time out in the parlour, Cowper brought treats of carrots. Tiney, always the most cautious and fearful, snatched his carrot and ran, nipping Cowper's hand in the process, but Bess and Puss stayed close by while they munched theirs. When they had finished their treat of carrot, they stood up by Cowper's chair, resting their front paws on his legs, clearly asking for more.

"There are no more, my dears," Cowper protested, spreading his hands to show they were empty. Puss stared him in the eye and once again jumped into his lap. Cowper stroked his back, murmuring endearments. Puss relaxed, allowing the caresses with obvious pleasure, and then rose on his hind feet and nibbled on the hair falling over the poet's forehead. After a few more nibbles he settled back down into Cowper's lap and fell asleep. Had Cowper's heart not already been entirely captured by his small friends, this expression of affection would have ensured it. Nor could he help loving sweet Puss the most, although he also loved Bess for her intelligence and drollery – and Tiney for his stubborn wildness.

Puss became more and more tame, and soon Cowper was able to carry him about in his arms. Every morning the poet would carry Puss out to the garden and set him down by his favorite cucumber vine. If he was tardy in doing this, Puss would jump into the poet's lap, sit up, look him in the eye, and drum on his knee with his hind foot. The message was unmistakable: "Garden, now." Should Cowper be immersed in writing or other business and fail to take the hint, Puss would grab hold of Cowper's coat with his teeth and jerk, hard: "I said, Garden, NOW."

Delighted with this show of intelligence the first time it was exhibited, Cowper laughed, "My Puss, you well know how to communicate. Could you but hold a pen, I've no doubt you would write as succinctly."

Despite the exemplary care Cowper gave his new friends, Puss became ill one day. Not knowing what ailed his beloved hare, Cowper did the best he could to restore Puss to health, treating him with various fresh herbs and tending him with great care. Finally one morning it became obvious from Puss's increased appetite and alertness that the hare had turned the corner and would recover. As Cowper gently stroked his fur, Puss turned his head and carefully licked every inch of the poet's hand, lapping between every finger. Cowper had no doubt this was an expression of gratitude, and became more convinced than ever of the hare's basic intelligence, affection, and understanding.

Over the next few years Cowper devoted himself to his hares, finding their behavior a constant source of learning and delight. His melancholy lifted and the words began to flow again. In addition to composing his poems and hymns, Cowper, anxious to share his insights into his hare companions, wrote articles for the popular Gentlemen's Magazine in which he extolled his hares' cheerfulness, amiability, gratitude, and enjoyment of life. He became well-known for his unusual companions, and was presented with a beautiful enameled snuffbox on which were painted the portraits of the three hares. The snuffbox became one of Cowper's most prized possessions.

Every evening the hares' gamboling on the Turkish carpet in the parlour enchanted him. Cowper never tired of watching the hares as they bounded about the room, kicking their heels, doing amazing jumps and turns, and finally flopping on their sides for a rest. The poet allowed nothing to disturb this established routine, going so far as to have a town official who came to call taken up the back stairs rather than allowing him to go through the parlour and disturb the hares during their evening frolic.

But the best of care is not always enough, and after five years bold Bess died. The tears flowed freely as Cowper buried her in his garden. But although a return of melancholy threatened, Cowper knew he had to continue to care for wild Tiney and gentle Puss and could not give in to the darkness.

So life continued much as before, barring the now-empty space Bess had filled. Every evening Puss and Tiney frolicked in the parlour, and early every fine morning they foraged through the gardens – until one August morning when Puss did not come back when Cowper opened the door and called for the hares to return to the house at the usual hour of nine.

"Richard," he called his servant, "have you seen Puss? Did you by chance allow her to slip into the house earlier?"

"No, your honour," the servant replied, "but you might ask Thomas in the kitchen. Sometimes he gives them a treat of parings."

At that moment Thomas himself came puffing up the garden walk. "Yer honour, yer honour," he blurted, face red with the exertion of hurrying his well-nourished body, "it's Puss. He's got away somehow! I was coming up the street and there he was! I tried to put me hat o'er 'im to bring 'im back, but he screamed, he did, and jumped clear o'er my back and is gone toward town."

Cowper's heart stood still. Not his beloved Puss! "After him, Richard!" he commanded the younger and fitter servant. "Find him and bring him back, whatever happens."

As Richard obediently ran down the street after the escaped hare, Cowper searched the garden for a place Puss could have gotten out. He had been certain the garden was secure. But there behind some foxglove the poet found a hole chewed in the lattice, just large enough for the hare to squeeze through.

"Oh Puss," Cowper sighed. "I kept you here for your safety, but you must ever try the boundaries." Sadly he patched the hole lest Tiney should also escape, and then awaited his servant's return in the parlour, pacing back and forth in his agitation. Should he have gone to look for Puss as well? It was true enough he could not have kept up with the young servant, but in verity he had stayed behind because he could not bear the thought of how Puss would be found. He truly had no hope the hare would be returned alive—not with the dogs and the children and the carts in the street. How could he have faced finding Puss's broken and mutilated body? He would have broken down before the whole town.

Cowper's agitation increased as the time passed and Richard did not return. Twenty minutes, forty, an hour passed. He could wait no longer. Grabbing a hat from the stand in the hall, he jammed it over his head and started down the street. Just then Richard came into view hastening along the road, a sack hanging at his side.

Cowper's heart sank as he gazed at the inert sack. No, his Puss could not be gone! He could not bear it! The poet was unable to tear his gaze from the unmoving sack. Then the sack twitched. Puss was still alive! God was merciful! Cowper ran to meet his servant, tearing the sack from Richard's grasp.

"Here he is, your honour, a bit the worse for wear, but I've no fear will be soon on the mend," Richard said as he released the sack to his master.

Cowper took the sack and hurried back to Orchard Side, Richard close behind. He gently placed the sack on the floor of the parlour, rolled down the sides, and carefully extracted a very wet, bedraggled hare. "Turkish towels, Richard, and warm them," Cowper commanded.

When Richard returned with the warm towels, he began to narrate his adventures while Cowper dried the wet hare off with great care and tenderness.

"A merry chase he led me, your honour! Right through town, and dogs and children after him as well. I managed to hold the dogs off, they was the greatest danger, but Puss got right away from me several times and clear through town we went, out to the tanning yards where what did he do but tumble into the tanning pit! I thought he was drowned, indeed I did, your honour, but a likely young lad pulled him out by his ears and seeing he was still breathing we dunked him in a bucket of water to rinse off the lime, and put him in the sack so he could not get away again."

"You did well, Richard," Cowper praised his servant as he continued to dry off the soaked hare, "and I shall not be forgetting it."

Over the next few days Cowper devotedly nursed his beloved Puss back to health. Amazingly, the only hurts the hare had taken in his adventures were a torn claw and scratched ear, both of which quickly healed. Soon Puss was as well as ever, once more frolicking with Tiney, begging for his carrot treats, sleeping in the poet's lap, and nibbling on his hair, always pulling Cowper back from the melancholy that occasionally threatened the poet and bringing a smile.

Tiney lived to be eight years old, and when he died, Cowper immortalized him in the poem "Epitaph on a hare." Puss lived to eleven years, a tribute to Cowper's understanding of wild creatures and the ever-vigilant, ever-tender care he took of his beloved hares. Although he is not named, it is most likely Puss who is referred to in Cowper's poem "The Garden." During the years the poet shared his life with his hares he never fully succumbed to the depression that haunted him throughout his lifetime, but within a few years of Puss's death he was once again in its grip.

Remembered now mostly for the church hymns he wrote in conjunction with John Newton (who wrote "Amazing Grace"), Cowper was a poet of some note, a skilled essayist/letter-writer, and a remarkable spokesman for wild creatures during an age when such thinking was neither common nor fashionable.

CONTRIBUTORS

Please note: The fact a person contributed to this book does not mean they agree with everything contained in it. Contributors hold many different opinions about animal-related issues, rabbit care, and rabbit rescue.

Judy Books offers outreach to people to benefit both rabbits and their caregivers, inspired to do so by the many unwanted and neglected rabbits for which she has cared over the years. Knowing the challenges of finding good homes for rabbits, Judith contributed the article "Going Beyond cute Photographs" the House Rabbit Society website as a resource for rescues and shelters. Readers of the article can see how to use text in addition to photos to better promote adoptable rabbits on sites such as Petfinder and social media such as Facebook (https://rabbit.org/going-beyond-cute-photographs/).

Today Judy volunteers as an administrator of the Facebook page of the New Jersey House Rabbit Society, a not-for-profit organization dedicated to helping others learn how to care for and appreciate house rabbits as companions. Her administrative work also includes assisting caregivers indirectly with re-homing rabbits and promoting adoptable rabbits from shelters and rescue groups. Judy is currently in training to become a House Rabbit Society educator.

Andrea Bratt owns and operates K9sBehave.com, a reward based dog training business in Santa Barbara California. She is a CPDT-KSA, (Certified Professional Dog Trainer- Knowledge and Skills assessed) and a member of IAABC (International Association of Animal Behavior Consultants). Although she mainly trains dogs at present, she began her animal training journey by clicker training rabbits for agility. Andrea is the Behavior and Enrichment Coordinator for Santa Barbara County Animal Services where she works with dogs, cats, rabbits and guinea pigs at three Santa Barbara County animal shelters. She volunteers for BUNS (Bunnies Urgently Needing Shelter) and teaches their monthly rabbit and guinea pig care and training classes. She enjoys volunteering with her therapy dog, Oli, and her therapy rabbit, Axel. Andrea lives in the mountains above Santa Barbara with her husband Paul and their five Nubian goats, (clicker trained of course.)

Meg Brown, LMT, has been rescuing rabbits for about 20 years. She is a member of the Bunny Bunch and was an active member of the NYS Chapter of the House Rabbit Society for 17 years. Meg's particular strengths and interest lie in working with special needs rabbits. She has been mentored by some of the most advanced rabbit caregivers in the country, including Caroline Charland, president of the Bunny Bunch, Lucile Moore, author of *When Your Rabbit Needs Special Care: Traditional and Alternative Healing Methods,* and Davida Kobler, Chapter Manager of the Upstate NY Chapter of the House Rabbit Society.

Meg has adopted and lived with over 30 house rabbits and currently lives with ten, including a tripod bunny and a partially paralyzed bunny. She has also rescued and adopted out numerous rabbits. Meg has cared for eleven paralyzed bunnies – who have lived long and happy lives – with the help of her very experienced exotics vet, Dr. Joy Lucas, of Upstate Animal Medical Center in Saratoga Springs, NY.

Meg enjoys educating others in how to properly care for their house rabbits and often assists with post-opping bunnies following spay and neuter surgeries. She is also an active member of North Country Wild Care, a non-profit organization dedicated to the rescue and rehabilitation of injured and orphaned wildlife. Meg has been a NYS licensed massage therapist for 24 years. Prior to that, she worked in the medical field. If you need advice on conducting a class on rabbit care or rescuing a rabbit, email Meg at megandbunnies@icloud.com

Lisa Carrara is a dedicated animal advocate who has a special interest in rabbits. She has volunteered with numerous rescue projects, including the Reno Rabbit Rescue in 2006 with Best Friends Animal Society, and she was asked to coordinate The Accidental Rabbit Rescue in Las Vegas, Nevada. Lisa does ongoing rescue work in Las Vegas, as rabbit abandonment and neglect are epidemic.

Lisa has a degree in Veterinary Technology and extends her love and knowledge to helping all species. Another passion Lisa shares is SCUBA diving. She says that being underwater is a magnificent place to let her mind relax and regroup.

Niki Chapman contributed a story about her family's experience adopting a group of 50 rabbits from a large rescue.

Caroline Charland is founder and president of the Bunny Bunch Rabbit Rescue and Bunny Bunch Boutique, founded in 1984.She has dedicated her life to making a difference in the lives of rabbits. Over the years she has fostered and cared for thousands of rabbits. Bunny Bunch has the Boutique. For more information visit the websites BunnyBunch.org and BunnyBunchBoutique.com

Anthony Cimino never had pets as a child; adopting a rabbit with his second fiancée to see if they could handle being parents was what brought bunnies into his life. (He says that was the best thing that came from that relationship.) Rescue became a focus for Anthony after a vet killed his rabbit Muffin by prescribing amoxicillin. All the bunnies he saves he saves in Muffin's name, for the life that was stolen from her.

Anthony currently lives with rabbits Doodle Bug and Peabody, who were adopted from Scotia's APF as a bonded pair. Anthony is a landlord and IT professional who has been involved with Electric Vehicles for 15 years.

Jeff and Katrina Cutter have been owned by their house bunnies since January 2008, when they got their first bunny who was rescued from being euthanized at a local animal shelter in New York. They successfully bonded Cherry Vanilla and Vanilla Bean in 2010. The bunnies and humans love to travel and go camping together with the bunnies having their own bunk space in the travel trailer, dubbed the "bunnymobile." Cherry Vanilla and Vanilla Bean were happily husbun and wife until Cherry Vanilla's passing in late 2016. Jeff, Katrina, and Vanilla Bean currently reside in New Hampshire.

Kim Dezelon has been a volunteer for Brambley Hedge Rabbit Rescue (BHRR; bhrabbitrescue.org) since the year 2000. Kim started volunteering after the devastating loss of her first bunny "Bun," when she realized the only way to heal was to devote her life to helping homeless rabbits at BHRR.

Kim's family currently lives with four rabbits and two very bunny-friendly dogs. Her responsibilities at BHRR include adoption screening, event coordination and educating the public. BHRR coordinates with other agencies in the Phoenix area to help with hoarding situations and abandoned rabbits plus assist with rabbits that need specialized medical care.

Throughout her years volunteering with BHRR, Kim has had the opportunity to care for many special bunnies and help find them forever homes. In addition, she has been exposed to a wealth of knowledge concerning rabbits, their well-being, and overall health and safety. Kim says that her dream now and always will be for all homeless rabbits to find loving and safe homes for their entire lives.

Anna Ehredt is an Educator with the House Rabbit Society and has been volunteering with rabbit rescues for the past 5+ years. Her first rabbit jujube was what she considers her "worst-best decision." "Worst" because at the time she was unaware of the motto "adopt-don't-shop" and bought Jujube on a whim from a pet store while in her junior year of college. "Best" because Jujube sparked Anna's love for rabbits and reminded her that "when we know better, we do better." After Jujube passed away, Anna was determined to dive head-first into learning everything she possible could about rabbits, and for lack of a better term, became obsessed.

Over the years Anna researched proper rabbit care and discovered the House Rabbit Society, devoted her time to volunteering at the local no-kill shelter helping to structure their systems and procedures for rabbits, and eventually started up her own small business selling all-natural handmade small pet treats and goods. These days she spends her time at home with her four bunnies (aka taste testers and quality control team) crafting up new healthy treats for bunnies and other small pets. She hopes to help revolutionize small pet care through her business, The Well Kept Rabbit. Find her at www.thewellkeptrabbit.com and on instagram@thewellkeptrabbit.

Tony Frier and Greg Gude are the founders of Broome Animal Sanctuary (BAS), located in upstate New York in the heart of Schoharie Valley. BAS, an IRS designated 501(c)(3) organization, is a sanctuary for at-risk farm animals and is a certified wildlife habitat. Tony and Greg have both had a lifelong passion to help animals, and it was their dream to retire to a farm where they could devote themselves to rescue full-time. They are committed to helping others understand that farm animals are very intelligent and emotional creatures that should never be exploited. BAS is home to approximately 200 animals, including Snowball (photo p. 102) and five other rabbits.

Broome Animal Sanctuary is 2 ½ hours from New York City and less than an hour from Albany. Visitors at BAS can stay at one of the sanctuary's two self-serve inns and experience the beauty of Schoharie Valley and the Catskills. From Wattles Inn it is just a short walk to BAS, where animal lovers and advocates and other guests can tour the sanctuary or pitch in and help muck some stalls (www.wattlesinn.com). Wattles Inn the Middle (www.wattlesinnthemiddle.com), located in the heart of the town of Broome, is another option for visitors. 100% of the proceeds from both inns go to benefit BAS.

Nancy Furstinger has been speaking up for animals since she learned to talk, and she hasn't shut up yet. She is the author of nearly 100 books, including many on her favorite topic: animals! She started her writing career in third grade, when her class performed a play she wrote. Since then, Nancy has been a feature writer for a daily newspaper, a managing editor of trade and consumer magazines, and an editor at two children's' book publishing houses.

She shares her home with big dogs, house rabbits, and a chinchilla (all rescued), and volunteers with several animal organizations. She also visits schools and libraries with her lovable NZ white bunny who stars in her picture book, *The Forgotten Rabbit*. You can visit Nancy, her pets, and her books at her website: www.nancyfurstinger.com

Caroline Gilbert started rescuing rabbits in the late 1960's, and soon afterward established a sanctuary for domestic rabbits on her 30-acre farm in Simpsonville, South Carolina, where rescued rabbits live in outdoor natural environments called "rabbitats." The rabbits – many from laboratories, commercial breeders, local authorities, and unfit homes – are not adopted out, but given a "Home for Life" at The Sanctuary, where they live as natural a life as possible. The Sanctuary was incorporated in 1986, at which time the virtual adoption program, Adopt-A-Rabbit, was begun, and in 2006 became a nonprofit organization. The Rabbit Sanctuary, Inc. is the first lifetime care rabbit sanctuary to receive verification from the Global Federation of Animal Sanctuaries. Learn more about The Rabbit Sanctuary, Inc. and their virtual adoption program at: www.rabbitsanctuaryinc.org

Amanda Gilmore contributed photos of her adopted rescue rabbit Zinnia-Gayl. Since adopting Zinnia, she volunteers with T.H.E. Rabbit Resource (Upstate NY Chapter of the House Rabbit Society) which is the organization that rescued and fostered Zinnia for two years prior to her adoption. Amanda has been a rabbit enthusiast and bunny mommy for 18+ years.

Stephen Guida was introduced to the world of domestic rabbits in 1995 as a volunteer at a local humane society. He joined Brambley Hedge Rabbit Rescue in January of 2001. Stephen has had experience with the care and feeding of rabbits, their medical issues, rescuing abandoned and unwanted rabbits, and in the adoption and bonding of rabbits. For a number of years he also did native cottontail rescue and rehabilitation. Stephen currently lives the retired life in Phoenix, AZ.

Linda R. Harper, Ph.D. is a lifelong animal lover and advocate, and has been a clinical psychologist in the Chicago area for over 30 years. As the founder of Blessed Bonds, a foster-based program that keeps people and pets together, she understands the physical, mental, and emotional stress that comes with this heart-driven work. Linda is a frequent speaker at animal welfare conferences; she gives workshops locally and throughout the country including the Best Friends Animal Sanctuary. Linda facilitates the pet loss support group sponsored by the Chicago Veterinary Medical Association. She is an author of four books including, *The Power of Joy in Giving to Animals* (with foreword and contributions by Best Friends' co-founder, Faith Maloney).

Davida Kobler has been an Educator and Fosterer for House Rabbit Society since 1993, and Chapter Manager since 1994. Her passion with rabbits began in 1982, and expanded when she moved to Upstate NY in 1983 and realized there were no resources there for information or for rescue. In late 1980s, she was founder of Rabbit Rescue, and then took the idea to the local shelter, offering to teach classes, do rescue, triage and provide vet care for rabbits in need. She trained a dedicated shelter worker in daily care, and then as she finished graduate school and went to work full time, she began the Upstate chapter of HRS (Thrennion's Hoppy Endings Rabbit Resource, Inc) to handle the bunnies that the shelter could not provide care for – whether medical or behaviorally needy. Many shelters in central and upstate NY have recognized the need for designated rabbit programs and Davida and her chapter members teach and assist.

Aside from meeting many phenomenal rabbits in her years in rescue, Davida has found many incredibly compassionate people who have become her friends. She manages the chapter and provides care for a houseful of sanctuary rabbits. She states she is also very fortunate to have made good connections with the veterinary world, relying on several local vets as well as Dr. Morrisey, Chief of Exotics Service at Cornell. The learning curve never ends.

Davida received her BA in Biology and BSN in Nursing from the University of Pennsylvania, and a MSW in Social Work from Syracuse University. She works as an LCSW-R at an outpatient clinic of a state psychiatric facility.

Adrienne Lang has been volunteering for Ohio House Rabbit Rescue since 2011. Her duties have been varied and many, including buncare, field rescue, fundraising, and community outreach. Adrienne also serves as the Rescue Partner Coordinator for Midwest bunfest, a festival and exposition celebrating rabbits as home companion pets.

Ellie Lesch contributed the first two photographs in the story on the Bunderground in Chapter Six. She adopted her first rabbit from the Wisconsin House Rabbit Society in 2004 and has been involved with HRS and rabbit rescue ever since, including when she moved to NC where she joined Triangle Rabbits Rescue in 2012. Ellie started out fostering but saw the great need for transporting rabbits and quickly became the go-to person for bunny transports. Recently she has begun helping with interstate transports, including rescues from Hurricane Irma and from the Las Vegas dumpsites.

Best known for her ghostly thriller *Her Keepers,* **Laura Camby McCaskill** has taken her love for writing and harnessed it to help others. In 2012, Laura published her first work, *Her Keepers,* which won outstanding reviews. In 2016 she published her second work, *Fallow,* a romance thriller which received equally stunning reviews.

In 2016 she became a foster parent for Brother Wolf Animal Rescue. After working with – and fostering – several sick and injured small animals, Laura found a way to mix her love of writing and her love for animals. In 2018 her first article, entitled "Belk's Silent Cry," was published in The House Rabbit Society's magazine, *The House Rabbit Journal.* The article focused on the struggles of one of her foster rabbits, who had been diagnosed with a severe abscess in his lower jaw.

She has written other articles on obstacles other foster animals have had to face, due to sickness or injuries.

Laura also writes for the SC United Methodist Advocate Newspaper and is a part of the planning committee for Grateful Steps Publishing's 2019 Asheville Book-Fest.

Laura's next novel is set to be published in 2020.

Faith Maloney is one of the co-founders of Best Friends Animal Society. She is a consultant in all aspects of animal care at Best Friends Animal Sanctuary in Kanab, Utah. Faith co-presents the How to Start and Run an Animal Sanctuary three times a year at the Sanctuary in Utah and co-presents with Dr. Linda Harper at the national No More Homeless Pets Conference on compassion fatigue and burnout in animal welfare. Faith was born in England and has a degree in fine art. She also writes articles on animal issues and animal care for Best Friends Magazine and other publications.

Elaine Miyabara is the volunteer Rabbit Coordinator at Precious Life Sanctuary and contributed two of the photographs in the story on Precious Life Sanctuary in Chapter Seven.

Mary Caitlin Morrison is a pastoral counselor working with persons who are experiencing grief, life-altering diagnoses and trauma. She has volunteered in animal rescue for over 25 years, working with rabbits, cats, dogs and wild mammals. Mary Caitlin is a big believer in learning from the love, hope and strength of our animal friends.

Phyllis O'Beollain has been gardening organically for over 30 years and has lived with house rabbits for over 14 years. A fan of herbal therapy, she uses her gardening experience to grow her own wild edibles, thus ensuring their quality and potency. She shares these same wild edibles via Elliot's Awesome Treats – E.A.T. and can be reached at
bunnybinks@gmail.com

Shari Olson was born and raised in Milwaukee, Wisconsin. She started volunteering in animal shelters when she was nineteen years old. Shari spent many years doing animal cruelty investigations in Southern California and is currently a volunteer wildlife rehabilitator in upstate New York. Altogether, Shari has been helping animals for almost thirty years and never tires of it. She is looking forward to another thirty years of volunteering.

Michele Page started working at Best Friends Animal Society in 2002 as a parrot caregiver. She also worked with Best Friend's wildlife department, caring for abandoned and injured animals ranging from cottontail rabbits to raptors. Michele later worked on the construction of flight aviaries, and after seven years at Best Friends moved to the Rabbits department as a rabbit caregiver. There her duties included giving medications, changing rabbit runs, and leading tours and educational programs. Michele remained with the Rabbit Department until her retirement in 2017.

Renée Phelps lives in Reno, Nevada with her husband of twenty-three years. Together they have a very large family of rescues. Over the years, that's included cats, dogs, rabbits, birds, Guinea pigs and a rat. She owns Heart to Heart Pet Services, a pet sitting and pet care company, and uses those funds to operate Briar Patch Bunny Rescue. Currently, Renée is writing a book about a feral cat socialization program that she has developed.

Donna Prindle began her teaching/coaching career at Long Beach City College in 1977. During that time she coached softball, volleyball and basketball until 2002. She coached eight All-Americans, fifteen All State Players, and had more than fifty student athletes received scholarships to four year universities. Donna was inducted into Long Beach State's 49er Hall of Fame in 1996, Long Beach City College's Hall of Champions in 2008, and California Community College Athletic Associates' Hall of Fame in 2013.

Outside of coaching, Donna has been a very accomplished and successful educator at Long Beach City College and Cerritos College. She was awarded the California Community College PE award for Adapted Physical Education in 2001 and for Physical Education in 2010.

For many years, Donna has also been involved with the care of the cats and bunnies on the campuses of Long Beach City College, helping out with the TNR and feeding of the cat colonies and with the Best Friends-supported rabbit project. Although now retired, she continues to volunteer with both programs.

Melissa Shelton contributed a story about her first rabbit rescue in the hope it will help others who might find themselves in a similar position.

Bob and Marie Sherman adopted their first rabbit in 2006, "Penny Anne." Penny was a neighbor's outdoor hutch rabbit and they rapidly learned a lot about rabbits. Penny quickly became a house rabbit and loved the attention and freedom. Bob and Marie were assisted by Portland Rabbit Advocates and Dr. Chris Wilson, of Beaverton Pet Clinic in learning how to care for their new family member. Since then they have had several rabbits as family members.

Bob and Marie began volunteering with Portland Rabbit Advocates. (rabbitsadvocates.org), and Bob began volunteering with the Oregon Humane Society in 2007. Bob was named Small Animal Volunteer of the Year for 2008.

Bob and Marie moved to British Columbia in 2009 and began volunteering with another rabbit rescue group, helping care for over 800 rabbits. In connection with this rescue they designed and built shelter buildings for hundreds of rescued rabbits. In 2011 they developed a relationship with the Kelowna, British Columbia, SPCA, and began volunteering, working in rabbit care, adoption counseling, home visits, rabbit fostering, and education. Bob and Marie worked with the manager and staff to develop best practices for rabbit care. They believe in the education of youth and have presented programs about rabbits and their care for several years at "Kid's Spring/Summer Camps" and have donated rabbit books to the local school system. They also present an annual "Bunny 101" class to the community, and formed a non-profit society, Kelowna Rabbit Advocates (KelownaRabbits.com), to promote proper care for house rabbits. Bob and Marie are currently active with the Kelowna BCSPCA. Their plans include moving back to the USA and offering boarding to people whose house rabbits need a place to stay in their absence.

Bob is a retired Portland Police Bureau Sergeant who believes that "Serve & Protect" also applies to the world of animals. Marie is a retired Telus Communications employee and an Architectural Drafting & Design professional.

Jean Silva has been a volunteer with Bunnies Urgently Needing Shelter in Santa Barbara CA since 1992. During that time she has been a medical and behavioral foster home, an adoption counselor, and instructor for Basic Bunny. She is a long time member of the House Rabbit Society and a clicker trainer.

Jacqui Steele is the co-founder and president of Big Ears Animal sanctuary, a not-for-profit registered charity in Longford, Tasmania. Jacqui has a Bachelor of Arts and a Bachelor of Social Work, and was a social worker for 12 years before leaving to dedicate herself full time to her one true passion – the animals. Jacqui and her husband Brett have been together since 1990 and are both vegan and have dedicated their lives to helping animals. Jacqui was diagnosed with terminal breast cancer in 2011 and continues to fight the disease and surprise her oncologist, who has credited her ongoing health to her work with the animals and her vegan lifestyle.

Big Ears Animal Sanctuary is home to around 500 animals, including 220 rabbits, which are Jacqui's passion. The other animals include cows, horses, ponies, donkeys, cats, dogs, birds, sheep, goats, poultry, etc. Jacqui credits her proudest work at the Sanctuary as the meat rabbit farm buyout of 2012 when 300 rabbits were saved and a meat farm shut down for good.

Big Ears Animal Sanctuary relies totally on donations from the public, particularly through their animal sponsorship scheme. For more information please go to www.bigearsanimalsanctuary.com

Carly Thorpe is a 30-year-old animal rights activist from Hamilton, Ontario. Both her professional and personal life are intertwined with animal rights activism. She works at a vegan café where she helps share delicious vegan food with the public, and often has the ability to talk to the customers about exciting and innovating cooking techniques. She is also a volunteer organizer of the Save Movement, a worldwide network of over 500 groups bearing witness to farmed animals headed to slaughter, advocating veganism, and promoting love-based grassroots activism. She plans and attends vigils throughout southern Ontario several times a week.

In her spare time, Carly volunteers at farm animal sanctuaries, where she cares for, feeds, and cleans up after the animal residents while assisting with behind-the-scenes tasks. Additionally, Carly volunteers at VegFests and other vegan events on behalf of sanctuaries and local businesses to fundraise and spread the word about veganism and activism. Although her work is often challenging and emotionally draining, it is Carly's genuine passion and enthusiasm for the well-being and liberation of animals that encourages her to continue these efforts.

Caryl and Ralph Turner founded Precious Life Animal Sanctuary, a non-profit 501© organization located in Washington State in 1999. Both Caryl and Ralph have been active most of their lives in local, state, and national animal protection issues. Their mission is to rescue and provide a safe home for abused, neglected and abandoned farm and companion animals. Among the residents at Precious Life are around 100 happy domestic rabbits.

Erin Urano is an independent feral bunny and community bunny rescuer. Visit her Facebook page: Rusty and Furriends, Vegas Dumpsite Bunnies.

Evonne Vey is an artist who specializes in painting pet portraits (www.evonnesartcreations.com). Evonne contributed the artwork on pages 4, 7, and 212. Her interest in nutrition and homeopathy led to the formation of the private e-group, The Natural Rabbit. Evonne lives with her husband and four cats, four house rabbits, and one little dog.

Lisa White has been a bunny mom and rabbit advocate since 1990. She has volunteered in rabbit rescue with many shelters and rescues over the years, and is currently Vice President of Bunny Lu Adoptions, Inc. Lisa started volunteering with the Bunderground Railroad in 2011 as a driver and in 2014 as a trip coordinator.

SELECTED BIBLIOGRAPHY

Alley Cat Allies. How to Implement an Organizational Trap-Neuter Return Program. www.alleycat.org/resources/how-to-implement-an-organizational-trap-neuter-return-program/(accessed 8/18)

Alley Cat Allies. Know Your Rights: How to Talk to Local Authorities. www.alleycat.org/resources/know-your-rights-how-to-talk-to-animal-control/ (accessed 8/18)

ASPCA. A Closer Look at Community Cats. www.aspca.org/animal-homelessness/shelter-intake=and=surrender/closer-look-community-cats(accessed 8/19)

Best Friends Animal Society. Community Cat Programs: Public Policy and Legal Considerations. https://bestfriends.org/resources/community-cats-public-policy-and-legal-issues(accessed 8/19)

Best Friends Animal Society. TNR for Stray Cats: Meaning, History and Statistics. https://bestfriends.org/resources/tnr-stray-cats-meaning-history- statistics (accessed 8/18)

Bickel, Heidi. 2004. TNR and the Law: What Feral Caretakers Need to Know.www.straypetadvocacy.org (accessed 7/18)

BMJ 2005;331:1256. www.bmj.com/rapid-response/2011/10/31/rabbit-parasite-poses-threat-humans (accessed 10/18)

Bowman, Anastasia. 2014. Cuterebra species. American Association of Veterinary Parasitologists. www.aavp.org/wiki/arthropods/insects/cuteribridae/cuterebra-species/ (accessed 11/18)

BSAVA Manual of Rabbit Medicine and Surgery. 2006. Second edition. Edited by Anna Meredith and Paul Flecknell. British Small Animal Veterinary Association.

Buhner, Stephen Harrod. Plant Consciousness: The Fascinating Evidence Showing Plants Have Human Level Intelligence, Feelings, Pain and More. Conscious Lifestyle Magazine. www.consciouslifestylemag.com/plant-consciousness-intelligence-feeling/ (accessed 11/18)

Carpenter, James. 2010. Research shows that selamectin is safe for rabbits and higher doses are needed to effectively treat fleas. https://www.k-state.edu/media/newsrelease/aug10/selamectin83010.html (accessed 12/18)

CDC. Plague. www.cdc.gov/plague/transmission/index.html (accessed 8/18)

CDC. Rabies. www.cdc.gov/rabies/pets/index.html (accessed 8/18)

CDC. 2018. Tularemia. www.cdc.gov/tularemia/ (accessed 8/18)

Cook, A. J. and E. McCobb. 2012. Quantifying the shelter rabbit population: an analysis of Massachusetts and Rhode Island animal shelters. *J Appl An Welf Sci.* 15(4): 299-312.

Cousquer, Glen. 2006. Veterinary Care of Rabbits with Myiasis. *In Practice* 28:342-349.

CWHL (Cornell Wildlife Health Lab). 2018. Mange. https://cwhl.vet.cornell.edu/disease/mange#collapse3 (accessed 11/18)

Ellis, C. F., W. McCormick, and A. Tinarwo. 2017. Analysis of Factors Relating to Companion Rabbits Releases to Two United Kingdom Rehoming Centers. *J App An WelfSci* 20(3): 1-10.

Fry, David. 2010. Brief Summary of Feral Cat Legal Issues. Animal Legal and Historical Center www.animallaw.info/article/brief-summary-feral-cat-legal-issues (accessed 7/18)

Gagliano, M. 2017. The mind of plants: Thinking the unthinkable. *Commun Integr Biol.* 10(2):e1288333. www.ncbi.nlm.nih.gov/pmc/articles/PMC5398210/ (accessed 11/18)

Hansen, O., Y. Gall, K. Pfister, and W. Beck. 2005. Efficacy of a Formulation Containing Imidacloprid and Moxidectin Against Naturally Acquired Ear Mite Infestations (*Psoroptescuniculi*) in Rabbits. *Intern J Appl Res Vet Med* 3(4): 281-86.

Harcourt-Brown, Frances. 2018. Rabbit haemorrhagic disease and its variants (Lagoviruses). www.harcourt-brown.co.uk/articles/infectious-disease/rabbit-haemorrhagic-disease (accessed 9/18)

Harkness, John E., Patricia V. Turner, Susan VandeWoude, and Colette l. Wheler. 2010. *Biology and Medicine of Rabbits and Rodents*. Fifth edition. Wiley-Blackwell.

Kazacos, Kevin R. 2010. The zoonotic threat of rabbits and other wild animals. *Veterinary Medicine*.

Kortis, Bryan. Feral Cats, TNR & the Law. www.neighborhoodcats.org

Kortis, Bryan. Implementing a Community Trap-Neuter-Return Program. The Humane Society of the United States. www. humanesociety.org>docs

Livni, Ephrat. 2018. A debate over plant consciousness is forcing us to confront the limitations of the human mind. Quartz. https://qz.com/1294941/a-debate-over-plant-consciousness-is-forcing-us-to-confront-the-limitations-of the-human-mind/ (accessed 11/18)

Lohin, Amanda. Cuterebriasis (a.k.a. Cuterebra – Bot Fly Larva) in Pets. MSPCA-Angell. www.mspca.org/angell_services/bot-fly-larva-in-pets/ (accessed 11/18)

McCaughey, C. and C. A. Hart. 2000. Hantaviruses. *J. Med. Microbiol.* 49: 587-599.

McClure, Diane, Frank Bossong, Eva M. Jaeger, and LuAnn Peterson. Rabbit Trap-Neuter-Release – Not Just for Cats Anymore. https://www.slideshare.net/mobile/dmccluredvm/rabbit-trap-neuter-release-not-just-for-cats-anymore (accessed 11/18)

McVeigh, Tracy. 2011. Pet rabbits are cruelly neglected and mistreated in Britain, survey finds. *The Guardian*. www.theguardian.com/world/2011/may/21/pet-rabbits-cruelly-neglected-mistreated (accessed 2/18)

Mancinelli, Elisabetta. 2018. Update on treating *E. cuniculi* infection in domestic rabbits. *Vet Times* 48.20.

Moore, Lucile C. and Kathy Smith. 2008. *When Your Rabbit Needs Special Care: Traditional and Alternative Healing Methods*. Santa Monica Press.

Moonamart, W., M. Tansakul, C. Kiewsiri, R. Walanaboonchai, W. Somrith, C. Yinharnmingmongkol and M. Tunhikorn. 2018. Haematological response in the treatment of naturally acquired parasite infestations in rabbits. *World. Rab. Sci.* 26(4): 313-320.

Moxidectin. https://www.sciencedirect.com/topics/agriculturaland biological:sc/moxidectin

Neville, V., K. Hinde, E. Line, R. Todd and R. A. Sanders. 2018. Rabbit relinquishment through online classified advertisements in the United Kingdom: when, why, and how many? *J ApplWelfSci*6: 1-11.

Nitenpyram – an overview. https://www.sciencedirect.com/topics/veterinary-science-and-veterinary-medicine/nitenpyram

Ohio Country Journal-Ohio AgNet. 2018. Rabbit hemorrhagic disease found in Ohio. http://ocj.com/2018/09/rabbit-hemorrhagic-disease-found-in-ohio/(accessed 9/18)

Oxley, J. A., A. Previti, A. Alibrandi, Briefer, E. F. and A. Passantino. 2015. A Preliminary internet survey of pet rabbit owners' characteristics. *World Rab. Sci.* 23(4): 289-293.

Rocchi, M. S. and M. P. Dagleish. 2018. Diagnosis and prevention of rabbit viral haemorrhagic disease 2. *In Practice* 40(1): 11-16.

Seattle Times staff. 2014. Q&A: Experts weigh in on the botfly and pets. www.seattletimes.com/life/pets/qa-experts-weigh-in-on-the-botfly-and-pets/(accessed 11/18)

Spickler, Anna Rovid. 2018. Hantavirus. www.cfsph.iastate.edu/DiseaseInfo/factsheets.php (accessed 1/19)

Thompson, L. and L. Benato. 2018. Toxicity: insecticide. Pyrethroid toxicity. *Vetstream Vetlexicon Lapis* www.vetstream.com/treat/lapis/diseases/toxicity-insecticide (accessed 12/18)

Ulfsdotter, Linnea. 2013. Rehoming of Pet Rabbits in Sweden. Swedish University of Agricultural Sciences. Epsilon Archive for Student Projects. https://stud.epsilon.slu.se/5998/ (accessed 2/18)

Varga, Molly. 2014. *Textbook of Rabbit Medicine*. Second edition. Butterworth Heinemann Elsevier.

Williams, Bruce H. 2013. Zoonoses of Small Mammals. *Clinician's Brief.* www.cliniciansbrief.com/article/zoonoses-small=mammals (accessed 10/2018)

Wogan, Lisa 2018. Virulent disease in rabbits surfaces in Ohio. VIN News Service. http://news.vin.com/doc/?id=8737748 (accessed 10/18)

Wright, Kevin. Treatment and Prevention of *E. cuniculi* in Rabbits. www.petcha.com/treatment-and-prevention-ofe-cuniculi-in-rabbits/(accessed 9/18)

INDEX